ON SUPERVISION

ON SUPERVISION

Psychoanalytic and Jungian
Analytic Perspectives

edited by
Ann Petts and Bernard Shapley

KARNAC

First published in 2007 by
Karnac Books Ltd
118 Finchley Road
London NW3 5HT

British Library Cataloguing in Publication Data

A C.I.P. for this book is available from the British Library

ISBN 978 1 85575 497 3

Edited, designed and produced by The Studio Publishing Services Ltd
www.studiopublishingservicesuk.co.uk
e-mail: studio@publishingservicesuk.co.uk

Printed in Great Britain

10 9 8 7 6 5 4 3 2 1

www.karnacbooks.com

CONTENTS

ACKNOWLEDGEMENTS

The Editors would like to thank all of the contributors to this volume for the generous way in which they have given so much time, thought, and care in the preparation of their chapters for publication. All have also shown great patience, as yet another draft needs attention after editorial correction of often very minor details, but all have submitted to the obsessionality that comes with the task of editing a volume such as this with good humour. We would also thank some potential contributors for the interest shown in this project and the work that they did, work that will hopefully find an opportunity to be shared at some point in time.

The Editors would also like to thank the two past chairs of the Supervision Committee of the British Association of Psychotherapists, Sue Johnson and Eve Warin, for their vision and support. We would also thank Stan Ruszczynski for his support and sound advice and also all the staff at Karnac Books.

All case examples in this volume are either given with the permission of the participants in the supervisory relationship, or are composites of actual cases made up to illustrate a point, or have been so disguised that it is very unlikely that individuals could be recognized. If any psychotherapist or counsellor reading this does recognize themselves, we hope they will remember the spirit in which this book has been written: to facilitate more widely supervisory thinking that might enrich the profession as a whole.

Chapter Three of this volume, "The ethics of supervision: developmental and archetypal perspectives", by Hester McFarland Solomon is a revised version of material that has been previously published in E. Christopher and H. Solomon (Eds)., *Contemporary Jungian Clinical Practice* (London: Karnac, 2003); H. Solomon and M. Twyman (Eds.), *The Ethical Attitude in Analytic Practice* (London: Free Association Books, 2003); and J. Cambray and L. Carter (Eds.), *Analytical Psychology: Contemporary Perspectives in Jungian Analysis* (Hove: Brunner-Routledge, 2004).

An earlier version of Chapter Nine of this volume, "The analyst's countertransference when supervising: friend or foe?" by Jan Wiener, appeared in the *Journal of Analytical Psychology* (2007) 52(1): 51–71.

ABOUT THE EDITORS AND CONTRIBUTORS

Jean Arundale, PhD, is a Senior Member and training and supervising psychoanalytic therapist in private practice and part-time in the NHS at the Co-ordinated Psychological treatment Services, Munro Clinic, Guy's Hospital. She teaches clinical and theoretical seminars at the BAP and other organizations. She came from a background in psychology and philosophy.

Maureen Chapman, MSc, has spent considerable time in primary care both prior to her training as an analytic psychotherapist and post qualification, working in and supervising therapists working in General Practice. She is also a seminar leader, supervisor, and assessor, and is in private practice in Surrey.

Lou Corner is in private practice in Reading, Berkshire having previously worked in higher education and the voluntary sector. Her work includes supervision of both psychotherapists and counsellors and she is a training supervisor for several courses. She is currently chair of the British Psychoanalytic Council and has been a past Chair of the BAP and Chair of the Association's Ethics Committee.

Margaret Hammond is a Senior Member of the Jungian section of the BAP, in private practice in Shepperton, Middlesex. She originally trained as a supervisor in Relate, and has practised for many years, with both individuals and groups. She has a special interest in the parallel process as it emerges in supervision, and thinking around this informs her practice.

Susan Howard works clinically in private practice as a psychoanalytic psychotherapist. She also works part-time at the University of Surrey on the Clinical Psychology Doctoral course, where she teaches psychoanalytic skills and is involved in supervisor training and support. She has supervised counsellors, psychologists, and psychotherapists in both the public and private sectors for a number of years.

Sue Johnson is a Full Member of the British Association of Psychotherapists and has a full-time private practice of psychoanalytic psychotherapy and supervision. With Stanley Ruszczynski she is co-editor of *Psychoanalytic Psychotherapy in the Independent Tradition* (Karnac, 1999) and *Psychoanalytic Psychotherapy in the Kleinian Tradition* (Karnac, 1999). She undertakes clinical and theoretical teaching on a number of courses for the British Association of Psychotherapists. She was instrumental in establishing the BAP Supervision Service.

Helen Morgan is a psychotherapist working mainly in private practice and a training therapist and supervisor for the Jungian Analytic section of the BAP. Her background includes working in therapeutic communities for adolescents and adults. Previous published papers include "Between fear and blindness. The white therapist and the black patient", and "Exploring racism".

Ann Petts initially trained as a social worker and worked for many years in outpatient psychiatry. She currently works primarily as a psychotherapist and supervisor in private practice, and also works and supervises on two post-graduate counselling courses. She was a Founder Member of the BAP supervision group and has held numerous posts in the BAP, including Chair of the Psychoanalytic Training Committee and Chair of the Modified Training Committee.

Joscelyn Richards is a consultant clinical psychologist who has jointly run an NHS Psychotherapy Clinic for twenty years. She is a Senior Member of the BAP and a member of the IPA. She has been involved with the training and registration of psychoanalytic psychotherapists and was the first Chair of the British Confederation of Psychotherapists. She is interested in working with borderline and psychotic patients and has supervised many therapists in this field.

Bernard Shapley is a psychoanalytic psychotherapist working in private practice and as a part-time member of the Counselling Service of Middlesex University. He supervises individuals and groups working in a number of settings, including education, the voluntary sector, and in training psychodynamic counsellors.

Hester McFarland Solomon is a training analyst and supervisor for the Jungian Section of the British Association of Psychotherapists. She has been Chair of the BAP's Council, its Training Committee, and its Ethics Committee, and is a Fellow of the Association. She has published widely and has co-edited three books: *Jungian Thought in the Modern World*, *Contemporary Jungian Clinical Practice*, and most recently *The Ethical Attitude in Analytic Practice*. She is currently President Elect of the International Association for Analytical Psychology.

Denise Taylor is a Fellow of the British Association of Psychotherapists. She served as Chair from 1989 to 1902, a watershed time for the association with the acquisition of its Headquarters building, organizational growth, and expanding Professional Trainings. She worked as a psychotherapist and supervisor, and was an early supporter of the supervision course and service She was a Founder Member of the British Psychoanalytic Council. Previously, she worked at the Tavistock Clinic as a psychologist, clinician, and tutor.

Mary Twyman trained at the Institute of Psychoanalysis. She co-edited with Hester McFarland Solomon *The Ethical Attitude in Analytic Practice* (2003). She has contributed to *Dilemmas in the Consulting Room* (Alfille and Cooper), and *Fairbairn and Relational Psychoanalysis* (Pereira and Scharff). She was formerly Principal Social Worker in the Adult Department of the Tavistock Clinic and an Honorary Lecturer in the Psychoanalysis Unit at UCL. She is in private practice in London.

Jan Wiener is Training Analyst and Director of Training for the Society of Analytical Psychology. She works as a consultant adult psychotherapist at Thorpe Coombe Hospital and in private practice. She is joint coordinator of a teaching and supervision programme in St Petersburg, Russia. She is author of a number of papers and chapters and is co-author of *Counselling and Psychotherapy in Primary Health Care* (1998) and co-editor of *Supervising and Being Supervised: A Practice in Search of a Theory* (2003).

Heather Wood is a clinical psychologist and psychoanalytic psychotherapist currently working at the Portman Clinic, Tavistock and Portman NHS Trust, and in private practice. She has supervised individuals and groups within psychoanalytic, cognitive analytic therapy, and generic psychotherapeutic models in a range of NHS settings and privately.

On what to do with the countertransference? Supervisory technique and the therapist's countertransference: a historical perspective

Bernard Shapley

In the past forty to fifty years, supervisory technique in the psychoanalytic and Jungian analytic world has come of age. We have moved from a position where supervision practice was barely thought about to the situation today, where a robust debate on supervisory style is possible, grounded in core theoretical concepts. For example, one supervisor might respond to some clinical material in which the therapist describes strong countertransference feelings by suggesting, or perhaps instructing the therapist, "take this to your therapy". Another supervisor could view a therapist's own therapy as a private and sacrosanct space that the supervisor has no right to invade by setting therapeutic agendas from the position of an authority figure. Another might take a quite different view of the material, seeing it as an opportunity to explore the inner world of the patient via a projective identification the therapist has become drawn into. Still another, as the supervisor finds himself drawn into his own countertransference to the patient, therapist, and material, might wonder about an enactment in the supervisory relationship as an intersubjective expression of the therapist–patient relationship. It could be that the same supervisor might respond in different ways on different occasions. The countertransference that is accessible to thought and reflection might be far more able to be dealt with in the manner suggested earlier in this paragraph than that which cannot be thought about, and therefore becomes enacted or repeated in the supervisory relationship. Freud's (1914g) concept of acting out being associated with repeating as opposed to remembering is of particular relevance here.

All positions have merit in them, have a theoretical grounding, and are contained somewhere in the chapters that follow in this volume. They show a rich evolution of thinking about the role of the supervisor in the psychoanalytic and Jungian analytic world that has often involved the question of where and how to work with the therapist's countertransference feelings. To put it another way, how much is the therapist's unconscious the province of supervision or of their own therapy?

Historically, formal supervision grew out of the need for early psychoanalysts, Freud included, to have dialogue with colleagues, in order to evolve their thinking. Perhaps this still remains the core task of any supervisory relationship. It could be argued that Freud's letters to Fleiss and later the "Wednesday Society" both contain acknowledgment of the need to think with others and not struggle in isolation. The need to step back from the therapeutic encounter and make sense of what felt confusing became formalized as training structures developed. In the Eitingon model and Berlin training, where supervision and personal analysis first became formally separated (Kernberg, 2000), the supervisor adopts an observational and authority role over "control cases". This stance helps the therapist to internalize their own observational stance in relation to the clinical work, an ability we continue to value to this day. There seems to be a hope or expectation that the therapist's unconscious processes, and certainly the supervisor's unconscious processes, should have little part to play in the relationship.

Rather by contrast, the other significant training model that developed in the psychoanalytic world, the French School, uses supervision in a less detached and more emotionally charged way, in which it is expected that unconscious processes will be activated in the supervisory relationship and used to further learning about the unconscious (Kernberg, 2000). Supervision becomes akin to therapy, a highly private matter open to little external scrutiny. It is surprising that, given the central gate-keeping role of supervision in this model and the growth of interest in intersubjective approaches to supervision elsewhere in the psychoanalytic world, little seems to have been written that is accessible internationally on the experience of this model of supervision.

However, both models, when used as part of a training, place great power and authority in the hands of supervisors. As Kernberg points out, the possibilities for regressive idealization of supervisors, infantilization of students, imitative technique, and a turning away from "other" thinking all become part of the supervisee's overall countertransference to the training (pp. 107–112). This can be to the detriment of a spirit of genuine enquiry and learning.

It seems as if attempts to "abolish" unconscious processes, the very phenomena we are most interested in, in favour of the notion of "dispassionate" enquiry, is a familiar entry point in psychoanalytic thinking. The change in Freud's initial attitude to transference and the changing attitude to countertransference (Sandler, Dare, & Holder, 1979) both involve an acceptance that the unconscious cannot be expelled as an inconvenience, it is going to be part of the picture, needs acknowledgment, and could be of great help to us. The evolution of thinking about supervision is no different. There has been a moving away from the initial position of observer and a growing interest in the unconscious processes that may get played out in the supervisory relationship. Early focus on the intersubjective relationship in supervision as a reflection of the therapeutic relationship began with Searles (1965) in the USA and Mattinson's (1975) work in the UK as they explored phenomena that have become known as "parallel process". Later workers have sought to place particular emphasis on the parallel process as the most significant material for a supervisor to focus on in helping to understand the therapist–patient interaction. In a recent paper by Zaslavsky, Nunes, and Eizirik (2005) it is suggested that three methodological models of supervision have developed, distinguished by their different ways of working with the countertransference. The first, the classical or demonstrative model, focuses on the patient and seeks to demonstrate technique and impart knowledge. The therapist's countertransference plays only a minor role. The second model they call corrective or communicative, and it focuses on detailed examination of the clinical material, including the supervisee's countertransference, in order to understand the unconscious communications taking place between patient and therapist. The third, that they call comprehensive, relational, or experiential, centres on the interaction of the supervisory pair, using the relationship, including transference and countertransference aspects, in order to understand the patient.

Perhaps in all technical development there is a danger of overuse, such as that style of supervision described by Berman (2000) or the case example described by Brown and Miller (2002). In this, an emphasis on the supervisor's and therapist's unconscious processes could, it might be argued, leave little space for the poor patient and his unconscious. Contributors to this volume, while acknowledging the value of parallel process phenomena when they occur, are often cautious about an over-reliance on the supervisor's unconscious and the parallel process as necessarily indicative of events in the therapeutic relationship. Caution has also been expressed elsewhere, notably by Sedlak (2003). However, parallel process clearly has a clinical value as well as allowing us to move away from the theoretically untenable position that, as supervisors, we are all so well analysed that we can stand above any unconscious resonance to patient material or our supervisees! There are two particular instances where parallel process seems to appear quite regularly in the supervisor–therapist relationship. Both have been drawn to our attention by clinicians who would not necessarily have seen themselves in the forefront of this approach to supervisory technique.

The first involves Robert Langs (1994) and what some can view as his excessive preoccupation with the frame of the supervisory relationship, which he advocates setting in precise detail and for a particular and important reason. His view is that it is common for boundary violations in the therapeutic relationship to become unconsciously acted out in the supervisory relationship. When they appear in a firmly framed supervisory relationship, they act to alert the supervisor to enquire about the state of the boundaries of the therapy and boundary anxieties, in a way that might be able to reinstate boundaries or attend to anxieties promptly. A supervisory relationship that is more collegial, often advocated in order to make a distinction between supervision and therapy, might, in his view, make the boundary issues more masked. These issues are discussed further in this volume in chapters by Corner and Wood in particular

(Chapters One and Two). Perhaps it is not so relevant precisely where we draw the line; lines will be drawn and, if there is an unconscious parallel process communication being played out, a mutually familiar boundary will be crossed. Langs contribution is to alert us to the possible meaning in terms of the patient–therapist interaction.

The other familiar clinical phenomenon that involves a parallel process and the therapist's countertransference is where the supervisee is unable to think about particular issues in supervision or when with the patient, however often the issue is pointed out by the supervisor, or colleagues if in a group. There may, of course, be some personal resistance needing attention more appropriate to therapy, but Heinrich Racker (1968) has left us a very useful example of parallel process thinking in the concept of counter-resistance. This occurs where the therapist's unconscious identifies with the defensive structure against thinking about certain issues that the patient has, and then holds back from those issues in the consulting room and in supervision. This defensive structure commonly becomes very apparent in supervision as the supervisee temporarily seems imbecilic, unable to see what is clear to everyone else. It is a prime function of supervision to break through such defensive collusions between patient and therapist. The therapist is then freed to think about what the patient cannot yet bear to think about.

References

Berman, E. (2000). Psychoanalytic supervision: The intersubjective development. *International Journal of Psychoanalysis, 81*: 273–290.

Brown, L., & Miller, M. (2002). The triadic intersubjective matrix in supervision. *International Journal of Psychoanalysis, 83*: 811–823.

Freud, S. (1914g). Remembering, repeating and working-through. *S.E., 12*: 145–156. London: Hogarth.

Kernberg, O. (2000). A concerned critique of psychoanalytic education. *International Journal of Psychoanalysis, 81*: 97–120.

Langs, R. (1994). *Doing Supervision and Being Supervised*. London: Karnac.

Mattinson, J. (1975). *The Reflection Process in Casework Supervision*. London: TIMS.

Racker, H. (1968). *Transference and Countertransference*. London: Hogarth.

Sandler, J., Dare, C., & Holder, A. (1979). *The Patient and the Analyst*. London: Karnac.

Searles, H. F. (1955). The informational value of the supervisor's emotional experience. In: J. D. Sutherland (Ed.), *Collected Papers on Schizophrenia and Related Subjects* (pp. 157–176). New York: International Universities Press [reprinted London: Karnac, 1986].

Sedlak, V. (2003). The patient's material as an aid to the disciplined working through of the countertransference and supervision. *International Journal of Psychoanalysis, 84*: 1487–1500.

Zaslavsky, J., Nunes, M., & Eizirik, C. (2005). Approaching counter-transference in psychoanalytical supervision: a qualitative investigation. *International Journal of Psychoanalysis, 86*: 1099–1131.

Introduction

Ann Petts

A considerable body of literature addressing the task of supervision as distinct from clinical practice is now in existence, with many different and sometimes contradictory views and models being expounded. A supervision working party was set up in 1997, which was led by Sue Johnson with a view to offering experienced BAP members as supervisors to individuals outside of our own organization. What we were met with were numerous requests for a course. From this the Supervision Group was established, and the first Supervision Course started in 1998. The aim of the course is not to offer a "training" in supervision, but to provide a forum to enable the participants to explore their own practice and to highlight aspects of technique in the practice of supervision. The course went to Dublin for ten sessions in 2003 and was repeated in 2006–2007.

The course, which is for BAP members and non-BAP practitioners, quickly flourished and is ongoing. The book is the outcome of considerable work by BAP members who have given a version of their paper to the Supervision Course members. This is not a comprehensive list, but we are indebted to all the members who have presented papers and led discussion groups for the course. It provides a stimulating environment in which to think and question theory and aspects of practice.

The papers offered here make reference to key theoretical concepts, ethical issues, and various concerns we encounter in the practice of supervision. They also address the work settings in which we practise as supervisors, such as in private practice, in organizations like the NHS, and in training organizations. For the purposes of this book we have linked the papers together in thematic Parts, and the first three chapters encompass some of the thinking on "The fundamentals of supervision practice.

In Chapter One, "On beginning a supervisory relationship", Lou Corner sets out some important considerations when starting with a new supervisee and addresses some of the issues that need to be thought through prior to entering a supervisory relationship. The primary focus of the chapter is where the supervisor is working with a supervisee (or with a group) from organizations other than their own that might or might not be familiar to them. Issues of group supervision and the importance of setting ground rules are explored. The initial interview, where that is possible, is addressed, and Lou Corner poses the questions we need to have in mind to attempt to gain a general picture of the supervisee and their potential for development. She raises a number of questions that are important for a practitioner to consider before offering supervisory services. These are elaborated later in this volume by both Jean Arundale and Mary Twyman, the latter introducing the concept of the supervisees' "model of mind".

In the second chapter Heather Wood writes on "Boundaries and confidentiality". She writes that boundaries relate to the formal arrangements between the supervisor and supervisee and she refers to the differing views in some of the literature about where boundaries should be drawn. She also explores some of the pressures on boundaries that the supervisor may face that could lead to dilemmas encountered in different settings, such as the NHS and private supervision, as well as some of the issues of confidentiality and ethics. In a later chapter in this volume (Chapter Ten) Joscelyn Richards writes about a particular pressure on boundaries and confidentiality when faced with a patient who is suicidal.

The third chapter, "The ethics of supervision: developmental and archetypal perspectives", represents many years of thinking and its development by Hester McFarland Solomon, who chaired the Ethics Committee of the BAP for a number of years, and has also chaired the Sub-Committee for Ethics Procedures of the International Association of Analytical Psychology. She discusses the significant role that ongoing supervision plays in helping to maintain ethical thinking and its practice in clinical work. What is significant in her writing is the linking of the ethical attitude to an archetypal and developmental position in which she explores the development of an ethical capacity and its possible origins in relation to the analytic attitude. This is further considered in relation to supervision as a triangular space. Various authors' contributions to both analytic practice and supervision with respect to triangular space are compared and contrasted in this chapter.

Part II of the book, is entitled "On supervisory technique", and in Chapter Four Susan Howard writes on "Models of supervision". She reflects on her personal experience of supervision and the lack of an explicit framework or model of supervision and wonders if her supervisors conducted supervision according to their own experience. She offers us a review of models of supervision and their strengths and limitations. Susan Howard considers that concrete experience is the most valued knowledge in the profession, a view shared by Jean Arundale in the subsequent chapter. Susan Howard illustrates the lack of a framework for those beginning as supervisors within a psychotherapy-based model of supervision as well as exploring some of the strengths and limitations of developmental models. She addresses the point that much has been written about the process and theories over the past fifty years, and in my view we could be seen as striving towards a model that is unique and different from clinical practice.

Chapter Four, by Jean Arundale, is entitled "Supervising trainees: teaching the values and techniques of psychoanalytic psychotherapy", which is based mainly upon her considerable experience of working and supervising trainees within the NHS. In the opening paragraph she questions the notion of technique and postulates that it is somewhat artificial, and goes on to say that it is more a matter of values internalized from the experience and study of psychoanalysis that counts. She gives a personal view of what is required for the job of a supervisor and queries whether it is possible to teach the job of supervision. She postulates that courses or lectures can be used as a context for thinking about the issues of becoming a supervisor, which was fundamental to our thinking in the Supervision Committee when the course was first being thought about. Jean Arundale addresses the importance of psychoanalytic values as being fundamental, not just to clinical work, but also in forming the psychoanalytic identity of the supervisor. She also writes of models of supervision and postulates that the practice of clinical work is an apprenticeship that involves learning on the job and from experience, together with careful overseeing by the supervisor. This is a model we are all likely to be familiar with. She also addresses management issues and boundaries and the bringing together of theory and practice. When exploring the teaching of basic building blocks of analytic therapy she offers a personal view of what she sees as most significant.

The following two chapters continue the theme of personal experiences of supervision. In Chapter Six, Mary Twyman's paper entitled "Some dynamics of supervision" focuses on her experience from the supervisor's point of view, and the complexity of the task for all involved in the process. She tells us of her approach to supervision and the attitudes that inform it. She considers the task of the supervisor is one of eliciting the therapist's implicit theory of mind. What informs this is our own experience of analysis, previous supervision, seminars and lectures, reading and whatever brought us into the field of psychotherapy in the first place. Mary Twyman illustrates her views with various examples and addresses the resistance in therapists to widen their framework of reference, and questions how far supervision may be a teaching and instructing activity.

The following chapter by Sue Johnson, "Some personal experiences of supervision", is a personal account of her experience of supervision from the perspective of the supervisee. She addresses some significant facets of the supervisory relationship and the personal style of some of the supervisors she has worked with, from the perspective of their technique and what she experienced as facilitating or unhelpful. She gives a detailed example of her own work with a particular supervisee.

The final section of the book addresses "Aspects of the supervisory relationship". Chapter Eight is by Denise Taylor and is entitled "The supervision triangle", where she explores the therapist–patient–supervisor triad from the perspective of "the third other". Using the nuclear family as a prototype, she describes balanced as well as skewed triangular functioning and applies this to supervision of a therapist's work with a patient. She elaborates this with sketches and many examples to illustrate the theoretical model. She discusses the disruptive effects of triangular distortions in organizations, often not identified and recognized, and where the concept of the triad with its wealth of symbolism holds much power in its potential for illuminating apparently puzzling or intractable situations.

Chapter Nine, by Jan Wiener, is entitled "The analyst's countertransference when supervising: friend or foe?" In this chapter she gives a detailed account of transference and countertransference dynamics in the supervisory relationship and how they can foster or hinder the task of supervision. She considers the concept of refracted countertransference to describe the complicated processes of projection, introjection, and projective identification that the supervisor will have to make sense of. Jan Wiener gives a brief historical perspective of transference and countertransference and the additional perspective of working in organizations, illustrated by detailed clinical examples from her work as a supervisor in the NHS and with two different training organizations.

Chapter Ten, by Joscelyn Richards, is entitled "The role of supervision (internal and external) in working with the suicidal patient", in which she explores in depth the situation where patients convey to the therapist, directly or indirectly, that they are experiencing compelling thoughts to kill themselves. She writes of the therapists' and supervisors' possible reactions, and the pressures and complexities of working in an organization together with the policies and procedures around patient care, including the commitment to confidentiality. She gives us two detailed clinical examples from her work in the NHS, one from her experience as the therapist and the perspective of the internal supervisor, and the other from a case she supervised. We are given an account of management issues and the collaboration with colleagues. In her conclusion she writes "the most appropriate way for therapists to respond . . . is to resist the desire to act and instead to allow themselves to be open to patients' communications". She suggests that through this process therapists, supported by their supervisors, can help their patients to understand and contain the pressure to kill themselves.

In the following chapter Helen Morgan writes on "The effects of difference of 'race' and colour in supervision". From my personal experience as a supervisor it is often an issue trainees would rather avoid. However, in her opening paragraph, the aspect of the supervisor's avoidance is addressed and Helen Morgan highlights the effect of this reaction on the supervisee. She goes on to give a detailed account of the literature on "race" and racism, together with a number of illustrative examples. She sees "silence" as a serious challenge that needs to be taken on more directly from within the profession. In her conclusion she writes, "On the one hand this whole matter is extremely complex and difficult to explore. On the other it is really quite simple as long as one is able to stay within the analytic frame".

In Chapter Twelve, Maggie Hammond's contribution is entitled "The many 'ifs' of group supervision". In my personal experience, many of us who work in organizations are aware that the work in a supervision group can be collaborative and rich and at other times can be one in which it may be difficult to maintain an atmosphere of learning and enquiry. This chapter explores the task of a supervision group and the factors that may affect it. Maggie Hammond discusses group dynamics and the impact on those dynamics imposed by the presentation of clinical material. She explores the frame of the group and the role of the leader and illustrates the chapter with clinical examples from her experience as a consultant, supervisor and supervisee.

In the final chapter, Maureen Chapman addresses the important role of assessment in her paper entitled "Janus as a metaphor for the assessment process", in which she addresses some issues illustrating the power of the unconscious, using myth and metaphor. She draws attention to the complexity and the confrontational nature of the supervisory relationship during the assessment process. Maureen Chapman looks at the Roman image of Janus in the task of the assessor, who needs to look in two directions at once; to the profession and the standards expected for entry, and to the supervisee and the level they have reached.

With the advent of more rigorous CPD requirements and the demands of regulation, regular and effective supervision will be a necessary and important part of our practice in our work as psychoanalytic psychotherapists and psychodynamic counsellors. We would hope this volume may offer a contribution to good supervision practice for the benefit of the profession, supervisees, and patients alike.

PART I

FUNDAMENTALS OF
SUPERVISION PRACTICE

CHAPTER ONE

On beginning a supervisory relationship

Lou Corner

W hile the subject of supervision and the role of the super-visor have been written about within psychoanalytic literature (Berman, 2000; Brown & Miller, 2002; Grin-berg, 1997; Sedlak, 1997, 2003; Wiener, Mizen, & Duckham, 2003), the issues addressed most frequently refer to the supervisory rela-tionship between a training analyst and a trainee. In such cases, the supervisor is familiar with the training that the supervisee is under-taking and has some idea in regard to the expectations upon him, the supervisor, and upon the trainee. It may be argued that super-vision should only take place when the supervisor is familiar with the training. However, as Sedlak (1997) states when writing about his experience of working with untrained therapists in a region of the country not well blessed with good trainings:

> The unavailability of personal therapy or analysis and of a good training experience does not stop people in the caring professions working in what they consider to be an analytic or dynamic way. Senior practitioners can of course choose to have little to do with this possible diminution of standards; alternatively they can explore in what ways they can help, while maintaining their profes-sional integrity. [p. 26]

Drawing upon my experience as a supervisor, and as a trainer of supervisors, I am going to focus upon the beginning of the supervisory relationship that a psychoanalytic psychotherapist may provide to trained counsellors, therapists, or others in the caring professions, or to those who are training as such. Some of the questions I raise may not be as relevant to the psychoanalytic psychotherapist who acts in their capacity as a training supervisor, supervising a trainee within their own or another familiar training organization. However, I would suggest that some of the issues will apply equally to these situations. For ease of writing, when appropriate, I shall refer to the supervisor as *he* and the supervisee as *she* as a means of distinguishing between the two. I shall also use the term "patient", as used by psychoanalytic psychotherapists, although I am aware that supervisees who are in related fields, for example, counsellors, more frequently use the term "client".

I shall address some of the issues that should be considered by the supervisor before a supervision contract is entered into, and the questions the supervisor might have in mind when meeting a potential supervisee for the first time. Supervisors who are more experienced may nevertheless find some of the issues helpful when re-evaluating their role. I shall not necessarily be providing answers as these will differ from supervisor to supervisor, in the same way that each chooses the model of supervision they will use. I hold the opinion that it is as important to think about such issues at this early stage as it is to think about the related issues when undertaking an assessment interview with a patient, in order to consider the appropriateness of undertaking treatment with them. To enter into a supervisory contract with a supervisee that we later consider falls into that category of practitioner who leads to a "diminution of standards", when it should have been clear from the outset that this might be a possibility, leads to the tendency to blame the supervisee for our own neglect of addressing some of the issues I shall raise.

Some considerations prior to beginning a supervisory contract

Before a practitioner makes himself available as a supervisor, he has to have in his mind some idea as to whom he will work with and whom he will not. If the purpose of supervision is to enable a learning process, facilitating the professional development of the supervisee, then the supervisor has the responsibility to create such a learning environment. This cannot be done if the supervisor continuously feels critical towards the supervisee because he considers the supervisee is not serious about the work, has not undertaken an appropriate training of good standard, has not had a suitable analysis and so on. Further, the supervisor will only serve to undermine the supervisee, thus ensuring no professional development can take place.

It may be very tempting, when first enthusiastically setting out to undertake a supervisory role, to begin with a supervisee without considering these questions. In my experience of supervising those who supervise, there often comes a point when, in retrospect, there emerges the wish that such thinking had taken place at the outset. Of course, nothing can preclude the situation when, in an initial session, the supervisor's countertransference response to the person before them is so negative that, not withstanding his thoughts about this, he decides he could not form a working relationship. However, it is important to consider the following questions before meeting a supervisee for the first time:

1. Are we willing to supervise a supervisee who considers herself to be trained, but has actually undertaken a poor training? Is this willingness based upon the hope that during the course of supervision they will come to see the inadequacies of their training and will seek to undertake further training? What will we do if this insight is not gained?

2. If a potential supervisee has not made good use of what might be a reasonable or even good training, but they now work as a qualified practitioner, do we think it is better to supervise their work so that they have this opportunity to improve? Do we take the view that, as there are patients working with this practitioner, we must consider offering supervision as a means of monitoring this work for the patient's sake?

3. Are we willing to supervise work that is not of our own orientation but with a supervisee that might make use of our insights to enhance their own understanding? This might be in terms of theoretical underpinning or in terms of working with, say, social workers or psychiatric nurses.

4.   Are we willing to supervise work that might be different from our own in terms of, for example, short-term versus long-term work, or once weekly rather than intensive work? Are we willing to adapt our usual way of working to accommodate the supervisee, or do we leave it to the supervisee to adapt our ideas to facilitate their work?

All of these questions have an ethical dimension. If we are uncomfortable about supervising under any of the circumstances above but nevertheless make our own needs to supervise the priority, we begin without the respect for the person before us. As put by Jacobs, David, and Meyer (1995), it is important to create an atmosphere in which learning can take place.

> This can only be done if the supervisee feels that his teacher is sympathetic to and in tune with the obstacles to learning he is encountering. The trainee must feel that the supervisor will help him identify and overcome those obstacles without judging him. [p. 54]

So, while it is appropriate to help a supervisee think about areas that are lacking in their training or understanding, if in this initial stage we cannot tolerate the gap between what we consider to be an appropriate standard and the stage our supervisee has reached, it would be better not to enter into the contract. Furthermore, if we think we are able to tolerate this difference, we may also have to reconcile ourselves to the fact that the supervisee may never reach the standard we would hope for.

Having drawn his own conclusions in regard to the above, a supervisor will then need to reflect upon other aspects which may affect the way he works that are important in regard to the possible expectations upon him from a supervisee.

A supervisor has to consider whether he is interested in working only with the confined clinical space, that is, with the case material presented by the supervisee, or whether he is willing and interested in thinking about the context in which the work takes place and how this might impinge upon it. The potential supervisee might work, for example, in a GP's surgery, a hospital, a university counselling service, or a voluntary agency. Any impingement might be upon both the supervisee and upon their patient.

For instance, a therapist working in a GP's practice may be regularly faced with patients who come with the expectation of an immediate *cure*. This is, of course, something many patients do, but it may be emphasized in this setting, particularly if it is the GP who has made the suggestion of counselling. A further complication might be that the therapist finds the room in which the consultation takes place is changed without warning, or that a receptionist handles their appointment diary and makes changes with the patient without liaising with the therapist. A supervisor might need to question whether the supervisee has been able to set their own parameters, enabling them to work in a dynamic way. Is the supervisee able to take up what might be going on for the patient or do they take it all at face value? If they have not fully understood the necessity for boundaries, have not yet grasped the nature of the transference relationship, will they need additional help to make sense of these occurrences? However, it may also require the supervisor to help the supervisee find ways in which they can facilitate their work, which includes negotiating with other staff in regard to a suitable, consistent room, perhaps making changes to the room to make it more conducive to a facilitating environment. It may be important for the supervisor to find out how their supervisee's appointments diary is kept and whether they can negotiate more control over it. Will the supervisee need to "educate" a receptionist, so that she can understand why it is not helpful to say certain things to a patient that she might ordinarily do. In other words, the supervisor may have to provide a training input with regard to some of the basic requirements that enable psychodynamic work to take place. The supervisor may also need to recognize that there may be limits to the level of analytic work that can be carried out in such a setting.

A supervisee working in an educational context might face different impingements. Students seeking counselling may assume that the counsellor will be assessing them in the way that the entire university is doing, perhaps talking about them with their tutors. They may express hope that the counsellor will get them off their essay deadline or will make excuses for the failure of their examination. How does the counsellor respond to such expectations? Issues of confidentiality in such a setting are complex, and the counsellor also has to consider that the likelihood of meeting the student in the university corridor is much greater than working in other settings. If a supervisor is not interested in these things, and wishes to concentrate solely on the therapeutic encounter within the transference–countertransference relationship, they need to have this clear in their mind because it affects the kind of supervision they offer. The potential supervisee also needs to be made aware of this to avoid frustration on their part, which occurs when they feel the context in which their work takes place is misunderstood.

The supervisor also needs to consider whether they are interested in institutional dynamics. Do they wish to supervise on issues of management or the undertaking of tasks beyond the consulting room? For example, the supervisee who has to liaise with those in authority or who wants help with the management or even supervision of their own staff team.

Of course, such considerations also arise in private practice. A supervisor has to be alert to hearing when a supervisee's family impinge upon the consulting room, or the way that a supervisee handles possible interruptions of the doorbell or, indeed, the telephone.

The initial interview: individual supervision

Beginning with a new supervisee has many parallels with starting with a new patient. Even those who are well trained and have experienced supervision before may have received this supervision from a supervisor who works differently. The relationship begins from the moment of initial contact on the telephone. It may seem trite to say that we should state that we would like to see the potential supervisee for an initial session so that we can learn a something about them, their experience, and way of working. They can use the opportunity to find out how we work and how we might work together. Yet, all too often, there is an assumption made that making the appointment is synonymous with forming a contract. Of course, sometimes we already know of the person and therefore have already formed opinions about them and they about us. It is still important to have this initial session and clarify the contractual aspects to ensure there are no misunderstandings that might cause later difficulties.

This includes, importantly, the transferential aspect of the supervisory relationship. Grinberg (1997) states: "There is also the possibility of some interference in the task of supervision due to transference and countertransference problems on behalf of the supervisee and supervisor" (p. 2). Brown and Miller (2002), however, have drawn attention to the fact that, while we may think about the supervisor's countertransference response to their supervisee's patient, the actual transference–countertransference between the supervisory couple can often be ignored, but, they argue, as a result useful material that might help to understand the patient is lost. At this early stage, these two positions can only be reconciled if the supervisor is able to recognize the transference, and his own countertransference, using it not to make interpretations, as with a patient, but to assist clarification in his mind as to the type of professional relationship that might evolve with the person before him. As Berman (2000) has pointed out: "The supervisor–supervisee relationship is always a rich and complex transference–countertransference combination, even if the supervision is utterly impersonal; teachers are always a major focus of transference feelings" (p. 276).

The fact that the supervisory relationship is more "relaxed" than that of the therapist/patient—we are, after all, working with a (potential) colleague—also means that it can be harder to handle our own countertransference feelings, which nevertheless we have to do.

From the initial telephone call, we may already gain some indication of the difference between the reluctant supervisee and those that see supervision as an important aspect of their work. In regard to the former, discovering what this reluctance is about when we first meet with a potential supervisee is an important factor when considering whether we want to form an ongoing contract. There can be a number reasons for this reluctance. For example, with the advent of Continuing Professional Development (CPD), many such schemes require some form of supervision or clinical presentation. Is the supervisee seeking supervision simply to fulfil such a requirement rather than seeking it as a way of developing their practice for themselves? A training requirement may be seen as essential by the course but as a hurdle to be got through by the trainee. Perhaps the supervisee has not yet developed, indeed may never develop, a serious attitude towards the work. We may experience this as a devaluing of our work, and our feelings in this regard may get in the way of our being open to alternative reasons for the reluctance. For example, is their reluctance a defence due to an unresolved transference to an authority figure? There may be anxiety about feeling judged by a supervisor, in particular one who is to write a report of their work at some stage. We have to be mindful of the fact that the supervisee may be nervous and may express this by appearing diffident.

In contrast to the reluctant supervisee is one who comes across as very enthusiastic about the work and keen to begin supervision, but may be engaged in an idealized transference. This, too, can be problematic, in that they then may be so anxious to please the supervisor that they are easily knocked back by what they perceive to be negative criticism, or that they exclude aspects of work that they consider might be judged badly. They may lose their own ability to question or evaluate, locating all the good aspects within the supervisor. Ultimately, this can serve to undermine their confidence in their own abilities.

Assessing the potential of the supervisee to use what we have to offer can be difficult, but there are questions we can have in mind that can help us ascertain the willingness or otherwise of a possible supervisee, even though this cannot be foolproof.

If we know the person professionally, perhaps we are familiar with their training, we may already have some knowledge of how they work, how they think, etc. If they trained some time ago, we may be more interested in their work experience than their training. The following checklist is offered as a guideline and will need to be adapted. As in an assessment with a potential new patient, questions are in our minds but are not necessarily asked directly. If we begin by asking them to say something about what brings the supervisee to us, what they might hope to gain, we are inviting them to tell us a great deal. By the end of this first session we will want to know the following:

1. Is the supervisee trained? If it was recent, how did they experience this training, what particularly excited them? Are they able to talk about it creatively or do they merely provide us with a list of subjects covered?

2. How do they describe their theoretical orientation? This is important because some potential supervisees will say they are psychodynamic but it quickly becomes clear that their conception of what it means to work psychodynamically and our own may be very different. We then have to assess whether this is a failure of poor quality training, or whether they undertook a good training but could not grasp the basic concepts essential to psychodynamic practice. It is obviously a help to know of the course personally so that we can form opinions more quickly. However, because I want to know how they have assimilated their training, I always ask them to talk about it as if I do not know the course. It may be that a supervisee is unclear about their orientation; perhaps they have little or no training at the time they present to us, or they have had an eclectic training. We may feel that this precludes them, as we are only interested in working with someone who can easily grasp our ideas. However, it can be easier to work with a supervisee who is unclear about their orientation but who is open to ideas, than to work with a supervisee who is convinced they already know all there is to know.

3. What work experience has the supervisee had since completing their training? How do they talk about this experience? Do we gain any sense of thoughtful reflection upon their work?

4. Have they been, or are they in, their own personal therapy? What is the orientation of the therapist? If the therapist (or their training) has not been analytic I will then ask why they have chosen to come to see me. Do they think there might be difficulties in having the contrast between the therapist and supervision and sometimes even the training? The way they answer this helps me to discover how they have internalized their therapy, supervision, and training, and whether they have any real understanding of a theory that underpins their work. It may be that they are beginning to want to move in a more analytic direction and this is a way of doing it. It may also be that they are coming to me simply because I am the name they have been given by someone else.

The issue as to whether one should ask the name of the therapist is an interesting one. If we know of the therapist it will help us gain a further understanding of the similarity or difference between what we might offer and what they have experienced from being the patient. This is particularly important if the supervisee has undertaken a course other than psychoanalytic psychotherapy training. Will we, the supervisor, be expecting our supervisee to work at a level that they themselves have not experienced within their own therapy? The supervision I have felt most comfortable about giving has generally been with supervisees who are or have been in therapy and, conversely, the difficulties I have encountered in acting as supervisor have often been when the supervisee needs therapy. I agree with the view conveyed by Sedlak (1997),

> a therapist's work will deteriorate at the moment at which he is unable to deal with the countertransference in a professional, psychoanalytic manner. More specifically, it is when a negative countertransference is being experienced and cannot be managed that problems most frequently arise. This can be a greater handicap to the therapist and pose a greater risk to the therapeutic endeavour than the therapist's lack of knowledge of the finer points of the theory of psychoanalysis. [p. 25]

In this first session we are concerned about how the supervisee talks about their work, their ability to reflect upon it. Can they use a language congruent with the theoretical underpinning they say they use? Do they show a respect for their patients, do they understand what I would call the sanctity of the consulting room and the relationship they have with their patient? What is their understanding about confidentiality, boundaries and so on? In this first session I do not necessarily require that they talk about actual case material. We have not yet agreed to work together and might not do so. At this stage I am trying to gain a general picture.

As supervisors, we may not be concerned with whether the supervisee has all the theory at their fingertips, or if they have fully understood the transference relationship with their patient, making a useful interpretation at every appropriate moment. Would we not all like to do this! They are coming to supervision to learn and to gain a further understanding in their work with patients, which is the task of the supervisory process. Newly qualified counsellors, or trainee psychotherapists or counsellors rarely understand just how important they are to their patients and although they think they understand the transference, they do not. They know from their training that, for example, they should interpret issues around breaks but it takes a long and intensive training to grasp the full impact of the transferential aspects of separation anxiety. However, we do need to know that they have the potential to develop and what we might do if we think they do not.

The supervisor also needs to consider the way in which they will work so that they can tell the potential supervisee. In a supervisory relationship both have responsibilities, and the contract needs to include a clear statement of these as well as business arrangements. So, does the supervisor wish to work with transcripts of sessions and if so, how often? On each occasion, or just from time to time? Is he interested in hearing a case history of the client? Does he want written notes or more freely associated thoughts? Does he want to talk about one patient each session or does he expect the supervisee to talk about a number? Will he want to know about all the supervisee's casework and therefore ask them to bring patients in rotation, or will he expect the supervisee to bring what is of concern to them at any point in time? The supervisor needs to be clear about his preferred supervisory style in order to inform the supervisee of what is expected. All too often a supervisor can feel frustrated with a supervisee because they do not present their material in the *"right"* way. But how will they know what is right for the supervisor unless they are told? The inexperienced counsellor may feel concern to present all their cases, seeing the supervision as a check to ensure that they are helping each patient appropriately. It takes time to understand that the learning that goes on in the supervisory relationship is transferable from one patient to another.

The supervisor will also be concerned to leave time to talk about the practicalities of the contract; for example, timing, fees, how they will be invoiced, and whether missed sessions will be charged for. There are two aspects of confidentiality that will need to be discussed. The first is that offered by the supervisor. This is particularly important if reports to a training course are required. The second is how the supervisee wishes to preserve confidentiality within the supervision, while still being able to present the material in its entirety. It may be a false assumption that for supervisees who are experienced, all this will be known. The contractual terms of supervisors may differ. The supervisee's training may not have covered all these aspects. Indeed, many of our own trainings do not, relying on the trainee to internalize the practice of their analyst or supervisor.

The supervisor also has responsibilities, which they need to think of in advance of considering a supervisory contract. What will he do if a supervisee's work with a patient is unethical? Is it his responsibility to inform the supervisee's employer, if they have one, or their professional association via its ethics committee? Or does he simply refuse to work with the supervisee should such a stage be reached? It is becoming increasingly understood that "turning a blind eye" is unacceptable. If, having first taken up the matter with the supervisee to no avail, action needs to be taken, the supervisor can seek advice from his own Ethics Committee if he is uncertain about what course of action to take. He has, of course, the opportunity when working with a trainee to take this up with a Training Committee either directly or in the form of a supervisor's report.

We cannot, of course, always be clear in this initial meeting whether a good supervisory relationship will form, although from my own experience I suggest that we can begin to make differentiations at this early stage. When considering those supervisees who cannot make use of our form of supervision, Sedlak (1997) states:

> One recognizes such people in a relatively short period of time. Most notably, they have a great resistance to bringing process notes and undertaking close scrutiny of their clinical work. If one is prepared to take this up with them and, if necessary, terminate their supervision, then it is possible – although at the time unpleasant – to extricate oneself from a situation in which one feels one is colluding with something false or indeed even corrupt. [p. 37]

It may be that we have to keep this thought in mind so that we do not feel that once we have started a supervisory contract, we have to go through with it to the, sometimes, bitter end. This would not be satisfactory for the supervisor, and would also serve to further undermine the supervisee.

Specific issues in the supervision of trainees

The requirements in regard to both personal therapy and supervision for some psychodynamic counselling trainings have increased in recent years. The standard of training a therapist and supervisor is expected to have undertaken in order to be considered suitable for such trainees is also now higher. In many parts of the country, where psychoanalytic psychotherapists, (or psychoanalysts and Jungian analysts), are in short supply, requests for supervision may be frequent.

As a past trainer of counsellors for a number of years, I was struck by just how often a student would contact a supervisor and the latter would agree on the telephone to supervise them. If they had worked with a course before then at least they were familiar with it, but this was not always the case.

On the other hand, as a supervisor I have sometimes asked a trainee in the initial session if I am to receive a copy of the course handbook only to find this has surprised their tutor, who is not sure why I would want it.

So why did I? Well, it is important to know what is expected of us in terms of reports on students' work. Do we pass or fail them or just provide our opinion on their work? Does the course expect us to share any report with the student or keep it confidential? Does this view coincide with our own? Will we be expected to attend any meetings with the course? How does the course view clinical responsibility? Are we to be paid by the course or the student?

Trainees are understandably anxious about the assessment process and can feel very let down if the supervisor does not provide the necessary report or provides it late. It can feel to them that they will now fail their training on the grounds that we have not carried out our responsibility. They may have fantasies that it is because we think they are below standard, and this may be very far from the truth. If we have reservations about writing a report, we need to be clear about this at the outset. It is also important that we can give balanced feedback about the trainees' work. While it is important that we do not demolish the trainee by constantly focusing upon the negative, it is also important that we can verbally provide them with our thoughts about their work rather than putting our negative criticisms in a report that we hope they will not see. This will not facilitate their learning and leads to a sense that the supervisory relationship has been based upon a false premise. It is important that the supervisor has thought about these aspects of their relationship to the training before entering into a contract with the supervisee.

I also find it helpful to look at reading lists and the curriculum, what is taught when, so that I can have some idea about what the student might be expected to grasp or whether I will be talking beyond their present capacity for understanding. What are the course expectations in regard to what the student will eventually be able to achieve, in terms of their relationship with the client, the technique, and theory, etc?

We have to remind ourselves that, however well we get on with the student, we are also assessing their work. We would also do well to remember that we are also being assessed: by the student and by the course. In sharing our report on a trainee with the trainee, we need to be open to their feedback about us. An ongoing process for all our supervisory work is the capacity to assess ourselves as supervisors. As Casement (1985) comments:

> Just as we can see our own errors more clearly in others, so too in supervising others. Here there are endless opportunities for the therapists to re-examine their own work, when looking closely at the work of the person being supervised. Not infrequently, supervisors will be seeing reflections of their own difficulties with techniques. We do not always do as we teach other to do, but we can learn a lot by trying to do so. [p. 33]

Some thoughts about beginning a supervision group

Supervision is often offered in groups, and they too have a beginning. I will now discuss some particular issues that affect this beginning, which are not present in the same way within the individual supervisory relationship. I am going to focus upon the group as a training supervision group, rather than as a clinical discussion group for those who are already qualified, as the latter often consists of those who meet together to discuss their work without the use of a supervisor. Supervisors may offer a group to qualified practitioners, and supervision may be offered to qualified practitioners in a work setting with an external supervisor. Many of the issues I raise here in regard to working with trainees will also apply to the qualified group.

There are counselling trainings that rely solely upon group supervision. This will often take place within the course itself with a person appointed purely as a supervisor. This is distinct from trainings (in counselling or psychotherapy) that require individual supervision but also have clinical discussion groups within the course. If the clinical work is carried out in a placement, as opposed to private consulting rooms, a placement may have a number of trainees who are not necessarily from the same course.

If the supervisor sets up a group, he may well have the facility to interview each supervisee individually and select those he wishes to work with. If he works within the agency offering a placement to trainees, he can ensure some form of selection. Other members of his staff team may carry out the initial interview, and selection is made after consultation. In the same way that I do not think an individual training supervision should begin without some form of initial interview, leaving open the possibility that we may not form an ongoing relationship, so, too, I think it is important to make some form of selection in an agency setting. The same issues apply. However, an additional consideration may be whether the supervisee will fit in with a group. This can be difficult to assess in just one interview, and the group may be well established by the time it is apparent that a supervisee has such difficulties. It could also be argued that a group is well able to contain such a member, given time.

What must also be considered is the number of patients a group can realistically hold in mind. As Scanlon (2002) points out, while it is usually established that the number of members in a group will be between four and six, the more important factor is how many patients each will present. He suggests that a group cannot realistically hold in mind more than eight to ten, so that each group member may only have two patients any one time that they present to the group. This can present problems if a course requires of its trainees that they have more than two patients at one time, as many counselling trainings do. This may be resolved if there is also an individual supervisor, so that the supervisee can elect which patients to bring to the group. However, this may not be the case, and the supervisor needs to consider his options, which might include informing the course of his own restrictions, excluding him from running such a group.

When a supervisor takes on a group within a course, it is more usual that others have selected the members of the group. As a result, a supervisor may frequently find that his first encounter with the individuals concerned is when he meets the group for the first time.

While members of the group may be undertaking the same training, this does not mean that all are at the same level of understanding. If the group consists of people from different trainings, this will have a further effect upon the group. Some of these effects will be positive. Depending upon the sensitivity of the group, less able supervisees can be helped enormously by others in the group without the feeling of being judged by the supervisor. However, it can also be the case that when there is someone who is clearly of limited ability, frustration can be experienced by other group members, who then look to the supervisor to resolve the disparity. This often consists of a messianic hope that the weaker member will be transformed. Such difficulties may not be apparent in an initial session.

What can be quickly detected in a first session is the rivalry between members, and this can also extend towards the supervisor. If supervisees are all from the same course, rivalry may already be well established. Again, the transference to the supervisor may be apparent, which might be different for each individual but will also be collective for the group. Rivalry will be present in any group, but this might be made greater if the group members are not from the same training, as if each member is carrying a flag for their course. The supervisor can then be caught up, or perhaps out, by appearing to favour one course over another. A supervision group is as susceptible as any other group to operating on a set of basic assumptions (Bion, 1961).

Although a supervisor may have met each individual beforehand, this does not help him escape this initial jockeying for position. Whether he has or has not met members of the group before, introductions have to be made. If the group members have not met, this will include informing others about their training and something of their experience. Even when they are all on the same course, discussing something about their placement setting, or the number of clients they have, or do not have, begins to distinguish them from each other. It is important that a supervisor is aware of the tensions rivalry can bring within a group, because if this is not addressed within his mind (though not necessarily at this stage within the group), this may lead to a destructive envy rather than a healthy learning from one another.

In this first session it is important for the supervisor to set the ground rules, to say something of how he expects the group to work, and what will be expected of the individual members of the group. Group members often express an uncertainty as to whether their notes should be copied to each member of the group or whether they should use the name of the patient. What if someone in the groups knows one of their patients? Should they tell their patients that they are presenting their material in supervision? These concerns may be based upon an anxiety about presenting their work to others, but it is also a healthy concern about the important issue of confidentiality. Indeed, we might even think that absence of such concerns should raise anxiety within the supervisor because an ethical attitude towards our work is essential.

Dilemmas such as these provide the supervisor with an opportunity in this first session to give space for a discussion about these important ethical issues. They may help new trainees consider how they might disguise the material without losing much of its meaning, and how they might respect patient confidentiality while also using patient material to learn. In my view, supervision groups provide a useful forum for an ongoing discussion of the ethical aspects of our work when they arise in the material presented, as they inevitably will. There are no easy right or wrong answers to many of the ethical dilemmas that occur in our work. However, ongoing discussion helps us to form an ethical attitude in the same way as it helps us develop an analytic attitude. The two are, of course, synonymous.

The supervisor also has to let the group know if he wishes one member to present each session, or whether he is expecting to hear from all members of the group each week. If it is the former, will he leave space for urgent matters of concern from those not presenting? It is often the case that group members are worried that they will have to wait a long time before their anxieties can be discussed. In individual supervision, a supervisee has more choice about what she presents and when, but in a group, she will need to wait her turn. This anxiety is increased when the group is the sole source of supervision. From my experience, this anxiety usually disappears once a group has been running for some time. However, a supervisor will need to be alert to apparently urgent issues being used as a defence, so that session material is not presented, or is squeezed into a small space with little time left for exploration or discussion.

I consider that there are other issues that also need to be explored in this first session. Presenting in a group can be experienced as quite persecutory for the supervisees. If a group works well, it will not only be the supervisor who will be commenting on the material but also the group members. It is important for the supervisor to be thoughtful about how to present criticism, or how to pick up on the aspect that the presenter has missed. However, other group members, in their eagerness to demonstrate their knowledge and skill, may not be so sensitive to the person presenting. They may not take account of the fact that it is easier to see aspects of the transference when listening to case material, when countertransference feelings are at one remove. This can leave the presenter feeling rather demolished, particularly in the initial stages of the group. It may be helpful to talk about this with the group, reminding them that each will have their turn. The more rivalrous the group members, the more this might need to be addressed. A supervisor needs to be mindful of how a presenter is left at the end of a session.

An important aspect of group supervision is the potential for members to learn from each other. They will hear how others present their work, have the opportunity to think about how they might understand the material, and, it is hoped, they will be able to learn how to convey their understanding in a way which facilitates learning. However, it is important that the supervisor curbs his own need to rival his supervisees. If the supervisor feels that only he has the knowledge and only he can impart it, he will undermine his supervisees. It also means that he closes his mind to the possibility that he might learn from his supervisees, the scope for which, when a group is working well, can be considerable.

Summary

I have raised a number of questions which I think are important for a practitioner to consider before he offers his services as a supervisor. I also think it is useful to revisit them from time to time as a means of re-evaluating our work.

As the profession becomes increasingly engaged with issues of regulation and public accountability, the type of contract we set up with our patients is under constant review. However, the contract we set up with a supervisee can be neglected. As we have all been supervised, we may simply pass on this process to others. Although being supervised is an important learning process for the would-be supervisor, nevertheless we should be questioning why we choose a particular model of supervision, rather than just repeating the one provided. We should also be considering our responsibilities as a supervisor rather than waiting until something happens, calling them into question. Our thinking should include the issues that influence us in deciding with whom we wish to work.

We will need to convey something about the way we work to a new supervisee, and state what we expect of them, in addition to informing them about practicalities. This will hopefully enable them to use the supervision sessions fruitfully. Above all we must remember that how we present ourselves, how we convey our thoughts about the supervisee's work and how we conduct ourselves professionally, are all part of the learning process for the supervisee. They will be internalizing what is being offered and will pass this on in some form or another.

References

Berman, E. (2000). Psychoanalytic supervision: the intersubjective development. *International Journal of Psychoanalysis, 81*: 273–290.

Bion, W. R. (1961). *Experiences in Groups*. London: Tavistock.

Brown, L. J., & Miller, M. (2002). The triadic intersubjective matrix in supervision. *International Journal of Psychoanalysis, 83*: 811–823.

Casement, P. (1985). *On Learning from the Patient*. London: Tavistock.

Grinberg, L. (1997). On transference and countertransference and the technique of supervision. In: B. Martindale, M. Morner, M. E. C.

Rodriguez, & J.-P. Vidit (Eds.), *Supervision and its Vicissitudes* (pp. 1–24). London: Karnac.

Jacobs, D., David, P., & Meyer, D. J. (1995). *The Supervisory Encounter*. New Haven, CT.: Yale University Press.

Martindale, B., Morner, M., Rodriguez, M. E. C., & Vidit, J. P. (Eds.) (1997). *Supervision and its Vicissitudes*. London: Karnac.

Sedlak, V. (1997). Psychoanalytic supervision of untrained therapists. In: B. Martindale, M. Morner, M. E. C. Rodriguez, & J. P. Vidit (Eds.), *Supervision and its Vicissitudes* (pp. 25–37). London: Karnac.

Sedlak, V. (2003). The patient's material as an aid to the disciplined working through of the countertransference and supervision. *International Journal of Psychoanalysis, 84*: 1487–1500.

Scanlon, C. (2002). Group supervision of individual cases in the training of counsellors and psychotherapists: towards a group–analytic model? *British Journal of Psychotherapy, 19(2)*: 219–233.

Wiener, J., Mizen, R., & Duckham, J. (2003). *Supervising and Being Supervised – A Practice in Search of a Theory*. Basingstoke: Palgrave Macmillan.

CHAPTER TWO

Boundaries and confidentiality in supervision

Heather Wood

Introduction

There are wide variations in supervisory practice in the establishment and maintenance of boundaries. At the beginning of the encounter, one supervisor will receive a supervisee in silence and will wait for the supervisee to begin the work of the meeting; another will commence by asking the supervisee how they are; a third will offer coffee and social pleasantries. Each of these supervisors may have a rationale, based in psychoanalytic theory, for behaving in the way that they do. Different aspects of psychoanalytic theory can be used to justify a range of actions. Supervisors, therefore, face choices about the boundaries that they establish to protect and frame the supervisory relationship.

The boundaries of the supervision relationship relate to the formal arrangements between supervisor and supervisee. There is considerable variation in the way that even the practical aspects of this arrangement are managed—the regularity of supervision, flexibility over fees, the setting of the supervision, and the response to cancellations. The subject of boundaries also encompasses more qualitative issues: the boundary between therapy and supervision, between a social relationship and supervision, and between a teaching relationship and supervision. The literature on supervision reveals markedly differing views about where these boundaries should be drawn.

Before exploring some of the factors that might influence a supervisor's attitude to boundary issues, and some of the dilemmas faced by supervisors, I will outline two assumptions. The first is that supervision can be very anxiety provoking. At times, supervision can be an emotionally engaging, thought-provoking dialogue with a fellow clinician who shares a passion for the work and a curiosity about the complexity of the task. There are other occasions when the supervisor feels morally responsible, and may be legally responsible, for the care delivered to a disturbed patient who poses a risk to himself or others; the supervisor has not met the patient and so has only "second-hand" knowledge of the patient; the supervisee may be inexperienced, unfamiliar with the model or therapy, defensive or unreliable, and provides a very "muddy" filter between the supervisor and the patient. It can be very hard to know what belongs to whom in this triangular relationship. The supervisor is unlikely to have access to personal information about the supervisee that would enable her[1] to start to disentangle this complex web.

While the therapeutic task is a complex one, the supervisory task is multi-layered and at times, dauntingly complicated. Thus, supervision takes place in a tension between the potential for pleasurable learning, and the potential for anxiety, confusion and concern.

A novice therapist reported in supervision that her patient had become markedly more withdrawn as winter closed in and was expressing suicidal thoughts. She wondered whether this was an expression of Seasonal Affective Disorder. The supervisor did not know that the supervisee's father had died when she was five. The residue of this experience may have left the supervisee insensitive at times to the patient's feelings of abandonment, particularly when she, as therapist, was the catalyst for those feelings. As the Christmas break approached, the patient seemed disturbed and uncontained. The supervisor inferred that this reaction was connected with the break, but was unaware of the supervisee's contribution to this matrix of feelings.

The second assumption is that neither supervisor nor supervisee functions all the time in a rational mode. Gee (2003), outlining aspects of a code of ethics pertinent to supervision, comments that "While in an ego-oriented state these rules may seem almost puerile but we should never underestimate the power of the unconscious" (p. 164). A psychoanalytic approach to supervision is illuminating because it recognizes that we are all subject to unconscious forces that may compromise our professionalism. Boundaries cannot then be regarded as static principles of engagement, but become a dynamic element in a complex interpersonal relationship.

One response to this anxiety and uncertainty may be to seek rules. A superego injunction may appear to relieve anxiety and uncertainty. Issues of boundaries and confidentiality lend themselves to this kind of rule making—always do X and never do Y. Moreover, we work within a culture that places increasing emphasis on accountability, regulation, and the monitoring of practice. Such a culture fosters the creation of rules, guidelines, and protocols. These may at times become persecuting ideals rather than constructive guides. Rigid rules rarely encompass all possibilities and may impede thoughtful reflection on the issues. It may be more fruitful to try to contain anxiety and uncertainty while seeking to become aware of the unconscious forces and anxieties at work.

Why do boundaries matter?

While the role of clear boundaries may seem self-evident to psychotherapists, it may be worth reiterating the importance of boundaries in supervision. First, boundaries offer a secure frame to supervision. As in therapy, clear boundaries may enhance the sense of safety and containment that allows the exploration of sensitive, anxiety-provoking, and personal material. The supervisee may not be disclosing details of her personal life, but she is potentially risking feelings of incompetence, inadequacy, ignorance, guilt, and shame as she talks about the detail of her work. The regularity, privacy, and reliability of the supervision contribute to the necessary sense of safety.

Furthermore, if we minimize intrusions into the therapeutic space, there is more chance of being able to ascertain the unconscious sources of a patient's feelings. A consistent, predictable arrangement, which would not normally upset, provoke, or irritate the patient, provides the neutral backdrop against which it may be possible to discern why the patient is upset or angry on this particular occasion. In supervision, a supervisor who is late, unreliable, or takes phone calls during supervision may find it hard to know whether a supervisee's reported feelings of irritation with a patient originate in the consulting room or in the supervisory relationship.

Second, Langs (1994) argues that behaviour by the supervisor that breaks boundaries, implicitly sanctions rule-breaking behaviour by the supervisee in relation to their patient. A supervisor who is unreliable and regularly rearranges or cancels appointments at short notice implicitly communicates to the supervisee that this is acceptable professional conduct. Thus, Langs argues that the supervisor has a responsibility to model professional behaviour.

Third, carelessness with boundaries may represent "the thin end of the wedge". Schoener (1997) notes that, in patient–therapist relationships, excessive self-disclosure is the single most common precursor to therapist–client sex, although he does not specify the source of this finding. Seemingly innocuous flexibility with boundaries may be on a continuum with more frank breaches of ethical codes, and for a small minority of supervisors there may be a "slippery slope" from informality towards social relationships and subsequent intimacy with, or exploitation of, the supervisee.

Dimensions of difference in supervisory relationships

The model of therapy and supervision

Supervision is not a standard commodity. Different models of therapy invite different models of supervision. Even within the psychoanalytic tradition, brief, focused work may invite a more active, focused style of supervision than longer-term exploratory therapy. A supervision group with people who are also colleagues may invite a more informal, interactive style of supervision than private individual supervision of intensive therapy.

Models of psychotherapy supervision seem to vary on a continuum from those that view supervision as primarily an educational activity to those that regard it as a quasi-therapeutic activity. The former "tutorial" model focuses on the transmission of skills, knowledge, and understanding, whereas the latter "therapeutic" model emphasizes the establishing of a space in which unconscious processes can be considered, leading to the personal and professional development of the supervisee (see, for example, Mollon, 1997).

Many authors acknowledge both educational and exploratory components to supervision. Martin (2003) describes supervision as "more than teaching, less than therapy" (p. 143), and describes it as both a didactic and an emotional exercise.

Supervisors vary in the amount of teaching and advice that they offer and the extent to which they focus explicitly on affect and unconscious factors in the supervisee, the therapeutic relationship, and the supervisory relationship. Where we locate ourselves on this spectrum may have implications for our view of boundaries and the frame in supervision. Those who stress the similarities between supervision and therapy are likely to insist on clear, formal boundaries in supervision. Those who stress the differences between therapy and supervision may deliberately pursue more flexible boundaries in supervision. Grinberg (1997) insists that supervision is different from psychoanalytic psychotherapy because it does not stimulate regression, and recommends that every meeting between supervisor and supervisee begin with a brief chat to establish that this is a relationship between colleagues. Gee (2003) acknowledges that the relationship may border on the social, and Martin (2003) refers to those supervisors who always offer refreshments because they claim that coffee helps differentiate between an analytic relationship and supervision. In contrast, Langs (1994, 1997) believes that the maintenance of clear boundaries and the frame is just as important in psychoanalytic supervision as in psychoanalytic psychotherapy. His views will be considered in more detail under the heading "Pressures to breach boundaries in supervision", below.

The supervisor's perception of the personal and professional maturity of the supervisee

A further dimension affecting the nature of the supervisory relationship is the supervisor's perception of the personal and professional maturity of the supervisee. At one end of the scale are those supervisees whose clinical judgment and professionalism we can probably rely on, the "experienced colleagues". As supervisors we regard them as colleagues whose work we respect while recognizing that there is always a potential for a fuller or different understanding of the work. At the other end of the spectrum are "novice therapists", who are inexperienced in therapy, may not be in personal therapy themselves, and have not internalized a guiding model of psychotherapeutic work. They cannot be relied upon to respect boundaries or psychotherapeutic principles and may have limited capacity to contain their own reactions to patients. At times these supervisees may need to be treated with the care, secure boundaries, and vigilance that we expect to offer to patients.

These groups at either end of the spectrum require different responses from the supervisor. I would suggest that some significant errors in supervision occur when we misjudge where our supervisees are on this spectrum. In my experience, a therapist's position on this spectrum does not correlate exactly with professional status, stage in training, or chronological age. The term "novice therapist" is therefore used here to denote a quality of the supervisee rather than an absolute lack of experience.

> B was an NHS clinician whose interest in psychotherapy had developed relatively late in her career. Her extensive experience in other roles was evident in her equanimity and broad knowledge and the supervisor, younger by some years, valued her supervisee's expertise in specific areas, at times deferred to her, and related with the informality of colleagues. However, the supervisee had shortcomings: years of coping with challenging clinical situations without the support of a psychotherapeutic framework may have diminished her sensitivity; the subtleties of interaction with patients were often hard for her to grasp. The lack of formality and role reversal that occurred at times in the supervisory relationship may have made it more difficult to address these issues.

The supervisee's level of experience and competence

Of course, people do not stay at a fixed point on this spectrum. We would hope that in the course of their work all supervisees move from novice to colleague, and it may be appropriate to adapt our supervisory style accordingly. While there are risks of being too informal or unbounded with a novice supervisee, there are also dangers of treating someone like a quasi-patient when they are ready to be treated as an experienced colleague. They are likely to feel infantilized, resentful, and perhaps intruded upon and de-skilled. Szecsody (1997) alludes to this when she describes the supervisor's task in "holding" the trainee as "the establishment of a *phase-specific* security in the working relationship" (p. 107, my italics).

Boundary dilemmas facing the supervisor

The source and assessment of patients

When working within an organization such as the NHS, referral pathways are usually established and agreed and there may be cases waiting for treatment that have already been assessed. The supervisor's task is then to select an appropriate case based on some estimation of the supervisee's capacity. With a new supervisee this may be hard to assess, and there may be conflicts between the pressure to see the patient who has been waiting the longest and the desire to select a more suitable case from some way down the waiting list.

In private practice, the supervisor may have concerns about the source of the referral, whether the patient has been adequately assessed, and whether the supervisee will be working within the range of her competence. Supervisor and supervisee may disagree about the ethics or wisdom of receiving referrals from a particular source, such as the supervisee's own GP, or a colleague who is a personal friend of the patient. I have always worked in NHS services, where it is seen to be unethical to transfer NHS patients into one's private practice. I subscribe to this view, and would not want to supervise private patients who had previously been NHS patients of the therapist. I am also uneasy about supervising private therapy unless the therapist is either qualified to provide this particular type of therapy, or has a generic qualification (such as Clinical Psychology) that enables them to practice in a range of modalities, or is in training and providing therapy under the auspices of a training organization. I would be unwilling to supervise a case where the therapist was charging for a type of therapy that they had no qualification to practise. On other occasions I have agreed to assess or supervise a case where the patient is known or related to a colleague, and realized, too late, that the connections were more complicated than I had realized and probably precluded an absolutely neutral perspective on the work. Each clinician will have idiosyncratic "rules" about whom they will not supervise and treat; yet it is unlikely that any rules will protect us completely from occasional errors or conflicts of interest.

In a relatively large psychoanalytic community it may be possible to maintain a distinction between the roles of assessor and supervisor and to attempt to have the potential patient assessed by a reliable third party. When this is not practical, the supervisor may consider it responsible to assess the patient herself, but if she then deems the patient unsuitable for the supervisee, there is a risk that she will be seen to be depriving the supervisee of work and may evoke feelings of resentment. Even when an assessor has deemed a patient suitable, the supervisor may disagree; the supervisee may be relieved or feel thwarted in her desire to get on with the work.

Self-disclosure

For most therapists who work psychoanalytically, self-disclosure is usually avoided. The risk is that self-disclosure may introduce reality material into the transference that confounds the therapeutic process, may burden the patient with our response, or it may assume an identification with the patient that is misguided. In supervision it is also the supervisor's role to help the supervisee struggle with and contain countertransference difficulties without rescuing them through reassurance. However, as a supervisee I have greatly appreciated supervisors' self-disclosure about their own difficult cases. At select moments this has not offered an escape from the difficulties, but it has been enabling. When struggling with a patient who evokes feelings of being useless and inadequate, or a patient who evokes punitive or sadistic feelings in the therapist, it can be freeing to realize that a respected supervisor has also endured similar feelings in relation to specific patients.

Nevertheless, it is the supervisee's time. If the supervisor starts to elaborate the complex details of one of her cases the supervisee may soon feel that the supervisor is claiming the attention that is her due.

Brown and Miller (2002) recommend the judicious use of self-disclosure as a means of elucidating the three-way intersubjective matrix between patient, therapist, and supervisor. Theirs is an important point, and the difficulties of unravelling the contributions to this matrix cannot be underestimated. However, their account could also be read as a cautionary tale about the material that may be neglected when supervisor and supervisee become caught up in mutual self-disclosures within a "playful atmosphere" (p. 816). They describe an adolescent patient who starts missing sessions four months prior to the ending of four-and-a-half years of therapy. The therapist addresses the patient's sadness about ending, but only recognizes the patient's anxiety about growing up after supervisor and supervisee have shared their own dreams and feelings about haircuts, bald spots, shaving, and "coming of age". If supervisor and supervisee start to play with the rules which frame psychoanalytic interaction it may sometimes be illuminating but the risk is that the focus on the patient is lost. Sedlak (2003) cautions against the "megalomania" that may result in therapy and supervision when a preoccupation with the countertransference becomes detached from a focus on the patient's material. In his view the patient's material can be used as a basis for understanding the countertransference, but self-disclosure on the part of supervisor or therapist can and should be avoided.

It is also important to understand the supervisee's relation to authority. Will there be some triumph for the supervisee in hearing about their supervisor's failings or limitations? The supervisee may hear the supervisor's disclosures as a flaunting of her ability to manage difficulties. Self-disclosure may have a different quality and function with experienced colleagues, and with the novice therapist. With novice therapists I find myself more likely to make impersonal comments than to share personal experience. I think this reflects both a caution about rescuing them from anxiety, and an uncertainty about what they may do with the information. I may be less reserved as the supervisee gains experience and we become two colleagues discussing the challenges of difficult work.

Money and telephone contact

The exchange of money does not have to be addressed if both supervisor and supervisee are employed by the same organization. Within private therapy, the fee, increases in the fee, and the way that bills are paid, can become the focus for important issues about honesty and dishonesty, entitlement and grievance, grandiosity or feelings of impoverishment, envy, compliance, and defiance. The same transactions take place in private supervision, but it can be much more difficult to explore their meaning in this context.

A supervisor of mine once said to me—quoting, I believe, a supervisor of hers—"better [to be] a greedy analyst than a guilty analyst". What I understand by this is: it is better to be an analyst or psychotherapist who can take care of his or her own interests and bear her patients' wrath and resentment, than an analyst who is self-sacrificing and then feels resentful of or exploited by her patients. The latter situation is more pernicious.

However, when setting a fee in the role of supervisor, the clinician's judgment may be influenced by subtle identifications with the supervisee. Psychotherapists have all undertaken lengthy professional trainings, usually at considerable personal expense, and may sympathize with supervisees struggling with the multiple costs of personal therapy, course fees, and supervision, often relatively early in their careers when they have limited incomes and/or family commitments. The supervisor is unlikely to have access to information about the supervisee that would enable her to gauge the meaning of money and fees to this person. Balancing "guilt" and "greed" and judging how much to charge and how much to compromise are, then, subtle tasks.

There may be times, particularly when supervising psychotherapeutic work by clinicians untrained in psychotherapy, when the supervisor may make it clear that she may be contacted between supervision sessions if there is crisis or an immediate concern. It would be easier to make strict rules about keeping supervision within the boundaries of the allotted time, but this may not always be professional or responsible. However, being more flexible may allow enactments on the part of both supervisor and supervisee. Occasional telephone calls to seek advice or containment of anxiety may be on a continuum with more extended calls that effectively serve as a substitute for paid supervision. It may be clear that the supervisor should not charge for a ten-minute call and should charge for one of an hour, but what about a phone call of half an hour? It may be difficult to set clear boundaries about the type and length of calls that are considered appropriate.

Informality

Different attitudes to informality have been outlined above (p. 24 "The model of therapy and supervision") There are those who regard informality or sociability in supervision as a virtue, distinguishing this relationship from a psychotherapeutic relationship; for others, such as Langs (1994, 1997), it contaminates the serious work.

In my experience there are situations that invite more informality (such as group supervision of assessments or time-limited work with people who are colleagues) and situations that invite more formality (such as individual supervision of long-term intensive work, particularly when the supervisee is a trainee whose work is being evaluated). There are also supervisees, particularly those who have been supervised for a long time, with whom one can be relatively informal and it does not appear to jeopardize the supervisory task. There are others who bring considerable informality with them and I think it is then my task to be professional, bounded, serious, and alert to what is being enacted. When the supervisee is a novice therapist one feels particularly concerned for their patient, and the responsibility of supervision is felt very acutely. Informality at these times may be distracting, potentially seductive and misleading. Over-friendliness may serve as a defence against the anxiety felt by the supervisee and supervisor about the patient, the clinical work, or the supervisee's capacity to use and learn from the supervisor. Anxiety in supervision is discussed further in "The place of anxiety in supervision", p. 38.

Personal issues of the trainee

To what extent should the supervisor address issues that are personal to the supervisee, such as impingements from the supervisee's personal life or character traits and their impact on the work? In individual supervision, as opposed to group supervision, there is at least the possibility of exploring more personal issues, but where do you draw the line? Berman (2000) proposes that there is no personal topic that is out of place in supervision, and that knowing of a supervisee's impending divorce, a relevant childhood event, or a dream may all inform an understanding of the counter-transference and the intersubjective matrix. Sedlak (2003), in contrast, describes how, even when supervisees do communicate personal information,

> I try to file them away in a mental space that I try not to refer to either internally or in further supervisions. I believe that what I lose in forgoing interesting and illuminating facts is more than made up for by the sense that there is a proper distinction between the super-vision and the personal analysis. [p. 1498]

Sedlak emphasizes that it is the patient's material that can illumi-nate the aspects of countertransference that are pertinent to super-vision, and that personal knowledge of the supervisee detracts from this focus.

If supervisor, supervisee, and the supervisee's analyst or thera-pist do not have a shared understanding about what does and does not belong in supervision, there may be difficulties. Berman (2000) apparently used to attribute difficulties in supervision to the super-visee's resistance to supervision, but has increasingly come to regard these difficulties as reflecting the lack of a shared agenda that suits both members of the supervisory pair.

> A supervisor had a difficult supervisory experience with a supervisee who had a conspicuous physical disability and thought that issues about her disability and its impact did not belong either in the consult-ing room or in supervision. For her, this degree of self-reflection was intrusive and inappropriate. The supervisor felt that she could not function as a psychoanalytic supervisor if she was being asked to deny such an evident reality and the work between the pair proceeded uneasily.

Conversely, the supervisor may want to limit the self-disclosure of an uncontained supervisee and redirect her to a therapist. If the supervisor is concerned that the supervisee is not able to function professionally at a particular time, and is not taking appropriate steps to care for herself and make safe provision for her patients, the issue may become an ethical one of whether the supervisee should be reported to her professional body.

Confidentiality

Confidentiality is a complex issue that warrants extensive consideration, but I will touch on three aspects: the confidentiality of the material the patient brings, the confidentiality of the supervisory relationship, and confidentiality when the supervisor or others in the supervision group recognize the patient being discussed.

The supervisee must understand that they should never promise absolute confidentiality to the patient, which would preclude them discussing material with their supervisor. In this respect there should be no boundary around the patient–therapist relationship that excludes the supervisor.

In terms of the confidentiality of the supervisory relationship, this is often broken where there is an obligation on the supervisor to report to a training body, or where the supervisor also has a managerial responsibility for the therapist or the therapeutic work. In my experience this is unproblematic while the supervisee is making progress and their work is of a good standard. Reporting to others about the supervisee's work may not be ideal, but can usually be managed when the supervisee is made aware of what will be reported. For members of a supervision group, this would, of course, need to take place in an individual meeting with the supervisor. When faced with a supervisee whose work evokes concern, the supervisor's role may be compromised. Assessing, reporting, criticizing, and "policing" work that is causing concern, may be at odds with creating a safe and bounded space in which difficulties and anxieties can be addressed in the service of development and learning.

Langs (1994) simply vetoes reporting on supervisory relationships. However, when working within an organization or on behalf of a training organization, many supervisors do not have this option and the conflicts are at times uncomfortable. A supervisor, by virtue of her role, may be seen to be a source of judgement and criticism associated with Oedipal authority, superego functions, or more persecutory anxiety. Where the supervisor is reporting to a workplace manager or a training organization, the anxieties aroused may be amplified and these dynamics are even more likely to impinge on the working relationship.

Confidentiality may also be jeopardized when the supervisor or others in a supervision group recognize a patient being discussed. There are some situations when we recognize the patient being discussed that call for healthy splitting. All clinicians learn the art of not batting an eyelid when they need to be discreet. For example, the patient being discussed may be unaware that her partner is also known to the service, but clinicians may feel that they can manage this knowledge without compromising the patient's treatment. In clinical seminars or referrals meetings when a patient is recognized, the clinician may opt for decisive action and leave the room. For supervisors, the most difficult situation is where there is a growing realization that they have a connection with the patient that impairs their neutrality; the patient may be a distant relative, the partner of a colleague, or perhaps have a connection with the supervisor's own analyst or therapist. The supervisor may not wish to disclose to the supervisee why she no longer feels able to supervise this particular case. She cannot erase that which she has already heard; thus, boundaries may have been breached unwittingly before the supervisor recognized the patient. In large professional communities alternative supervisors might be available; in small communities this may be problematic. The supervisor may feel a conflict between her curiosity and professionalism. If the supervisor feels she has no choice but to terminate the supervision without explanation, the supervisee's curiosity will be aroused, fantasies may be stirred up and the supervisor risks being seen to be unprofessional. These are very difficult situations.

Pressures to breach boundaries in supervision

A psychoanalytic perspective casts light on some of the unconscious pressures to breach boundaries. Curiosity, perhaps founded on an early curiosity about the Oedipal couple, may be one of these forces. Langs (1994, 1997) places unconscious pressures to breach boundaries at the centre of his model of supervision.

For Langs, supervision requires a well-secured frame as much as psychotherapy. He looks for confirmation of this in the encoded, unconscious communications of the supervisee. In his view, the importance of interventions that secure the frame—refusing to change a supervision time, or to agree to a reduced fee—will be unconsciously confirmed when the supervisee proceeds to talk about safe and creative spaces, well-functioning individuals, and so on. He insists that secured frames are containing, holding, and growth- and health-promoting. They also arouse anxiety; being within a securely bounded space can evoke fears of entrapment and annihilation. Thus, there may be constant pressures to break the frame.

Langs believes that the basic ground rule is that life is bounded by death. He argues that rule-breaking has unconscious reverberations, creating illusions of omnipotence and immortality. "The rule-breaker unconsciously believes that he is the exception to all rules, especially the fundamental existential rule of life—that death is the inevitable outcome" (1997, p. 131). In Langs' view, frame-breaking behaviour by a supervisor disturbs the work and the learning of the supervisee and implicitly encourages and sanctions the supervisee to break the frame in his or her therapeutic work.

Langs (1994) writes quite emphatically that supervision should always occur on an individual basis; he discourages the use of consulting rooms in the home or in a place of work shared with the supervisee; he would prefer that there had been no prior contact between the supervisee and supervisor; he argues that no written record of the supervision should be preserved, confidentiality should be absolute, and efforts on the part of the supervisee to renegotiate the fee or the time should be resisted. Self-disclosure on the part of the supervisor is seen as "human but hurtful" to the supervisory process and to be avoided.

Langs appears to be describing the supervision of qualified, responsible analysts or psychotherapists, where the supervisor has no formal responsibility to maintain standards, no legal responsibility for the care delivered to the patient, no obligation to report on the work of the supervisee, and no pressure to accommodate the demands of an organization.

Many of us work in settings where it is impossible to adhere to these exacting requirements. Supervision often has a managerial component. We may be asked to supervise people who work for the same organization as we do, whom we see in meetings and other contexts as colleagues. Often, group supervision is the norm for reasons of economy; there are also significant gains from shared learning. Failure to keep some documentary record of the supervision might be seen to be unprofessional or careless. If a patient makes a complaint to the organization about the treatment they have received, the supervisor's notes may be important in ascertaining what may have gone wrong and whether the supervisee was acting according to advice.

Even if Lang's recommendations are not followed to the letter, his ideas are valuable in alerting the supervisor to the latent content of the supervisee's communications.

> A supervisor extended her summer break by a week because she was unwell. On her return, a supervisee, C, brought to supervision a patient whom she felt she had lost contact with over the summer, who seemed very withdrawn, and who, in his withdrawn state, failed to arouse C's interest or to engage her. Supervisor and supervisee talked about the therapist's lack of availability to the patient over the summer and the supervisor pointed out her lack of availability to C, and how this might have left C feeling forgotten and uncontained. C verbally endorsed this, but then went on to provide unconscious confirmation of this idea. Rather abruptly, she changed the subject and told her supervisor about someone she had been trying to assess who kept cancelling sessions. She was exasperated with the patient, who had phoned after the last missed session to say he was unwell. C found this unconvincing, and was tempted to close his file and not to persevere with him. The supervisor was left wondering whether *her* illness had been "unconvincing", leading to C becoming disheartened about being held and contained in her work, with consequent loss of interest in her patients. Through exploration of these issues C's characteristic interest in her work was quickly restored. If this resentment had not been articulated, C was a supervisee who probably would have recovered her interest and commitment spontaneously, but this might have taken longer, she might have given up on the errant patient in the meantime, and an opportunity for understanding would have been missed.

Langs focuses on the anxieties about and the denial of death as the principal pressure to breach boundaries in supervision, but there may be other pertinent issues. Martin (1997) cites Money-Kyrle's (1978) stipulation that there are three "supremely important" facts of life: the existence of the breast as a good object, the fact of parental intercourse, and recognition of time and the inevitability of death. Martin focuses on the supervisor's role in helping the therapist to help the patient to recognize these primal facts of life. It may be valuable to reflect on how these facts of life may impinge on the supervisory relationship.

A supervisee who had accepted the existence of the breast as a good object would presumably be able to use and internalize the expertise of the supervisor in a constructive "feeding" relationship without feeling envious, humiliated, or wanting to spoil, attack, or denigrate what is offered. A supervisee who had fully accepted the implications of parental intercourse would presumably be able to accept the authority of the supervisor, the procedures he or she recommends, and the private relationship that may exist between the supervisor and the training organization or manager without wanting to intrude into this relationship and without feeling persecuted by being excluded from it. Someone fully able to recognize time and death would presumably be able to tolerate being in the "juvenile" position of a learner, knowing that they will grow and develop although they will never be omnipotent or omniscient.

In the likely event that a supervisee had not fully worked through these facts of life, their own unconscious struggles may impinge on the supervision. Grinberg (1997) lists a number of problems that may occur with the supervisee: manic attitudes, envious attacks, rivalry, omnipotence, or defences against the "intrusions" of the supervisor's contribution. It is possible to see many of these problems as related to the anxieties aroused by these "facts of life". Because of the nature of the supervisory relationship we often never know what lies behind a particular supervisee's difficulty in learning or accepting the boundaries of the supervisory relationship. We may be aware of chaotic behaviour, heightened anxiety, and defensiveness or rivalrous challenges to the supervisor. The dynamics underpinning these behaviours usually remain obscure.

Supervisors are, of course, not exempt from these pressures. A colleague recently reflected that she had wondered whether a former supervisor used to talk so much because she had had to be so silent with her patients. In a profession that calls for self-restraint and "abstinence" on the part of the therapist, providing supervision may seem like a welcome opportunity to be more spontaneous, interactive, and talkative. It may offer an opportunity to exercise our knowledge and understanding, thereby providing a relief from the helplessness and lack of comprehension that may prevail in the consulting room in the immediacy of the session. Beyond this, there is undoubted narcissistic gratification in demonstrating our insight and expertise, and some satisfaction in being the Oedipal "authority" or the "good breast", and not the vulnerable "child" in relation to these two. The supervisor may be prey to the manic denial of boundaries and constraints, and think that, on this occasion, there would be no harm in breaking a "rule", whether it be to change a supervision session for her own convenience, to be more personal and self-disclosing than usual, or to deliver a speech on a favourite subject.

Langs insists that the repercussions of these boundary violations are always severe and far-reaching. In my experience, there are some supervisees with whom they seem to matter considerably more than with others. Caruth (1990) notes two of many potential mismatches that can occur between supervisee and supervisors: when a supervisee who is passive and idealizing is matched with a supervisor who is driven to demonstrate their omniscience; and when a supervisee who is covertly engaged in Oedipal rivalry is matched with a supervisor who is eager to be "pals" and to eliminate the generation gap. The subtle intermeshing of the supervisor's failings and the supervisee's vulnerabilities may amplify the impact of any boundary violation.

The place of anxiety in supervision

Nerwith (1990) suggests that one of the primary concerns in supervision is to assist the supervisee in overcoming their anxiety in the psychotherapeutic situation. Nerwith discusses three types of anxiety: "schizoid" anxiety, evoked by feeling abandoned by the supervisor and alone in the room with the patient, "paranoid" anxiety as boundaries between patient and therapist become permeable and the therapist becomes the recipient of projections, and "depressive" anxiety when the therapist recognizes their own hostile feelings towards the patient.

This raises the question whether it is our role as supervisors to contain our supervisees' anxiety, or to address uncomfortable issues that may lead to them becoming more anxious. A colleague recently told me that in her first year of training as a Clinical Psychologist she had had two supervisors. With one she had an adult-to-adult relationship, the supervisor gave good advice, strengthened her confidence, and reduced her anxiety. The other supervisor she described as more maternal. This supervisor behaved more like a therapist, drawing out her anxieties so that the trainee felt more anxious and vulnerable. I was curious to know with whom she felt that she had learned more: with the maternal therapist–supervisor, the one who "taught" her less.

I suspect that this supervisor recognized that this was a resourceful trainee who could cope with a degree of regression in this supervisory situation, enabling her learning to be anchored in affective experience. In contrast, Mollon (1997) recognizes that there are supervisees for whom anxiety interferes with reflective thinking. He then sees his role as fostering a sense of safety, so that the supervisee will feel able to think and talk freely about her experience with the patient without fear of humiliation.

I would suggest that one of the ways in which this is achieved is through the subtle regulation of the boundaries of the supervisory relationship. At times the supervisor may shift to a formal, challenging, therapeutic style of interaction, potentially increasing the supervisee's anxiety; on other occasions, or with other supervisees, a creative space may be achieved through the establishment of a more informal, supportive, or educational style of interaction. But where there is room for discretion, there is scope for error. The risk of exercising discretion is that the supervisor misjudges the optimal conditions for a particular supervisee, and fails to offer sufficient challenge to a highly defended supervisee, unwittingly endorses frame-breaking behaviour by an unbounded supervisee, or offers an environment that is experienced as persecutory, claustrophobic, or inhibiting by the highly anxious supervisee. Part of the challenge and pleasure of supervision is that it is highly complex work requiring subtle judgements, vigilance, and care.

Conclusions

To conclude, I would make three observations. The first is about contracts. Should we use contracts with supervisees, in which ground rules about boundaries and confidentiality are clearly established? The message that Langs communicates very clearly is that we are all subject to unconscious pressures to break the frame, to breach boundaries, and to break out of a safe but potentially "trapping" secure relationship. It is only when we recognize and understand these pressures in ourselves that we can exert some conscious choice and behave in a bounded way. An explicit contract might help us to keep boundaries in mind and on the agenda, but it is not a substitute for self-awareness and constant self-scrutiny. A contract might be helpful in as much as it draws attention to the importance of boundary issues; it can be unhelpful if it fosters the illusion that boundary issues have thereby been dealt with.

Second, I have learned from my supervisory experiences to err on the side of caution, especially in a new supervisory relationship. If, as a supervisor, you commence with informality and excessive flexibility, it is very hard subsequently to introduce formality and restraint.

Finally, I would agree with Langs that, with a supervisee who can tolerate an increase in anxiety, a formal, bounded supervisory space might allow the most profound learning. I also hold that for some supervisees at some points in time, a more informal, adult-to-adult supervisory relationship has a place in fostering personal development and expertise in psychotherapy.

Acknowledgements

I would like to thank members of the BAP's Supervision Courses in London and Dublin whose comments about these issues have contributed to my thinking. Also, thanks to Ruth Berkowitz, Eric Karas, Alessandra Lemma, and Stephen Blumenthal for helpful comments on an earlier draft of this chapter.

Note

1.   For convenience, and to reflect the fact that women are more numerous in the profession of psychotherapy, feminine pronouns will be used to refer to all supervisors and supervisees and male pronouns will be used to refer to all patients.

References

Berman, E. (2000). Psychoanalytic supervision: the intersubjective development. *International Journal of Psychoanalysis, 81*: 273–290.

Brown, L. J., & Miller, M. (2002). The triadic intersubjective matrix in supervision. *International Journal of Psychoanalysis, 83*: 811–823.

Caruth, E. G. (1990). Interpersonal and intrapsychic complexities and vulnerabilities in the psychoanalytic supervisory process. In: R. C. Lane (Ed.), *Psychoanalytic Approaches to Supervision* (pp. 181–193). New York: BrunnerMazel.

Gee, H. (2003). Boundaries in supervision. In: J. Wiener, R. Mizen, & J. Duckham (Eds.), *Supervising and Being Supervised. A Practice in Search of a Theory* (pp. 151–166). Basingstoke: Palgrave Macmillan.

Grinberg, L. (1997). On transference and countertransference and the technique of supervision. In: B. Martindale, M. Morner, M. E. C. Rodriguez, & J.-P. Vidit (Eds.), *Supervision and its Vicissitudes* (pp. 1–24). London: Karnac.

Langs, R. (1994). *Doing Supervision and Being Supervised*. London: Karnac.

Langs, R. (1997). The framework of supervision in psychoanalytic psychotherapy. In: B. Martindale, M. Morner, M. E. C. Rodriguez, & J.-P. Vidit (Eds.), *Supervision and its Vicissitudes* (pp. 117–134). London: Karnac.

Martin, E. (2003). Problems and ethical issues in supervision. In: J. Wiener, R. Mizen, & J. Duckham (Eds.), *Supervising and Being Supervised. A Practice in Search of a Theory* (pp. 135–150). Basingstoke: Palgrave Macmillan.

Mollon, P. (1997). Supervision as a space for thinking. In: G. Shipton (Ed.), *Supervision of Psychotherapy and Counselling* (pp. 24–34). Buckingham: Open University Press.

Money-Kyrle, R. (1978). *The Aim of Psychoanalysis: The Collected Papers of Roger Money-Kyrle*. D. Meltzer & F. O'Shaughnessey (Eds.). Perth: Clunie Press.

Nerwith, J. W. (1990). The mastery of countertransferential anxiety: an object relations view of the supervisory process. In: R. C. Lane (Ed.),*Psychoanalytic Approaches to Supervision* (pp. 157–164). New York: BrunnerMazel.

Schoener, G. R. (1997). Boundaries in professional relationships. Paper presented to the Norwegian Psychological Association, September 1997. www.advocateweb.org.

Sedlak, V. (2003). The patient's material as an aid to the disciplined working through of the countertransference and supervision. *International Journal of Psychoanalysis, 84*: 1487–1500.

Szecsody, I. (1997). (How) Is learning possible in supervision? In: B. Martindale, M. Morner, M. E. C. Rodriguez, & J.-P. Vidit (Eds.), *Supervision and its Vicissitudes* (pp. 101–116). London: Karnac.

CHAPTER THREE

The ethics of supervision: developmental and archetypal perspectives

Hester McFarland Solomon

Introduction: integrating the ethical attitude in analytic practice

This chapter argues that the provision of ongoing supervision, peer supervision, or consultation helps to ensure, among other important functions, reliable access to ethical thinking in analytic practice. This does not in any way preclude the importance of, or suggest the lack of, an ongoing, active internal capacity for ethical thinking or an internal supervisory function that comes through the processes of internalization of the analytic attitude during the course of training and post qualification professional development. I am, however, advocating the expectation that analytic practitioners be aware of the need for constant attention to the ethical dimensions of their clinical work, and that this may best be fostered by supervision as a present factor in clinical practice.

The struggle to keep ethical thinking integral to clinical work and the theory building that develops out of clinical experience requires sustained diligence and is particularly needed in those areas of our analytic and therapeutic practice where we are likely to be the most tested as clinicians. The function of the ethical attitude in clinical practice is not simply a matter of a set of rules that can be forgotten as long as they are not contravened in the clinical setting. I have argued in other contexts (Solomon, 2000b, 2002) that the ethical attitude is integral to all our activities and relationships as human beings as well as clinicians, and especially to that most intimate, intense, and demanding of relationships, the analytic relationship. Since the time of the Hippocratic Oath, professional Codes of Ethics and Codes of Practice state the practitioner's commitment to ethical practice and the principles that underpin it.

In this chapter I will explore the role of supervision in helping to maintain ethical thinking and practice in clinical work. I refer to the terms supervision (in which a younger practitioner, often a trainee, seeks regular, often weekly, supervision on one patient seen intensively, and where a fee is paid to the supervisor by the trainee), consultation (which usually refers to two colleagues, one senior and one junior, who discuss, regularly but not necessarily weekly, patients or clinical issues, and where the senior colleague receives payment from the junior one), or peer supervision (often in a small group of colleagues who are more or less at the same level of clinical experience and where payment is not involved, who meet regularly but not necessarily weekly). Unless there is a specific point of differentiation to be made between these modalities, for the purposes of this chapter I will use the term "supervision" to cover all three.

Crucial to my argument is the view that the analytic attitude is in essence an ethical attitude, and that the achievement of the ethical attitude is tantamount to the achievement of a developmental position. Here, "developmental position" is meant in much the same way that Klein or Bion had in mind when they referred to the paranoid–schizoid or the depressive positions as stages in the developmental process. Much of the argument of this chapter will revolve around the notion that the ethical attitude, like the paranoid–schizoid and depressive positions, is not a once-and-for-all achievement, but rather is part of an internal human dynamic that is experienced alongside and in relation to more primitive and sometimes more dangerous states of mind. Hence, just like the depressive position, the achievement of an ethical attitude can be considered in developmental terms, which requires mental effort, in particular, conscious effort, to sustain. This perspective has much to offer when we think of the importance of an ongoing supervisory function in the practitioner's clinical work as offering a place where that conscious effort is shared and reinforced.

The view that I set out in this chapter incorporates the role of both developmental and archetypal perspectives in the understanding of the achievement of ethical thinking through the supervisory function. Alongside the triangular developmental perspective of achieving an ethical attitude, in whatever way that may be accomplished (this chapter focuses on the role of supervision in this achievement), there lies the archetypal nature of the triangular relationship underpinning the achievement of the mental capacity for ethical thinking.

Achieving an ethical attitude: a developmental model

It is a truism that it is not possible to be ethical in a vacuum. The ethical function is a relational function involving the assessment of subjective and intersubjective states. Jung pointed out (Jung, 1958 [1964], pars 371–399) that it is ubiquitous and hence has a collective dimension, while at the same time being experienced most vividly at the personal level. In thinking about the development of the young mind and how an ethical attitude might come into being, the Kleinian model shows that, because of the massive onslaught of internal and external stimuli on its limited mental capacities, the infant is at first suffused with psychotic states of mind that may cause profound anxieties, particularly if the holding environment is deficient and unable to process such states. These anxieties are primarily managed defensively through splitting and projection. Communicating, relating, and using the other psychodynamically often take place through projective identification (Klein, 1946). Hence, self and other are mixed up, and parts of each are allocated to different and separate psychic locations, either internally or externally, in the self or in the other. Klein called this the paranoid–schizoid position, where the perception and experience of the bad and good parts of the self and the other are not psychically found together, and where relating is at the level of part objects, because the young mind is not as yet capable of holding together opposite affective states. In a later development, called the depressive position (Klein, 1935), the infant or child is more able to experience the other as a whole object, separate from the self, and containing both good and bad aspects. Thus, the child's feelings of love and hatred for the object, which had previously been split off and experienced as separate, are now capable, at times, of being held together in the infant's mind, giving rise to feelings of ambivalence towards the object, as well as feelings of guilt and the wish to repair the damage that the self might have wreaked on the object in the previous, part object mode of relating. In elaborating how this dynamic occurs, Britton (1998) has made a helpful contribution in offering a model which involves the circularity of the dynamic movement between the paranoid–schizoid and the depressive positions, such that each new cycle builds on the experience of the previous ones. Schematically, this has similarities with Fordham's model of deintegration and reintegration (Fordham, 1957).

In thinking in developmental terms about what are the conditions that foster an ethical capacity (Solomon, 2000a,b, 2002), I have suggested that it is through the combination of the infant or child's earliest experiences of devotion and reflection by the parental couple, who maintain the ethical attitude in relation to their infant or child, and that it is this combination that is eventually internalized by the child and is activated as the self and ego develop in dynamic relation, eventual internal parents in the psyche. The first stirrings of a nascent ethical capacity occurs as the infant experiences being the recipient of the non-talionic responses of the parental couple in face of his or her various states of distress, including rage and dread. Under the right conditions, the infant's experience of the parent's non-talionic responses is eventually internalized and identified with, and becomes the basis for gratitude. The idea of the ordinarily devoted parent, mother or father, represents a deeply ethical mode in their instinctual and unconditional devotedness to another, their infant, overcoming their narcissistic needs and frustrated rages, their shadow projections, and resisting by and large the impulse to skew their infant's development through requiring undue acquiescence.

Later they will leave this state of primary preoccupation and devotedness and will begin the processes of socialization that are so necessary a part of ethical development—the capacity to say, in different ways, "no", thereby establishing boundaries and expectations of self regulation, including those in relation to others. Thus, with the image of ordinary devotedness to a nascent self I am combining the notion of the discriminating and thinking function of the masculine principle, evoking a notion that appears in various guises in psychoanalytic and Jungian analytic literature, that of the creative potential of the third, whether a third person, a third position, or a third dimension. The activation of an archetypal potential for eventual ethical behaviour thus will be reinforced in ordinary good enough situations by caregivers capable of sharing acts of thoughtful devotedness and of empathic and devoted thinking about their infant. This has a clear parallel with what happens in the consulting room, where the analyst's willingness to go on sacrificing their own narcissistic needs through the sustained activity of thoughtful devotedness to the patient that we call the analytic attitude protects the patient so that they may develop and grow according to the needs of their self.

From dyad to triad: the eventual achievement of triangulation

I am conjecturing that the internalization of and identification with the agapaic function of the parental figures in their empathic holding as well as their thinking and discriminating aspects can trigger or catalyse a nascent ethical capacity in a young mind, the first steps of which include those primitive acts of discriminating good and bad that constitute the foundations of splitting and projection. Early (as well as later) splitting and projecting may be, therefore, instances of primitive moral activity, what Samuels (1989) calls original morality—the expulsion from the self of what is unwanted and felt to be bad into the other, where it is identified as bad and eschewed. Even in situations where the good is split and projected, it is in the service of maintaining a discriminating, but highly defensive, psychic structure. This is a two-dimensional internal world, in which primitive psychic acts discriminate good from bad experience and split the bad from the psyche by projection into the caregivers—a first, primordial, or prototypical moral discernment prior to the state where there is sufficient ego strength for anything resembling mature moral or ethical behaviour to arise. This constitutes the very preconditions for the creation of the personal shadow, which eventually will require a further ethical action of reintegration when the person has achieved an internal position of moral and ethical capacity.

As we posit, following Fordham (1969), the self as a primary integrate, autonomous but very much in relation to another or others, so we are alone as moral beings while at the same time finding our moral nature in relation to others. To truly find another represents a transcendence of narcissistic ways of relating in which the other is appropriated for use in the internal world, denying the other's subjective reality. To live with the implications of this capacity to recognize and relate to the truth of the other is a step in the development of—and perhaps eventually beyond— the depressive position. The depressive position is usually considered to contain acts of reparation through guilt and fear that the object may have been damaged and therefore may be unable to go on caring for one's self (Hinshelwood, 1989). As such, acts of reparation remain contingent on preserving the other for the benefit of the self. The ethical attitude envisaged here goes beyond this contingency and suggests a non-contingent realm of ethical behaviour. This situation has direct implications for what transpires in the consulting room between the analytic couple (see previous discussions in Solomon, 2002).

This represents a two-stage, dyad-to-triad process that reflects the two-stage developmental process in the infant (the neurophysiological implications are also considered in Solomon, 2000a) in which the neural development of the infant's brain post partum must be matched by a parallel nurturing provision such that (i) at first infant and mother are highly attuned (a "me–me" relationship); and (ii) where, later, there follows complementary and compensatory discriminations (a "self–other" relationship). The differentiation would then be between when to be "caring" and flexible and when to be "tough" and resilient, both of which have implications for the interactions in the consulting room. Just as the analyst can have a two-stage developmental relationship with their patient, so the intensive dyadic work would have a counterbalancing relationship created by the triangular space of supervision.

In this developmental framework, it is evident that there evolves a gradual demarcation between self and other, including an enquiry about how the self individuates from out of a projective and identificatory mix-up between self and other, through to a fuller experience of the reality of the self's subjectivity in relation to the reality of the subjectivity of another. This is the beginning of the capacity for triangulation, that "theory of mind" (Fonagy, 1989) that the child has achieved when he or she is aware that their thoughts and those of the other are separate and not available directly to each other (as assumed in states of fusion or identification), but only through reference to a third perspective. As Cavell has described:

> . . . the child needs not just one but two other persons, one of whom, at least in theory, might be only the child's idea of a third . . . the child must move from interacting with his mother to grasping the idea hat both his perspective on the world and hers are *perspectives*; that there is a possible third point of view, more inclusive than theirs, from which both his mother's and his own can be seen and from which the interaction between them can be understood. [Cavell, 1998, pp. 459–460]

Jungians would amplify this view by addressing the difficult but necessary work on the withdrawal of the projections of those negative aspects of the self, called shadow projections, through to a gradual capacity to view the self along with the other as separate but interrelated subjectivities with multivariate motivations, including shadow motivations that project the bad outside one's self. The withdrawal of shadow projections, predicated on the realization that the other is truly other and not assumed to be a function or aspect of the self, which otherwise might sully the gradual more mature experiences of intersubjectivity, underpins the ethical attitude. As such, it is a developmental achievement that derives from an innate potential, activated at birth, and fostered by the continuous "good enough" experience of living in an ethical environment. It represents a constant struggle through acts and attitudes that are against the natural selfish inclinations of the self, acts which are *contra naturam*, forgoing insistence on the self's limited perspectives in order to encompass a wider view, including the recognition of that which is not ethical within the self. In Jungian terms, that recognition represents the integration of the shadow back into the self, steps towards incremental advances in the self's movement towards greater states of integration and wholeness. This is the individuation process, and it is predicated on a teleological view of the self in which the self's capacity for change, growth, and development are understood and experienced as being suffused with a sense of purpose and meaning.

Triangulation: the archetypal third

In 1916, a short time after the split between Freud and Jung, when he was suffering what might be described as a psychotic regression in the face of his loss of Freud, who represented the centrally organizing psychic function of the father figure he had never had before, Jung wrote two landmark papers that can appear to be diametrically opposite in content and form: "VII Sermones ad mortuos" ("Seven sermons to the dead") and "The transcendent function". The former was published at the time, but not in a separate English edition until 1982, whereas the latter was not published until 1958, only a few years before Jung's death in 1961. Both reflect, in different ways, the immediacy of Jung's distressing and threatening psychic experiences that arose from Jung's self analysis, undertaken, as Freud's self analysis, on his own. At the same time, Jung continued to function as Clinical Director of the Burgholzi Hospital in Zurich and also fathered a growing family. If the tone of the "Seven sermons" was that of a chilling account of the horrifyingly vivid psychic experiences he endured at the time of his "confrontation with the unconscious" (1961, p. 194), that of the "Transcendent function" was of a measured, scientific contribution to analytic theory building, which he compared to a "mathematical formula" (Jung, 1916 [1958/1960], par. 131), and which we could interpret as a dispassionate exteriorization of his highly emotive internal state at the time; a kind of self supervision. In this paper, Jung set out an archetypal, deep structural schema of triangulation in which he demonstrated that psychic change occurs through the emergence of a third position out of an original conflictual internal or external situation, the characteristics of which cannot be predicted alone by those of the original dyad. In relation to this idea, it is interesting to note that the philosopher and psychoanalyst, Marcia Cavell, who has recently put forward the idea of triangulation in a psychoanalytic context, refers to Polanyi's notion of "emergent properties" in much the same manner as that pertaining to the dialectical nature of the transcendent function, that is, as "properties that in a developmental process arise spontaneously from elements at the preceding levels and are not specifiable or predictable in terms of them" (Cavell, 1998, p. 461).

Whether or not he consciously drew on its philosophical origins, Jung's notion of the transcendent function is based on the idea of the dialectical and deep structural nature of all change in the living world expounded by the nineteenth century German philosopher, Hegel, in his great work, *The Phenomenology of the Spirit* (see Solomon, 1994). Hegel posited a tripartite schema as fundamental to all change, including psychic change, a situation in which an original oppositional pair, a dyad, which he called thesis and anti-thesis, struggle together until, under the right conditions, a third position, a synthesis, is achieved. This third position heralds the transformation of the oppositional elements of the dyad into a position with new properties that could not have been known about before their encounter—the *tertium quid non datur*, in Jung's terms. Hegel called this ubiquitous struggle dialectical, because it demonstrated how transformations in the natural world happen through the resolution of an oppositional struggle and can be understood to have meaning and purposefulness. This was a deep structural patterning of dynamic change that was archetypal by nature and developmental as a dynamic movement in time.

This archetypal schema can also be thought of as the basis of the tripartite Oedipal situation, where transformation from out of a primordial pair, mother and child, can be achieved through the third position afforded by the paternal function, whether this be a real father, or a capacity of mind in the mother or in the child, or both, as Fonagy illustrates (Fonagy, 1989). It is in this sense that we might speak of the emergence of the mind of the child, the child's identity, as separate from his or her mother, through the provision of a third perspective. For Jung, this would be thought of as the emergence of the self, through successive states of transformation and individuation via the transcendent function. In the context of the function of supervision with which we are concerned in this chapter, we could say that it is through the provision of the supervisory third that both patient and analyst are helped to emerge from out of the *massa confusa* of the analytic dyad. Both change as a result as individuation progresses.

In psychoanalytic theory, the importance of the negotiation of the Oedipal threesome, that archetypal triad *par excellence*, constitutes much of the psychoanalytic understanding of developmental achievement. Freud first used the term "Oedipus complex" in 1910, following Jung's scientific researches on the complexes using the Word Association Test (WAT). At that time, the Oedipus complex was considered to be one of many organizing complexes of the psyche, but soon became the core psychoanalytic concept. Britton sums up concisely the Oedipal situation:

> ... we notice in the two different sexes the same elements: a parental couple . . .; a death wish towards the parent of the same sex; and a wish-fulfilling dream or myth of taking the place of one parent and marrying the other. [Britton, 1998, p. 30]

Britton stresses the necessity of working through the Oedipus complex in order to resolve the depressive position and of working through the depressive position in order to resolve the Oedipus complex (*ibid.*, p. 29). He evokes the notion of internal triangulation, which requires the toleration of an internal version of the Oedipal situation in order to do this. He describes "triangular psychic space" as "a *third* position in mental space . . . from which the *subjective self* can be observed having a relationship with an idea" (*ibid.*, p. 13). He concludes that "in all analyses the basic Oedipus situation exists whenever the analyst exercises his or her mind independently of the inter-subjective relationship of patient and analyst" (*ibid.*, p. 44).

In developing Britton's idea of the Oedipal triangle as present through the internal events and relationships that occur in the analyst's mind, as links to an internal object or to psychoanalytic theory, I wish to reiterate that the external manifestation and facilitation of this internal triangular state is quintessentially present in the supervisory or consultative relationship. Here, two people, the analyst and the supervisor, are linked in relation to a third, the patient.

Within psychoanalysis, the current debate about the implications of intersubjectivity— that the analyst and patient are acting together within a treatment relationship, in which the analyst's countertransference to the patient's transference as much as the reverse (for example, Atwood & Stolorow, 1993, p. 47) offer essential information—has been enhanced by Cavell's (1998) notion of "progressive triangulation". Rose summarizes her notion succinctly: ". . . in order to know our own minds, we require an interaction with another mind in relation to what would be termed objective reality" (Rose, 2000, p. 454). I hold that the provision of supervision, including the internal supervision that happens when the analyst thinks about aspects of the patient and the analytic relationship, is an important instance of "progressive triangulation", in that it allows for ongoing interaction with another mind in relation to a third, the patient, who can be thought about because differentiated from the dyadic relating of the patient–analyst couple.

Triangular space and supervision in analytic practice

The provision and function of supervision of analytic and psychotherapeutic work with individuals, children, couples, or families, creates a needed triangular space essential to the care and maintenance, the ongoing hygiene, of the dyadic relationships. I use the term "hygiene" in the sense that, through its provision, supervision keeps constantly activated the awareness of the analytic attitude, including its ethical component, in and through the presence of a third person (the supervisor), or a third position (the supervisory space), and that it acts as an aid in the restoration of the analytic and ethical attitudes when at times they might be lost in the maelstrom of clinical practice. Supervision is itself the representation of that attitude through the provision of a third area of reflection. The treatment, at profound levels, of the psyche in distress always involves a regressive and/or narcissistic pull back into part object relating, those primitive either/or dichotomous states of mind that Jung and others have shown are dominated by the internal experience of the archetypal warring opposites at the basis of the defences of the self (Kalsched, 1996; Solomon, 1997). Ensuring the provision of the sustained triangular space of the supervisory situation creates the necessary opportunity for analytic reflection, where two people work together to think about a third, whether the third is an individual, a couple, or a family, or an idea or aspect within the therapist or analyst, that is relevant to their clinical work. The provision of triangular space through internal or external supervision, or both, is essential to the maintenance of the analytic attitude in the face of the multitudinous forces and pressures at work within the analytic and therapeutic situation, arising from the conscious and unconscious dynamics within and between patient and analyst alike, and the consequently inevitable, often unconscious, intersubjective exchanges between them as a pair, that would seek, for defensive reasons, to undermine analytic achievements.

To the extent that this triangular space created by supervision is necessary to the hygiene of the analytic couple (just as the paternal, reflective principle is essential to the hygiene of the mother–infant dyad, providing the space for psychological growth to occur), then supervision has an ethical as well as a clinical and didactic role to play in all analytic and therapeutic work, notwithstanding the years of experience of the practitioner. Whether supervision is provided in the same way as during training, with weekly meetings in a one-to-one situation with a senior practitioner, or in consultations with a senior practitioner at agreed intervals, or whether peer supervision in small groups is selected as the means of providing the triangular space, these are questions that are up to each clinician to decide upon, according to personal need and inclination.

In the case of the analysis and supervision of training candidates, where there are particular ongoing boundary issues and other pressures inherent in the training situation that do not usually pertain in work with non-training patients, such as the need to see a patient under regular supervision at a certain minimum intensity (three, four, or five times per week), over a certain minimum amount of time (often for a minimum of either eighteen months or two years), supervision will help to identify and work under these constraints without foregoing the analytic attitude. This will, in turn, foster in the candidate their own ethical attitude, as they internalize the expectation that all analytic work, including the work of their own analysts and supervisors, is in turn supervised. The trainee will then know from the very outset of his or her training that there is always a third space created in which he or she as a patient or as a supervisee will be thought about by another supervisor–practitioner pair.

Fostering the ethical–supervisory expectation is more likely to engender a generationally based commitment to the analytic attitude within a training institution, as the tradition of good clinical practice is passed down across the analytic and therapeutic training generations. Currently, there is an assumption that the aim and goals of training can often be summed up in almost the opposite way: that is, that the success of the candidate's progress through his or her training is assessed according to whether he or she is judged to be ready to "work independently". Of course, the assessment of the trainee's capacity for independent judgement and a sense of their own viable autonomy is an important, indeed crucial, factor in the process of assessing whether someone is ready to qualify to practise as an analyst or therapist. I am arguing here that, included in this assessment should be a judgement about the candidate's awareness of the need for, and usefulness of, the provision of a triangular space in which to discuss their clinical practice, in order best to insure against the risks inherent in working in such intimate and depth psychological ways, including the dangers of mutual identificatory states or the abuse of power.

My contention is that, as well as its obvious advantages, the expectation that the practitioner will ensure that they have ongoing supervision or consultation on their clinical practice is a sign of maturation, both on the part of the practitioner as well as that of the training institution, as they assess their own and others' clinical competence. This is part of the assessment process that results in the authorization to practise as members of the training institution. There is the added dimension that some members go on to become eventual trainers, that is, training analysts, supervisors, and clinical and theoretical seminar leaders, entrusted with the responsibility for training future generations of analysts and therapists. The expectation in the trainee of ongoing supervisory and consultative provision is modelled by the trainers, fostering the candidate's respect for, and understanding of, the conditions that create and sustain the analytic and ethical attitude. This includes attention to boundary issues that can arise within and through the intensity of the intersubjective dynamics within the analytic and therapeutic relationship. (See Gabbard and Lester, 1995, for a detail discussion of boundary issues in analytic practice.) These intersubjective dynamics are inevitably released by the interpenetrative, projective, introjective and projective identificatory exchanges within the transference and countertransference.

The recommendation that (1) members of analytic training institutions seek to establish an ongoing supervisory ethos to discuss their work, even if the provision is not systematically maintained, and that (2) all training analysts and supervisors of the institutions have regular consultations regarding their training cases (including patients, supervisees, or training patients) represents a further development of those ubiquitous triads created by the training situation: the trainee–training analyst–supervisor; the trainee–training patient–supervisor; and the trainee–supervisor–Training Committee. The expectation of providing a space for reflection with another would benefit all parties concerned and, at the same time, increase clinical awareness. Without this benefit, we run the risk of identifying with those narcissistic and other pathological processes and pressures, inevitable in analytic practice, as we are liable to treat those aspects in our patients that correspond and resonate with our own internal issues and personal histories. Hence the importance of clinical "hygiene", of creating the third space of supervision, that can help us to maintain our connection to genuine object relating and to staying alert to the pitfalls of intense dyadic relating.

Conclusion

I have explored some aspects of the supervisory function in analytic practice in relation to developmental and archetypal perspectives. The provision through supervision of a triangular space in which clinical work with patients can be thought about creates the necessary dimensionality for psychological transformation to occur and has resonance with developmental reality and archetypal truth. The ethical aspect of supervisory provision is predicated on the notion that genuine object relating arises out of such dimensionality, in which one mind is aware of the subjective reality of another and chooses to take ethical responsibility towards the other, as the parent in relation to the child, and the analyst or therapist in relation to the patient. This is fostered in the supervisory setting, where the triangular relationship of supervisor–analyst/therapist–patient makes manifest in concrete form a universal triangular and deep structural situation which is necessary if psychological development is to occur.

It may be that the emergence of an ethical capacity represents a development from the depressive position, in that it seeks to provide for and protect a non-contingent space or place for reflection about another, be it a person, a relationship, or an idea. Such reflection may result in decisions taken with respect to another, and may be followed by actions, which include the content, form, timing, and other characteristics of interpretations, as well as other, more subtle, modes of being in the presence of another, that will have a direct impact on the quality of their internal world. It is for this reason—because of the possibility of doing harm to the vulnerable interior reality of another—that the Hippocratic Oath was first established two thousand five hundred years ago with its main premise, *nolo nocere*, and why we, as practitioners, continue to seek to hone its ethos.

References

Atwood, G., & Stolorow, R. (1993). *Structures of Subjectivity*. Northvale, NJ: Analytic Press.

Britton, R. (1998). *Belief and Imagination*. London: Routledge.

Cavell, M. (1998). Triangulation, one's own mind and objectivity. *International Journal of Psychoanalysis, 79*: 449–468.

Fonagy, P. (1989). On tolerating mental states: theory of mind in borderline personality. *Bulletin of The Anna Freud Centre, 12*: 91–115.

Fordham, M. (1969). *Children as Individuals*. London: Hodder and Stoughton.

Fordham, M. (1957). *New Developments in Analytical Psychology*. London: Routledge and Kegan Paul.

Freud, S. (1910b). Leonardo da Vinci and a memory of his childhood. *S.E.*, 9: 252. London: Hogarth.

Gabbard, G., & Lester, E. (1995). *Boundaries and Boundary Violations in Psychoanalysis*. New York: Basic Books.

Hegel, G. W. F. (1807/1977). *The Phenomenology of Spirit*. A. V. Miller (Trans.). Oxford: Oxford University Press.

Hinshelwood, R. (1989). *A Dictionary of Kleinian Thought*. London: Free Association.

Jung, C. G. (1916)[1958/1960]. *The Transcendent Function. C.W., 8*. London: Routledge & Kegan Paul.

Jung, C. G. (1958)[1964]. *A Psychological View of Conscience. C.W., 10*. London: Routledge & Kegan Paul.

Kalsched, D. (1996). *The Inner World of Trauma*. London: Routledge.

Klein, M. (1935). A contribution to the psychogenesis of manic-depressive states. In: R. Money-Kyrle, B. Joseph, E. O'Shaughnessy, & H. Segal (Eds.), *The Writings of Melanie Klein*, Vol I. London: Hogarth, 1975.

Klein, M. (1946). Notes on some schizoid mechanisms. In: R. Money-Kyrle, B. Joseph, E. O'Shaughnessy, & H. Segal (Eds.), *The Writings of Melanie Klein*, Vol I. London: Hogarth, 1975.

Rose, J. (2000). Symbols and their function in managing the anxiety of change: an intersubjective approach. *International Journal of Psychoanalysis, 81*: 453–470.

Samuels, A. (1989). *The Plural Psyche*. London: Routledge.

Solomon, H. M. (1994). The transcendent function and Hegel's dialectical vision. *Journal of Analytical Psychology, 39*(1).

Solomon, H. M. (1997). The not-so-silent couple in the individual. *Journal of Analytical Psychology, 42*(3). Also in *Bulletin of the Society of Psychoanalytic Marital Psychotherapists*, 1994, Bulletin 1, Inaugural Issue.

Solomon, H. M. (2000a). Recent developments in the neurosciences. In: E. Christopher & H. M Solomon (Eds.), *Jungian Thought in the Modern World* (pp. 126–137). London: Free Association.

Solomon, H. M. (2000b). The ethical self. In: E. Christopher & H. M Solomon (Eds.), *Jungian Thought in the Modern World* (pp. 191–216). London: Free Association.

Solomon, H. M. (2002). The ethics of supervision: developmental and archetypal perspectives. In: H. M. Solomon & M. Twyman (Eds.), *The Ethical Attitude in Analytic Practice*. London: Free Association.

Solomon, H. M. (2003). The ethical attitude: a bridge between psychoanalysis and anaytical psychology. In: H. M. Solomon & M. Twyman (Eds.), *The Ethical Attitude in Analytic Practice* (pp. 21–30). London: Karnac.

PART II
ON SUPERVISORY
TECHNIQUES

CHAPTER FOUR

Models of supervision

Susan Howard

I n the course of my career as a psychoanalytic psychotherapist I have been supervised by a number of different people. All were senior members of the profession and thus very experienced; most were helpful and I learned interesting and valuable things from each of them. There were some that I felt did not supervise me well, and from whom I learned less than I might. However, none of them made explicit whether they structured their supervision within any particular framework or model of supervision and, if so, what that model was. I wonder whether they supervised me, as I myself supervised later, according to their own experiences of being supervised and on the basis of their later experience of supervising. In other words, they may not consciously have had a model that framed their thinking. Likewise, when I first began to supervise I did it the way I had learned from my own supervisors. It was, therefore, something of a surprise to me when I discovered that there is a burgeoning literature about the supervisory process and theories about supervision, which has been developing for the past fifty years. These theoretical models can help in thinking about our role as supervisors as well as how we structure supervision sessions.

Some models have been developed specifically for psychoanalytic supervision, and some models have a more general application throughout the helping professions. In this chapter I examine not only the psychoanalytic-specific models but also some of the generic ones that might be useful to psychoanalytic supervisory practice. First, though, I want to consider the different, but related, issue of how we learn as adults. This issue is important because there tends to be an implicit assumption that one style of learning suits all, rather than that we might need to discover and then take into account our adult supervisees' learning styles and supervise them accordingly.

Kolb's Experiential Learning Theory (ELT)

David Kolb's Experiential Learning Theory has been influential in a number of professions that are skills based, including management training, teaching, counselling, nursing, and social work. He identified four ways of learning in adults, which he mapped on to four different learning stages (Kolb, 1984). The first stage is concrete experience, which is learning through involvement with tangible, relatively concrete issues. The second, reflective observation is learning through contemplation and reflection. The third, abstract conceptualization is learning that involves a more abstract and analytical approach. The last stage is active experimentation or learning through "applying" and taking an active role.

He further proposed that students have preferred learning styles that match the learning dimensions he identified. These he called "intuition" (from concrete experience); "reflection" (from reflective observation); "theorizing" (from abstract conceptualization) and "doing" (from active experimentation). Previous learning theories had tended to privilege abstract thinking over concrete experience, whereas Kolb argued that each style of learning had its strengths and weaknesses and that each was valuable in its appropriate place. He argued that students learn most easily using their preferred learning style. However, he warned that there are dangers in always prioritizing a preferred learning style; learning can become skewed or incomplete if one learning style is always privileged at the expense of other styles.

Kolb suggested a four-step learning cycle that students should go through in a given sequence in order for complete learning to take place (Smith & Kolb, 1986, cited in Raschick, Maypole, & Day, 1998). He proposed that all learning should proceed through the same order, starting with concrete experience, followed by reflective observation, abstract conceptualization, and, last, active experimentation.

The strength of the model lies in the fact that it draws our attention to different aspects of the learning process, how those interrelate and the necessity of including all types of learning for complete learning to take place. It also helps to structure our thinking about what a student might be lacking in their learning. However, later writers (for example Raschick, Maypole, & Day, 1998) have argued that requiring students to move through the learning experience in the same order is too limiting as it assumes that everyone learns best in the same way and does not allow for individual differences in preferred learning style.

They propose that the most important application of the Kolb learning cycle lies in identifying and then utilizing a student's preferred method of learning. They argue that some students will learn better if they begin the process of learning by using inductive methods such as concrete experience, while others will benefit from using deductive methods, such as abstract conceptualization. We could apply this proposal to learning basic therapy skills among psychotherapy students. Students who learn best through inductive learning could start with concrete experience by undertaking an initial session with a patient in which they made an attempt to engage them. Following this, they could reflect on what they had done (reflective observation). This would lead to a theoretical discussion about the conceptual issues related to engagement and hypotheses could be developed (abstract conceptualization). Last, the students would have a further experience in which they could try out some of their newly developed hypotheses of basic engagement skills in the next session with their patient (active experimentation). The cycle would then begin again with the next experience of seeing a patient.

By contrast a deductive learning cycle might start with a conceptual discussion of basic therapy skills (abstract conceptualization); using some of these ideas in a role-play (active experimentation);

undertaking a session with a patient (concrete experience); last, reflecting on the whole learning experience (reflective observation).

A number of studies have demonstrated a learning style preference for concrete experience among students and supervisors in different fields within the caring professions. Van Soest and Kruzich (1994) discovered that student teachers found it difficult to form relationships with supervisors who were significantly different from them in the importance they ascribed to concrete experience. They recommended that supervisors should adapt their method of supervision according to the learning style of their trainees, rather than that supervisors and trainees be matched for learning style.

Raschick, Maypole, and Day (1998) make a number of recommendations as to how we might utilize an understanding of the four learning stages to facilitate supervision. They recommend that students observe or shadow qualified staff as a part of concrete experiential learning; that they use reflective journals and supervisory discussion to promote reflective observation; that they discuss theoretical concepts in supervision to facilitate abstract conceptualization. They further recommend that supervisors should encourage students to use different approaches to working with their clients as a part of active experimentation. Raschick and his colleagues reported considerable initial resistance to their attempts to encourage students and supervisors to apply Kolb's concepts to supervision. However, there were a number of positive outcomes from their research. First, supervisors and students began to engage in discussions about their respective learning styles, and second, students were more aware of the aspects of the learning cycle they needed to develop in order to maximize their learning.

How does this map on to supervision within a psychoanalytic framework? Interestingly Kolb argues that different professions privilege different learning styles, which reflect the kind of knowledge that is valued in the profession. Although I know of no formal study that identifies the kind of knowledge valued by our profession, anecdotally there is quite a lot of evidence that we privilege inductive over deductive knowledge and learning. Ask most psychoanalytically trained therapists what they found useful in their training and they will reply in the following order: "My personal analysis/therapy, supervision of my patients, and the theoretical seminars". Although each of Kolb's four stages is built into our training and continuing professional development in different ways, concrete experience is privileged in the sense that we have to have had personal therapy and some relevant experience with patients before training can commence. Concrete experience also comes through the work we do with our patients. Reflective observation is given a prominence in the way in which we advocate the development and use of the countertransference and in the use we make of clinical seminars and supervision to explore our reactions to our patients and our work. Abstract conceptualization occurs during theoretical seminars, meetings or conferences, and through private reading. Most of us can attest to being influenced by a seminar or supervision or piece of work we have done with another patient in generating and testing new hypotheses with a patient and thus engaging in active experimentation.

However, I wonder about the extent to which we bring them all together in thinking about how we supervise. In my own experience, supervisors vary considerably in the extent to which they link theory to practice in clinical supervision, and this raises a number of questions. How often do we focus almost exclusively on the concrete experience of clinical material and the accompanying reflective observations but not include very much abstract conceptualization? Would a relative lack of theory–practice linking inhibit supervisees from generating alternative hypotheses that would facilitate active experimentation? And, by doing so, do we inhibit our supervisees' development, if, as Kolb advocates, we need to be able to engage in all the different aspects of the learning cycle in order to maximize learning?

We could profitably think about what we would sacrifice or gain if we used a model of supervision that was more overtly influenced by Kolb's theory. One change might involve a more collaborative relationship between supervisor and supervisee as they discussed issues such as each other's preferred learning styles. This could prove a significant challenge in a profession where hierarchy still plays an important role in determining relationships between its members, and where there are at times complaints that supervisors can behave in supervision as though the supervisee was a patient rather than a colleague. Also, how would we feel about using role-play or other experiential methods to facilitate active experimentation? Another challenge would involve how we work with supervisees whose preferred learning style is abstract and deductive. How many supervisors would be prepared to adapt their own supervisory style to accommodate such a learner, given my hypothesis that concrete experience is the most valued knowledge in the profession?

Models of supervision

A number of writers have proposed different ways of categorizing supervisory models. I have found Beinart's (2004) dual categorization useful in thinking about psychoanalytic supervision. She divides models into those that are based on and are an extension of psychotherapy theories and those that have been developed specifically for understanding what happens in supervision. Therapy-based models of supervision were the first of the supervision models, and probably most of us have experienced being supervised in this framework. The way in which supervisors supervise within these models reflects the therapeutic model they espouse. So a supervisor whose theoretical model is psychoanalytic will focus on different aspects of the work undertaken by the supervisee from someone who supervises from a cognitive–behavioural, systemic, or humanistic therapeutic model. I think it is fair to say that most psychoanalytically orientated supervisors practise within a psychotherapy model of supervision rather than using a model that has specifically been developed to account for what happens in supervision itself. I will therefore begin by examining psychoanalytic theories of practice models before looking at some of the models that are specific to supervision.

Theories of practice models

As Carroll (1996) notes, Freud was the first supervisor, and he set the tone for how supervision was conducted and, in some ways, still is. Freud supervised in a way that conveyed knowledge downwards; he was the arbiter of truth, knowledge, and power, and he inducted more junior members of the profession into the norms and mores of psychoanalytic work. His was essentially an apprentice model and much psychoanalytic training and supervision still retains that model.

Psychoanalytic models of supervision have developed in tandem with, and therefore reflect, developments in psychoanalytic theory and therapeutic practice (see Brown and Miller, 2002; Frawley-O'Dea & Sarnat, 2001; Langs, 1994). In other words, supervision theory has moved from a one-person to a two-person orientation and then a relational orientation reflecting changes in psychoanalytic theoretical models. Frawley-O'Dea and Sarnat have developed a model of supervision that reflects recent developments in psychoanalytic practice. They also devised a tripartite typology, which I think is very helpful in thinking about therapeutic models. They compared each of the three types of therapeutic models through examining the nature of the supervisor's authority in relation to the supervisee; the supervisor's consideration of what data is considered relevant to supervisory processing; the supervisor's primary mode of participating in the supervision.

One-person models

One-person models are based on patient-centred theories where the emphasis is primarily on the patient and the workings of his mind. They reflect classical theory in psychoanalytic thinking where the emphasis is on understanding the individual patient, and where use of the countertransference is limited to what it tells us about the workings of the patient's mind. According to Frawley-O'Dea and Sarnat, in this model the supervisor's authority in the supervision comes from the (conscious or unconscious) agreement between supervisee and supervisor that the supervisor is a relatively uninvolved expert who is the primary judge of the quality of the supervisee's work. The relevant data for supervision are the contents of the patient's mind. Any difficulty the supervisee may have in the countertransference would be referred to the supervisee's personal therapy. This model of supervision expects the supervisee to maintain as objective a distance as possible from his countertransference reactions to the patient and from his transference reactions to his supervisor. It does not take into account the supervisor's contribution to what goes on in the supervision; in fact the supervisor can become like the blank screen that Freud (1912e) advocated in his work with patients. Frawley-O'Dea and Sarnat argue that the supervisor's primary mode of participating in the supervision process is didactic. If the supervisee was unable to use the supervisor's understanding of the work then the problem was his rather than his supervisor's.

Two-person models

Frawley-O'Dea and Sarnat then go on to describe a number of supervisee-centred (two-person) models that began to develop in the middle of the twentieth century. In these models the psychology of the supervisee becomes a central concern in the supervisory process, reflecting the changes in psychoanalytic theory to a two-person psychology that had become increasingly influential at that time. Supervisee and patient are seen as a system in which each regulates the other. Although the supervisor's authority continues to rely on her role as the uninvolved expert, there are significant changes in the other two dimensions. The data relevant for consideration and processing in supervision now include the supervisee's mind as well as that of the patient. Patient and supervisee are seen as a dyad in which the internal world of each contributes to the unfolding therapeutic drama. The supervisor's primary mode of participation is less didactic and more experiential in this model. The authors examine three supervisee-centred models, one based on an ego-psychology clinical model, another based on the self-psychology clinical model, and the third based on the object relations clinical model. I will examine in more detail only the object relations model, as it is the one that supervisors in the UK are most likely to use.

Frawley-O'Dea and Sarnat call this model "the supervisee-centred anxiety-focused (object relations) model", indicating that a primary function for the supervisor is the containment and bearing of the supervisee's anxiety in relation to his work with his patient. In this model the supervisor derives her authority from her position as the expert who facilitates the supervisee in becoming aware of primitive anxieties present in his therapeutic work and in helping him to deal with them. Relevant data for processing during supervision include understanding the patient's inner world and the supervisee's psychology. Frawley-O'Dea and Sarnat identify two aspects of the supervisee's psychology that are particularly relevant: first, how the supervisee's unconscious anxieties in relation to the patient manifest themselves in the supervisory relationship; second, how the supervisee enacts his identification with the patient's internal object relationships in the supervision. The supervisor participates in supervision through the containment and interpretation of the supervisee's anxieties and enactments and by enabling him to process them into symbolic representations.

The theory base underpinning the supervisee-centred anxiety-focused model of supervision is drawn from object relations theorists such as Winnicott and Klein (see Jarmon, 1990 and Nerwith, 1990, both cited in Frawley-O'Dea and Sarnat, 2001). In Winnicottian theory the notion of holding is quite central. A primary maternal function is that of holding the baby, while a primary paternal function is to hold the mother to enable her to hold the baby. This tripartite relationship is necessary for adequate containment of the primitive anxieties present in the mother and baby relationship. In the same way, in a Winnicottian object relations framework the supervisor's role can be seen as holding and containing the supervisee's anxieties in order for him to contain his patient's. To facilitate this, the supervisor needs to create a safe space in which "the supervisee can be helped to bear the anxieties and unsymbolised experiences evoked in the therapeutic relationship" (Frawley-O'Dea & Sarnat, 2001, p. 40). In Kleinian-influenced theory the anxiety is seen as more influenced by paranoid–schizoid processes and the fear of abandonment. Other Kleinian concepts such as coping with hatred and the guilt associated with it are also transposed into the supervisory relationship where the role of the supervisor is, in part, to contain and metabolize the supervisee's anxieties.

Langs (1994) proposed a model of supervision that bridged the two-person model and the more fully relational model proposed by Frawley-O'Dea and Sarnat detailed below. He called his model the "self-processing supervision model". He emphasized the importance of integrating the supervisee's conscious and unconscious experiences into supervision so that the two are held together, thereby maximizing his learning experiences. This is concordant with a standard two-person model. However, Langs also advocated that "Full attention is paid to the transactions between the supervisor and the supervisee" (p. 42). This brings in the person of the supervisor, whose contribution to the supervisory process indicates a more relationally founded model. However, this model does not fully include the contribution of the supervisor to the supervisory process, as does that of Frawley-O'Dea and Sarnat, which I will now describe.

Three-person or relational models

Frawley-O'Dea and Sarnat (2001) call their own model the supervisory-matrix-centred (relational) model. They note that the model could not have been conceived before the relational school of psychoanalysis had achieved the level of maturity necessary for it to support a supervisory theory. Relational theories of the self emphasize dissociative rather than repressive mechanisms, in which there are multiple self-systems. Psychological health is therefore characterized by managing the paradox of contradictions in relationships both between different self-states and relationships with others. Relational theory emphasizes the way in which therapeutic relationships are co-constructed and the importance of the effects of relationships on relationships. The individual is therefore no longer seen as a unitary self, but rather as a "self [that] is primarily motivated to express its variety of self-experiences through relationships with others" (*ibid.*, p. 52).

In the same way the supervisory relationship in this model is also seen as co-constructed. Not only does the therapist become a full partner rather than an observer in the construction of the therapeutic relationship, but also the supervisor becomes a full partner rather than an observer in the construction of the supervisory relationship. Consequently the minds of all three participants (patient, supervisee, and supervisor) are understood to contribute to the process of supervision, including enactments. Thus, all three are the subject of reflection and discussion in supervision.

In the supervisory-matrix-centred model the supervisor derives her authority in the relationship from her engagement in the supervisory relationship and her "capacity to participate in, reflect upon, and process enactments, and to interpret relational themes that arise within either the therapeutic or supervisory dyads" (*ibid.*, p. 41). The supervisor's authority is therefore based less on her expert knowledge of theory and technique and more on her ability to reflect on and process what happens between herself and her supervisee. Frawley-O'Dea and Sarnat advocate that the supervisor, in setting up the supervisory contract, makes an explicit invitation to the supervisee to raise issues about the supervisory relationship and his experience of supervision and his supervisor in order to facilitate such processing.

Issues discussed in supervision therefore include parallel processing, the process by which themes and conflicts in the therapeutic relationship become manifest in the supervisory dyad (and vice versa). In an interesting article that examines the "interlocking unconscious processes of the patient, analyst and supervisor" (p. 814), Brown and Miller (2002) give a graphic example of how the sharing of unconscious material between supervisor and supervisee enabled the supervisee to work with his patient to unlock an analysis that had become stuck as the therapeutic dyad worked towards termination. This could only be achieved once the supervisory dyad had faced the unconscious conflicts associated with the ending in their own relationship.

It is also expected that organizational issues and themes, as well as themes from the supervisee's own therapy, will enter the supervisory relationship. Indeed, according to Frawley-O'Dea and Sarnat, all aspects of the participants' experience, including dreams, affects, somatic experiences, and other unconsciously motivated material are considered relevant to discussion within supervision.

Although Frawley-O'Dea and Sarnat anticipate that the supervisor's role will include informing about theory and therapeutic technique and containing anxiety, they understand the supervisor's primary mode of participation in supervision as a "highly experiential approach to teaching and learning" (2001, p. 41). This occurs through the exploration of the unconsciousness engagements of the various actors in the supervisory and therapeutic process. Supervision is considered to be an analytic endeavour in its own right. Supervisor and supervisee agree to identify and discuss analytic material such as transference and defences as they arise within the supervisory relationship that might facilitate or impede the supervisory process and therefore the clinical work with patients. Supervision is therefore seen as a much more mutual interaction than it has been in previous models of supervision, and Frawley-O'Dea and Sarnat acknowledge that, for inexperienced supervisees, this may be difficult, as they generally long for more direction than is implicit in this model. However, they argue that, by sharing her experience of both the clinical data and the supervisory experience, the supervisor demystifies the process of supervision and enables the supervisee to witness her internal analytic processing at work. This becomes an additional opportunity for learning for the supervisee, as well as a model for collaboration and negotiation that the supervisee can use in a relationally influenced therapeutic relationship.

They stress that in emphasizing mutuality in the exploration of the supervisory relationship they are not advocating a symmetrical relationship in which power relationships and differences in the roles of supervisor and supervisee are denied. Rather, they see mutuality in the context of asymmetry. After all, there is an asymmetry in the degree of power and influence each exerts in the relationship. They have different roles, functions and responsibilities in the process of supervision, which are also asymmetrical. However, as Frawley-O'Dea and Sarnat note:

> The relational supervisor holds his awareness of these asymmetrical aspects of the relationship in active tension with acknowledging and valuing the qualities that both members of the supervisory pair share in common. He acknowledges that, in many respects, he is more like his supervisee than he is different from her. Both parties participate in regressive experiences. Both participate in enactments and in processing the data thus generated. Both have blind spots and areas of narcissistic vulnerability. Both have particular interests at stake and operate from particular contexts that affect their participation. Neither party is "objective", since each is embedded in the situation in a particular way. [2001, p. 81]

Strengths and limitations of therapy models of supervision

Dynamic psychotherapy training has traditionally operated within an apprentice model (also called "psychotherapy-bound models" by Bernard and Goodyear, 1998) in which the less experienced supervisee acquires the skills of therapeutic practice from a combination of his own therapy or analysis and his supervision with an experienced practitioner. There are a number of strengths associated with the apprentice model. First, in focusing on those processes in supervision that are concordant with the therapeutic model being taught, the supervisee has the opportunity to experience for himself how the model works at an intellectual and emotional level. Second, as Feltham and Dryden (1994) note, those training in the profession benefit from a congruence between the therapeutic orientations of therapist, supervisor, and supervisee, since it minimizes confusion.

Also, the supervisee has the opportunity to observe an expert in the field putting theory into practice. This is true as much for supervision that focuses on the individual psychology of the patient as it is for supervision that operates within a relational model. Theories of dynamic psychology are complex, and Kolb's theory of adult learning points to the significant advantage of a method of supervision that gives the supervisee a concrete experience of the theory he is using in his therapeutic practice. However, as Carroll (1996) notes, there are problems associated with the fact that psychotherapy training occurs within an apprentice model of learning.

Carroll describes a number of drawbacks to therapy models of supervision. First, that there is a narrowness of learning because it is based on the skills of the "apprentice-master", who hands down what has been inherited without adequate attention to the individuality of the apprentice or consideration of his learning needs (or, as noted above, learning style). His second criticism is that because supervisors are appointed rather than trained, the notion of the supervisor as the expert who hands on the skills of the craft of psychotherapy is reinforced. This leads to the assumption that supervisors are suitable to supervise because of their expertise in the consulting room rather than because of their ability to think about the learning needs of their supervisee and to adequately supervise. Indeed, in psychotherapeutic institutions there is a tendency for training supervisors to be drawn from the ranks of those who have demonstrated advanced competencies in their therapeutic work or shown loyalty to the organization and its values rather than those who have specifically demonstrated their ability to supervise. This increases the potential for supervision to become a method of indoctrination rather than a forum for learning. Carroll also argues that the apprentice model is of limited value because psychotherapy is a profession "where the main tool used is the person of the individual, rather then simply the skills that he/she has, and where the focus of the training is to enable the beginner to practise in his/her own way" (p. 26). This contrasts with craft apprenticeships, where there are more clearly defined right and wrong ways of performing a technical skill, and where the person of the apprentice has less effect on the performance of the skill.

Another disadvantage of therapy models is that they have encouraged a division of labour within dynamic psychotherapy trainings in which didactic or formal teaching (reading seminars for example) takes place separately from the practical aspects of doing therapy. It is a very individual matter as to the extent to which supervisors recommend reading, courses, or conferences, or discuss academic papers within supervision. Therapy models have also tended to ignore methods of supervision that are discordant with the method of therapy being taught. So, for example, role-plays, explicit skills training, and other experiential methods of teaching are not routinely included in most psychotherapy supervision, because such direct methods are not used in therapy. The consequence of this skewedness in teaching means that it is more difficult to include the whole of Kolb's learning stages within psychotherapy supervision as it is currently practised. And, as Bernard and Goodyear (1998) note, as therapy and supervision are different endeavours, using therapeutic models to understand supervision may have restricted the evidence base because directions given for research and practice in supervision have been narrowed.

Last, Matthews and Treacher (2004) point directly to one of the limitations of psychodynamic models of supervision, which is that there is insufficient attention paid to alliance building. They argue that psychodynamic approaches to supervision are still too hierarchical, and that even Frawley-O'Dea and Sarnat do not adequately pay attention to contract making, which they see as a foundation for a good supervisory relationship. Along with Hawkins and Shohet (2000) they argue that a supervisory alliance should be built on

> openness and clarity ... [about] ... the methods to be used ... and why they are used, the style of supervision, the goals of supervision, the kind of relationship it is helped to achieve and the responsibilities of each partner in the supervisory relationship. [Hunt, 1976 cited in Hawkins and Shohet, 2000, p. 28]

Models developed specifically for supervision

While therapy-based models of supervision have a role in the acculturation of the supervisee into a method of therapy, Beinart (2004) argues strongly that the main problem with psychotherapy-based models of supervision is that they do not provide a framework for training those beginning as supervisors. Like others in the field (Carroll, 1996; Hawkins & Shohet, 2000; Scaife, 2001), she proposes that there is a need for models of supervision that have been specifically developed to explain the complexity of the supervisory process, and which therefore provide a framework for developing as a supervisor. Such frameworks also enable supervisees to understand their role in the supervisory process and facilitate them in what is happening in supervision. A number of the new models have been developed for counsellors or clinical psychologists, for example Scaife's (2001) general supervision framework or Carroll's (1996) generic integrative model. These models take into account the tasks and functions of supervision. I shall now look at two major types of supervision-specific models that are relevant to psychotherapy supervision: developmental models and Hawkins and Shohet's process model of supervision, which owes much to psychodynamic theory.

Developmental models

Developmental models were the first models that dealt specifically with the process of supervision without allegiance to a specific model of therapy. They attempt to explain how the supervisee makes the transition from novice therapist and supervisee to experienced clinician. In 1998, Bernard and Goodyear estimated that there were over twenty-two different developmental models, an indication of the extent to which they became "the zeitgeist of supervision thinking and research" (Holloway, 1987, p. 209).

Developmental models pay attention not only to the development of the supervisee but also to the development of the supervisor, and there are complementary models that account for the development of each (e.g., Watkins, 1993). As Watkins (1995), in a review of the research noted, developmental models share some key identifiable assumptions.

a) That therapists in training or supervisees develop and grow, provided they are not exposed to a pernicious supervision/training environment; b) that their development proceeds through a sequence of stages, from less to more developed; c) that during those stages, they struggle with various developmental issues and concerns (e.g., competence, identity); and d) that supervisors would do well to consider the developmental level of their supervisees and structure supervision accordingly. [p. 647]

The integrated development model (IDM)

An example of a dependency model is that of Stoltenberg and his colleagues (Stoltenberg & Delworth, 1987; Stoltenberg, McNeill, & Delworth, 1998). The IDM takes a stage approach to supervisee development, identifying four stages: (1) dependency; (2) dependency–autonomous; (3) conditional dependency; (4) master professional.

In stage 1 (dependency), supervisees are likely to experience high levels of anxiety and insecurity which can make it hard for them to attend fully to the patient and process material in the session; indeed, they can often be focused on just surviving the session. At the same time supervisees are highly motivated to work and to be successful in what they are doing. The supervisee is seen as having little autonomy at this stage and looks to the supervisor to offer guidance in regard to casework. The supervisor's role is to provide structure, safety, and containment, and she may need to be contactable outside normal supervision times. She will almost certainly take the major responsibility for the supervisory session. The supervisor will encourage development at this stage by making facilitative interventions that are intended to convey support, through giving positive feedback and listening attentively. They propose that it can be helpful for supervisees at this stage to see the supervisor struggling so that the supervisor models a "coping" rather than an "expert" model of her own practice. They suggest that dependency can manifest itself in a number of ways, including those supervisees who have to appear very knowledgeable and those who appear to know nothing. The former can lead to avoidance in supervision while the latter can evoke too much help from the supervisor, which can reinforce feelings of incompetence.

Stage 2 (dependency–autonomy conflicts) is characterized by the supervisees fluctuating between feelings of over-confidence and being overwhelmed. They have developed a range of intervention skills, though these may not yet be fully integrated into the theoretical framework they are working in. Their motivation is likely to suffer and they may question their decision to work in this way. Although no longer anxious about surviving the session with the patient, supervisees can find it difficult to participate in the session while monitoring their own countertransference or other process issues. They tend to focus principally on the patient's perspective and become therefore quite identified with the patient in a way that can ignore discrepancies in what the patient says and other information such as their own countertransference. They can easily feel discouraged and angry about the work and their own capacities, and these feelings can be directed at the supervisor. Stage 2 supervisees are considered the most difficult to supervise, and therefore not suitable for beginning supervisors. Supervisors need to be able to offer a "secure base" (Bowlby, 1988) at this stage and to be able to normalize the fluctuating motivations and confidence that the supervisee experiences. Stoltenberg and his colleagues recommend that supervisors provide a highly autonomous supervision space in which a persuasive rather than an authoritarian supervisory stance is used.

In stage 3 (conditional dependency) supervisees have a more consistent level of skill and confidence in their work and are able to focus on process issues and their own countertransference within the session while remaining empathic towards the patient. Their motivation towards the profession stabilizes, and they become more confident in their ability to do the work. They become more spontaneous and creative in their work and are more able to acknowledge both their strengths and weaknesses as therapists. Because they are more autonomous they are not so easily threatened when they have crises in their work, and are less dependent on their supervisor. When they are dependent it is because there is a clearly identified issue where they have developmental needs. Supervision at this stage will rarely focus on strategies for surviving a session. There will be a greater orientation towards the thinking and feeling that informs the work and their relation to the theoretical framework and less need to focus on technique. A supervisor who lacks confidence or experience can find herself feeling anxious or redundant with supervisees at this stage, since they are autonomous, and may be better therapists than the supervisor! It is suggested that supervisors need the quality of wisdom at this stage and the ability to use joint exploration as the preferred method for conducting supervision. Also the supervisor needs to balance supporting the supervisee with challenging him. Supervisor disclosure is considered appropriate and even helpful at this stage in order to facilitate a more collaborative relationship.

Stage 4, or master professionals, are characterized by their autonomy, insightful awareness, and their ability to confront personal and professional issues. The work of supervision is described as "process-in-context" centred and the relationship between supervisor and supervisee becomes much more collegial and consultative. There is a shared responsibility for the structure and process of supervision, and, since the supervisee is probably supervising himself by now, the content of supervision may include issues to do with his own supervision practice.

The IDM assesses issues such as self and other awareness, motivation and autonomy across a number of domains. Specifically these are: intervention skills competence; assessment techniques; interpersonal assessment; patient conceptualization; individual differences; theoretical orientation; treatment goals and plans; professional ethics. Stoltenberg, McNeill, and Delworth (1998) argue that few, if any, therapists reach Stage 4 in all domains of clinical practice, so that there is never a time when the task of development is complete and supervision becomes a redundant process.

The supervisor complexity model (SCM)

As noted earlier, developmental models can also be applied to the practice of supervision, and indeed Stoltenberg and his colleagues propose that there is a complementary IDM model for supervisors. However, I wish to include Watkins (1993) model, which he calls the supervisor complexity model (SCM) as it goes beyond a description of stages to consider other factors influencing supervisor functioning. Like the IDM above, it identifies four developmental stages.

The first is *role shock*, in which the supervisor is acutely aware of her weaknesses, questions her abilities, lacks confidence, and feels overwhelmed and unprepared. She has limited awareness about her supervisory strengths, motivation, or style, or her impact on her supervisees. She also has little sense of identification with the supervisory role and looks to others for help and guidance.

The second is role *recovery/role transition*, in which the supervisor has gained some confidence in the role and recognizes some of her strengths and abilities, though she can still be easily shaken if confronted by supervisory problems. She has begun to develop an awareness of her impact on her supervisees. She has also acquired a limited recognition of what behaviours, ideas, and beliefs characterize her style of supervision, and is beginning to develop her personal theory of supervision. Her identification with the role of supervisor is as yet unconsolidated, but she relies less on others for help and guidance.

The third stage is that of *role consolidation*, in which there is an increasing confidence in her supervisory skills and a more accurate perception of herself and her supervisees. She is not as easily shaken by supervisory problems. She also gains confidence in the favourable impact she has on her supervisees, as well as being aware of her weaknesses. Her personal theory of supervision becomes consolidated and she now has a professional identity that includes that of supervisor. She now is fairly autonomous, though will seek support if necessary.

Role mastery, the fourth stage is characterized by consistency and coherence. The supervisor has a solid sense of her skills and abilities, and she handles supervisory problems effectively. She has a consistent awareness of her supervisory strengths and weaknesses and an image of herself as an effective supervisor. Her theory of supervision, which is personalized and theoretically consistent, consistently guides her practice. She has a well-integrated sense of her identity as a supervisor, and is self-reliant.

Watkins generates a number of variables that he considers salient in developing the model in addition to developmental stage: how supervisors deal with issues in their own development; how the personality of the supervisor impedes or facilitates the supervisory relationship; how much supervisor training or supervision the supervisor has had; how experienced the supervisor is; what environmental supports the supervisor has.

Strengths and limitations of developmental models

As Bernard and Goodyear (1998) note, these models have proved appealing in part because they are meta-theoretical (that is, not tied to a particular theory, but able to be used across theories). They have certainly increased sophistication within supervision because of their direct implications for practice and training. They have also provided a conceptual framework for research. Additionally, they facilitate thinking about supervisor and supervisee development across a professional lifetime. They make intuitive sense for supervisors, who can identify their own developmental progress and that of their supervisees in these models. Importantly, they identify complementary processes in the development of both supervisor and supervisee, which is absent from the theory-bound models of supervision.

Developmental theory has been implicit in psychoanalytic supervisory practice. Scaife (2001) proposed that "the theory of learning in psychoanalytic supervision is of a developmental progression that takes place through the establishment of a learning alliance" (p. 192). She describes how analytic supervisees begin by being heavily reliant on the supervisor to guide them through their work with their patients. As the supervisee introjects the qualities of the supervisor and identifies with her, he becomes more independent and increasingly reflective, so that eventually he becomes more autonomous through the development of what Casement (1985) calls the internal supervisor. Casement argues that with developmental maturity there should be a more equal dialogue between the supervisee's internal supervisor and the person of the external supervisor.

Despite the intuitive attractiveness for supervisors and their heuristic qualities, there has been quite a lot of criticism of supervision models, not least that they are simplistic. Holloway (1987) also argues that they do not provide an adequate developmental explanation from the standpoint of developmental psychology, which is the theory base on which they were predicated. Most people tend to think of themselves as improving with experience, but in fact Worthington, in a review of the research in 1987, suggests that while there is some evidence that some supervisor–supervisee dyads change as supervisees increase in experience, supervisors do not necessarily become more competent with experience. Watkins (1995), in an update of Worthington's paper, concludes that there is some support for the model, but that the research remains flawed. There has been insufficient attention paid, for example, to the actual behaviours of both supervisor and supervisee in supervisory sessions and there are many unanswered questions about how supervisees develop over time. It is only in recent models (such as the IDM) that the supervisory relationship itself has become a focus; in this respect most developmental models share some of the limitations of the early therapy models. As Beinart (2004) notes, given the amount of theories and research in the area, the findings are disappointing.

A process model of supervision or the seven-eyed model of supervision

Hawkins and Shohet's (2000) model has elements in common with Frawley-O'Dea and Sarnat's (2001) model in that it encompasses the relationship between supervisor and supervisee as well as that between supervisee and patient. The model pays attention to six interlocking foci: the session content; the therapist's strategies and interventions; the therapy relationship; the internal experience of the therapist; the supervisory relationship; the internal experience of the supervisor. Hawkins and Shohet's model further sets these foci in the context in which supervision takes place.

The session content: Shainberg argued that "it is the task of the supervisor to enable the supervisees to become more aware of what actually takes place in the session" (1983, cited in Hawkins and Shohet, 2000, p. 71). This involves not only an accurate description of the patient and what happened in the session, but also an avoid-ance of premature theorizing and interpretation of what has happened. Other tasks involve an exploration of the connections between one part of the session and another, and of the presented session with previous ones. It is in this part of the model that the conscious and unconscious mind of the patient is attended to.

Strategies and interventions: in this mode of working the focus is on what interventions the supervisee made in the session, how and why they made them, and what they would do now on reflection.

Hawkins and Shohet advocate brainstorming and active role-playing, including supervisor and supervisee role-reversing. They caution against the supervisor offering her own interventions on the basis that there is a danger of the supervisee introjecting the intervention and with it the supervisor's mode of working rather than developing the quality of his own interventions.

The therapy relationship: Hawkins and Shohet view the therapeutic dyad as a system and advocate that the supervisor focuses on the conscious and unconscious interaction between them. It is in this mode that the patient's transference is attended to. Hawkins and Shohet argue that the job of the supervisor is "listening to how the unconscious of the client is informing the therapist about what the client needs and how the therapist is helping or getting in the way" (p. 76).

The therapist's process: the supervisee's countertransference is one aspect of the process. Hawkins and Shohet distinguish between four different types of countertransference: the therapist's own transference feelings stirred up by the patient; the therapist's response to the patient's transference; feelings in the therapist used to avoid or counter the patient's transference; projected material from the patient that the therapist has taken in. Hawkins and Shohet suggest ways in which the supervisee's countertransference can be elicited, including asking "who does this person remind you of?" and asking the supervisee to describe how their patient is like the person and what is unfinished in their relationship to that person.

The supervisory relationship: in this mode the focus moves away from the client and therapist and to the supervisor focusing on herself. Hawkins and Shohet identify parallel processing as an important focus in the supervisory relationship. They note that in managing this skilfully the supervisor needs to be able to process her own reactions and to feed her observations back to the supervisee in a non-judgemental way.

The supervisor's process: in this mode Hawkins and Shohet focus on the disruptions that the supervisor might experience during supervision; for example, boredom when a particular patient is being discussed. They argue that the unconscious material of the therapist is being received by the supervisor, who then processes it and makes it available for exploration. They also draw attention to the supervisor–patient relationship, and how her fantasies about the patient may alert the supervisor to previously overlooked aspects of the therapeutic or supervisory relationship.

The wider context: here Hawkins and Shohet draw our attention to the fact that therapy and supervision take place in a contextual field. This includes the organizations to which one or both are contracted, as well as the professional bodies to which they are affiliated.

Hawkins and Shohet argue that good supervision should pay attention to all seven modes, and that training with supervisors should help them identify which processes in the model they most frequently use and which they are less confident of or neglect. They recognize that for many supervisors the supervisor-focused modes are the most difficult to access, particularly new supervisors, who are less confident of their supervisory skills.

Strengths and limitations of the Hawkins and Shohet model

Although this model uses quite a number of psychodynamic principles, it is not specifically a therapy model, and has therefore been used by those who are not psychodynamically trained as a way of understanding supervision. It is a practical rather than an heuristic model, and as such makes intuitive sense to supervisors, particularly those who are psychodynamically orientated. It is also a flexible, accessible, and pragmatic model; for example, Hawkins and Shohet suggest that the dominant mode of focus should shift according to a number of factors. One of these is the developmental level of the supervisee: they suggest focusing on modes 1 and 2 with beginning therapists and only later including modes 3, 4, 5 and 6. They also pay attention to individual issues that are often neglected in other models, such as the supervisee's personality, learning style, work style, and cultural background. Another strength of the model is that, unlike a number of models of supervision, it can be used for group as well as individual supervision.

However, there are significant limitations. The model is not well elaborated and it does not easily lend itself to rigorous evaluation. Consequently, there is a paucity of research, so establishing the efficacy of the model is almost impossible. Like other models, it does not attend sufficiently to how the supervisory alliance is built, and seems to assume it. It does not look at the tasks and functions of supervision nor what actually happens in supervision, including the behaviour of the supervisory dyad. Thinking in terms of Kolb's learning theory, it does not pay sufficient attention to the different learning styles or needs of supervisees and does not explain the process by which the supervisee progresses in supervision.

Conclusion

These models illustrate some of the many models of supervision that are in current use. As well as exploring therapy models I have drawn on models that use psychodynamic ideas to explain the supervisory process in order to widen the frame of reference within which we can think about how, why and to what effect we supervise.

References

Beinart, H. (2004). Models of supervision and the supervisory relationship and their evidence base. In: I. Fleming & L. Steen (Eds.), *Supervision and Clinical Psychology: Theory, Practice and Perspectives.* Hove: Brunner-Routledge.

Bernard, J. M., & Goodyear, R. K. (1998). *Fundamentals of Clinical Supervision* (2nd edn). London: Allyn & Baker.

Bowlby, J. (1988). *A Secure Base: Clinical Applications of Attachment Theory.* London: Routledge.

Brown, L. J., & Miller, M. (2002). The triadic intersubjective matrix in supervision: the use of disclosure to work through painful affects. *International Journal of Psychoanalysis, 83:* 811–823.

Carroll, M. (1996). *Counselling Supervision: Theory, Skills and Practice.* London: Cassell.

Casement, P. (1985). *On Learning From the Patient.* London: Tavistock.

Feltham, C., & Dryden, W. (1994). *Developing Counsellor Supervision.* London: Sage.

Frawley-O'Dea, M. G., & Sarnat, J. E. (2001). *The Supervisory Relationship: A Contemporary Psychoanalytic Approach.* New York: Guilford.

Freud, S. (1912e). Recommendations to physicians practising psychoanalysis. *S.E., 12:* 111–120. London: Hogarth.

Hawkins, P., & Shohet, R. (2000). *Supervision in the Helping Professions: An Individual, Group and Organisational Approach.* (2nd edn). Buckingham: Open University Press.

Holloway, E. L. (1987). Developmental models of supervision: is it development? *Professional Psychology, 18*(3): 189–208.

Kolb, D. A. (1984). *Experiential Learning: Experience as the Source of Learning and Development.* Englewood Cliffs, NJ: Prentice-Hall.

Langs, R. (1994). *Doing Supervision and Being Supervised.* London: Karnac.

Matthews, S., & Treacher, A. (2004). Therapy models and supervision in clinical practice. In: I. Fleming & L. Steen (Eds.), *Supervision and Clinical Psychology: Theory, Practice and Perspectives.* Hove: Brunner-Routledge.

Raschick, M., Maypole, D. E., & Day, P. (1998). Improving field education through Kolb's learning theory. *Journal of Social Work Education, 34*(1): 31–42.

Scaife, J. (2001). *Supervision in the Mental Health Professions: A Practitioner's Guide.* Hove: Brunner-Routledge.

Stoltenberg, C. D., & Delworth, U. (1987). *Supervising Counsellors and Therapists.* San Francisco, CA: Jossey-Bass.

Stoltenberg, C. D., McNeill, B., & Delworth, U. (1998). *IDM Supervision: An Integrated Developmental Model for Supervising Counsellors and Therapists.* San Francisco, CA: Jossey-Bass.

Van Soest, D., & Kruzich, J. (1994). The influence of learning styles on student and field instructor perceptions of field placement success. *Journal of Teaching in Social Work, 9:* 49–69.

Watkins, C. E. (1993). Development of the psychotherapy supervisor; concepts, assumptions, and hypotheses of the supervisor complexity model. *American Journal of Psychotherapy, 14*(1): 58–74.

Watkins, C. E. (1995). Psychotherapy supervisor and supervisee: developmental models and research nine years on. *Clinical Psychology Review, 15*(7): 647–680.

Worthington, E. L. (1987). Changes in supervision as counsellors and supervisors gain experience: a review. *Professional Psychology: Research and Practice, 18:* 189–204.

CHAPTER FIVE

Supervising trainees: teaching the values and techniques of psychoanalytic psychotherapy

Jean Arundale

W hen I was asked to talk about supervision technique, for the BAP course on "Developing supervision skills", my initial response was "I'm not sure what the technique is, but I can think about what I do and maybe find out." Thinking of supervision as having a technique with a set of skills to be learned seems a natural approach in our technical culture, so I accepted the invitation. However, I soon had second thoughts about the notion of technique. Is supervision a matter of laying out procedures of good practice to be followed, or something deeper? I have now come to believe that the concept of technique in supervision is somewhat artificial, a view of the surface, and that it is much more a matter of values internalized from the experience and study of psychoanalysis that counts.

So I begin with some questions that are perhaps heretical in view of current trends towards training in supervision. Is it possible to teach the job of supervision, as such? Is supervision a group of skills or a process that can be transmitted in a training course? Is it necessary to provide training for the position of supervisor? Is training a necessary requirement for the job?

I am not at all sure that the answer to any of these questions is "yes". Whether in private practice or NHS work, I feel that a capacity for supervision and knowing the best way to go about it grows organically out of having had, first of all, a good personal analysis; then, one needs a firm grip on reality, wide reading of the psychoanalytic and psychotherapy literature, opportunities to discuss early cases with experienced practitioners, followed by a substantial experience of working as a therapist, perhaps 5–6 years, in treating a wide variety of patients in clinical practice. After training and entering independent practice, or acquiring a job as a therapist, it is usual to seek further supervision, or perhaps be required to have it, to advance one's own development, particularly when we encounter patients with pathology we cannot understand, with therapies that are stuck, or with very disturbed and disturbing patients. Now, with CPD requirements, one can expect frequent returns to supervision throughout a professional career, or regularly seeking what is now termed "consultation", which may be a brief version of supervision of around 4–6 sessions.

As practising therapists deepen their understanding of unconscious processes through study of their own cases and those of others, through peer group discussions, journals, books, or conferences, they may feel ready to begin to supervise. It seems to me that this point comes when a therapist has internalized psychoanalytic values and concepts sufficiently well, and begins to trust him or herself to know enough to start supervising others. I do not think that supervision courses can provide a short-cut or substitute for "maturing in the vat", so to speak, although courses and "how to" manuals, can provide food for thought after an overall level of experience and confidence has been reached. Courses or lectures can be used as a context for thinking about the issues and putting one's mind in order, yet, without a deeply felt commitment to psychoanalytic values, internalized, digested, and made one with core beliefs, supervision methods acquired by simply following rules of technique or by imitation can lead to supervision that rings hollow, or falters in confusion.

When I speak of psychoanalytic values, a number of elements come to mind, the first being a belief in the existence of an unconscious, with dreams, free associations, parapraxes, and enactments as the main paths to its discovery. A conviction that the unconscious exists is not something to be taken for granted. To be slightly provocative, it is said that one's first analysis is to convince one of the reality of the unconscious in oneself, and one's second is to fully analyse it. Further, the belief that unconscious psychic reality is the source of neurosis and personality disturbance, and that this involves sexual and aggressive urges, defences that protect a vulnerable, angry, or libidinal inner self and cherished or hated objects, and that this inner self can be reached in the therapeutic relationship, is vital in analytic work. The belief in insight as a condition for change is important, and that it is necessary to expend time on understanding transference and countertransference as the foundation and vehicle for insight and meaning. There are other values in the analytic corpus without which a supervisor is likely to be ineffective, such as honesty, professionalism, a real empathy for human suffering, and an epistemophilic drive towards understanding and truth. A genuine keenness and satisfaction when insight is found, whether by the patient, therapist, or supervisor, cannot be simulated, and represents a coming together of the highest psychoanalytic values: that is, an emotional, cognitive, and symbolic understanding of symptoms and neurotic patterns in the patient. Together with the capacity for reflection, making links and connections, thinking, remembering, and working through, all of these values form the psychoanalytic identity of the supervisor who will help to form the psychoanalytic identity of the trainee.

Much has been written about the "learning alliance" in the psychoanalytic education literature (Dewald, 1987; Fleming & Benedek, 1966). In the early years, supervision was through a so-called "control analysis", with a senior, experienced analyst laying down the rules of psychoanalysis and dictating how the therapy should proceed. This was challenged by proponents of a more *laissez-faire* approach, those who felt the candidate needed to learn at his own pace without so much control on the part of the supervisor. It is now agreed that the trainee needs freedom to discuss work in a place where it is safe to explore problems and discuss mistakes with a supervisor who is trusted, while at the same time keeping within a disciplined learning alliance. A recent researcher, Nicholas Ladany (2004) has studied the learning alliance and finds empirical evidence that it is the foundation stone for effective supervision. He defines the supervisory working alliance as a mutual agreement on goals and tasks of supervision together with an emotional bond between supervisor and supervisee, suggesting that attention to the development of a strong alliance in the first three to five sessions is significantly related to a satisfactory supervision experience. Thus, establishing a good relationship with the trainee and clarifying the goals and tasks early on will increase and facilitate learning.

Once a good supervisory alliance is formed, regular feedback to the trainee on his performance and functioning as a therapist is necessary. It is bad practice not to confront the trainee with learning problems, mistakes, or inadequacies as they come up, though this can go against the grain for those who feel supporting the trainee is primary. One of the worst mistakes a supervisor can make, in my view, came to my attention a few years ago when, after two years of supervision during which there was no mention by the supervisor of any problems with her work nor any critical feedback, the time came for qualification and the supervisor said, to the surprise and shock of the trainee, that she could not give permission. This, I think, is inexcusable. The supervisor, in my view, has a didactic responsibility to teach the supervisee, to explain if something is going wrong, or where the supervisee is falling short.

There was another debate in psychoanalytic training institutions in the 1930s concerning whether the supervisor should also have a therapeutic role, as was the practice up until then, since the supervisor is particularly well placed to see a therapist's pathology as it appears in supervision or in interaction with the patient (Eckstein & Wallerstein, 1958). There is now a consensus amongst psychoanalytically-based trainers that supervision should not include therapy for the trainee and that all trainees should have their own therapist or analyst. Nevertheless, in view of the fact that many supervisees have limited experience of being in therapy or analysis, particularly in NHS settings, often a concise remark by the supervisor, either arising spontaneously or carefully thought out, can help the trainee to be aware of where his own personality is interfering with the therapeutic process. Trainee problems might be such tendencies as too much rigidity, intellectualism, wanting to be liked by the patient, a tendency to mother or nanny, guilt about not giving the patient more, fear of the patient's anger, or conflicting states of mind or blind spots in the trainee that the supervisor can help resolve. Nevertheless, principally, supervision should be firmly patient-orientated and, when the supervisee's problems leak into the supervision or the therapy, it is appropriate, I feel, for the supervisor to suggest that the problem is taken to the therapist's own analysis or therapy.

In my view, supervision is an apprenticeship in which learners attach themselves to an experienced clinician to become proficient in using the tools of their trade. The apprenticeship method involves learning on the job and learning from experience, together with careful overseeing by the supervisor, who monitors the therapy, correcting technique when necessary, giving support and encouragement. Supervision input depends on the stage of the trainee: supervisors will need to be more didactically active at the beginning of training, then, over time, less active as the trainees find their feet and develop their own style.

However, others take a different view of supervision, seeing it as an evolutionary process in which two equals come together bringing many influences, life experience, and knowledge from the past, joining up to understand and treat a third person, the patient. Whichever view is taken, the foundation and core theories, the values and principles, the tried and true fundamentals of psychotherapy, will need to come into the equation, to be clarified, discussed, and absorbed until some level of proficiency is reached, and the supervisor can feel confident that the trainee has a grasp of his patient's dilemma and is a safe-enough pair of hands.

Methods and techniques of supervision

Management of supervision

Management issues include keeping watch over the boundaries of the setting, keeping to the regular time and place, and generally overseeing the relationship with the outside world, which may include reporting the progress of trainees to professional organizations, writing letters to referrers or to the patient, or seeing that trainees keep NHS records up to date on patient contact.

Supervision begins, optimally, with a written report from an assessor who has evaluated the patient's suitability for an analytic approach. After discussing the assessment report, the supervisee is then prepared for the first session with the patient and asked to make notes, as verbatim as possible, and to read them out in supervision. Note-taking is essential, not only to enable the supervisor to understand what is going on in the therapeutic process, but also as an essential part of the training of the aspiring therapist's mind, to hone his associative memory and to help internalize not only this particular patient, but psychoanalytic thinking as a whole.

The supervisor is responsible for knowing about and discussing issues of confidentiality and ethical practice with the trainee. Also, it is the duty of the supervisor to act responsibly whenever there are crisis situations, seeing that GPs, psychiatrists, or CPNs are contacted, when appropriate.

Environment of the supervision session

Although there is a basic discipline to be learned, most supervisors agree that supervision is generally an enjoyable experience, easier and less emotionally demanding than therapy, where one is on the firing line of strong positive and negative transferences or uncomfortable projections. Supervision is a place where the supervisor can allow his or her thoughts and imagination to flow in ways that are not possible in therapy sessions. Although the relationship in supervision is as apprentice to master craftsman, it is important to foster a shared search for meaning and understanding, to get the best learning environment. In an atmosphere of enquiry, with enough time to discuss issues that come up, trainee and supervisor can explore larger questions such as the meaning and purpose of symptoms, the forms and sources of human anxiety, the curious workings of the unconscious, the structure of the mind, and what it means to be a human being.

Having said that supervision can be a pleasure, none the less a main function of the supervision session is the toleration and containment of anxiety, uncertainty, and ambiguity. Therapist anxiety about competence is multiplied by having to function as the container for the patient's anxiety. The supervisor has constantly to work at identifying and interpreting sources of anxiety, exercising a developed capacity for containment.

One may need to be a model of patience in tolerating the length of time it takes for the therapist to learn and for the patient to change, and not to be irritated or bored (as supervisees sometimes are) by repetitious behaviour, reversals, or refusal to change in the patient. When there are puzzling transferences, dreams, or behaviours that cannot be understood after being worked on in supervision, the supervisor will indicate a need to wait for more material to emerge and to think together in future sessions until things become clearer. A wound to self-esteem is often involved, for it can be painful to admit to not knowing something and to take in something new, so that praising the trainee for a piece of good work is helpful as a counterbalance. In my view, some humour is important as a leavening and to help regulate tension, for the work can sometimes be demoralizing when there is severe disorder, self-destructiveness, or tragedy in patient's lives.

The environment of supervision in a group can have distinct advantages over individual supervision in several ways. There is the opportunity to learn from the cases of others, to enter into enriching group discussions of patient material; and the shared experience helps to reduce anxiety and gives a sense of collegial friendliness. Even though envy and competition sometimes arise, the collegial opportunity for co-learning outweighs the risk of rivalries or group tensions, always present in professional situations at any rate. In NHS work, where Honorary Psychotherapists on training courses are mixed in with Junior Doctors getting experience of psychotherapy to fulfil the requirements of their psychiatric training, I believe it is important for all therapists in the group to report on at least one of their patients each week. It is an advantage if the supervisor does the assessing of patients so as to have first hand knowledge of them.

Bringing together theory and practice

A crucial, ongoing task of supervision is to link events in the therapy with psychoanalytic concepts. Whenever material in the session illustrates a concept, the supervisor can point this out and discuss the theory, formulating a hypothesis to be tested in the next session. Then, it is often helpful to discuss how different theorists, Freudians, Kleinians, Winnicottians, Bionians, or cognitive–behaviourists, for example, would handle the material, and one can include examples from one's own practice. It is usual for the supervisor to suggest articles or books to read as they come to mind in relation to the material. I find David Malan's book *Individual Psychotherapy and the Science of Psychodynamics* (1979) useful with beginning NHS therapists, as it simply and clearly describes transference links in present and past relationships, with many interesting case vignettes.

What about the charge by our critics that we impose theories on the material rather than working with what emerges from the patient? Ideally, we want, as Bion (1970) suggests, to be without memory or desire, to be in a state of "not knowing", fully tuned into the patient in the present moment, hearing and learning something entirely new, but much of the time we will respond to the patient's spontaneously produced associations with interpretations linked to mental patterns organized by our theories based on past experience of this patient or previously known ones. I firmly believe that there is no such thing as value-free or theory-free perception, thought, action, or practice. One's theories, whether tacit or explicit, are always involved in every therapeutic intervention we make, so it is far better to be aware of the theoretical framework we use, helping supervisees to keep it in mind in work with patients. This will offer some proof against unconscious contradictory theories or insidious ones creeping into the work.

Teaching the basic building blocks of analytic therapy

The basic model for supervision, in my view, is a structuring that takes place in the supervisor's mind, based on Ronald Britton's (1998) concept of "triangular space"—the supervisor observes the therapeutic pair from a third position, identifying with the situation of the patient and then with the therapist in turn, and trying to make each position clear to the supervisee. The term "identifying" here embraces the term "empathy", that is, putting oneself inside the mind of the patient, then the therapist, and feeling and thinking along with each of them. Then, central to the psychoanalytic approach, the supervisor observes the interaction of the therapeutic pair in order to clarify their relationship, which is part and parcel of the therapeutic process. It is also necessary to have a grasp of the social and cultural realities of the patient, bringing these into the discussion when appropriate. When the supervisor speaks of his observations he will convey how his mind works in understanding the therapeutic process, and by this means, get across the principles of analytic therapy.

Active listening skills cannot be overemphasized. Listening well with what is commonly called "free-floating attention" is actually quite difficult. To help the trainee to attune to the patient's unconscious and to really hear and feel the emotional/thought patterns, while keeping in touch with associations to the patient's recent and past history, is no small task, so that the cultivation of receptivity and listening will need to be frequently stressed.

I tell trainees at the beginning that the work of supervision will be to create a picture of the patient's personality and mental functioning, and to continue to elaborate this, embroidering as one does a tapestry, as new information emerges. Then, attention will be focused in detail on the fine-grained processes in the session, as through a magnifying glass, in order to illuminate the present internal state of the patient and the immediate relationship between the therapist and patient. Although emphasis on one or the other of these aspects of the patient, micro or macro, present moment or whole personality, may reflect the theoretical orientation of the supervisor, I believe that attention to both areas is essential. Good supervisors are intuitively responsive to the need for both, understanding what is happening in the here and now and how this links to the bigger picture, flexibly giving each attention in the supervisory process.

In teaching trainees how to frame interpretations, the wording is of the utmost importance. Telling the supervisee how to put things to the patient is often the best way to teach certain concepts and techniques, particularly in relation to timing, dosage, linking past with present, and interpreting the transference or countertransference. However, although saying what you would say at a given moment is a useful teaching tool, it has its drawbacks as it can produce dependency and imitation in the supervisee. Using the supervisor's words to patch on to work with a patient, as in a collage, is a temporary solution to difficulties but may not foster the higher aim of integrating new learning, so that the trainee needs to be encouraged to develop his own style.

Quite a lot has been written about the so-called "parallel process" in supervision; that is, when the projections and evacuations of the patient into the therapist are then projected into the supervisor or supervision group, giving rise to disturbances in supervision. These are sometimes powerful, sometimes subtle, unconscious, undigested or possibly indigestible emotional states that have not been understood or verbalized in the therapy session. These feelings or enactments can, one hopes, be brought to consciousness and discussed and understood in terms of the patient's pathology, then relocated in the patient's experience and used therapeutically. The parallel process is a convincing way to teach the operation and uses of countertransference, although it must not, in my view, be used as the main source of information about the therapeutic process, as some supervisors may insist. Persistent appearance of a parallel process in supervision can indicate that the therapist is overwhelmed by the patient's projections, unable to process them, and probably confused about what went on in the therapeutic session, and this will need to be addressed. Yet, at times, countertransference can effectively pick up the patient's background states that are unavailable to consciousness in either therapist or patient. An example is one of my trainees who actively dislikes her patient, coming in each week to complain about her and express anger in relation to the patient's ingratitude, her frequent messing around with session times and low-fee payments, her feeling that she never gets enough, and her obstinate refusal to value what the therapist gives.

Even though I try to point out patiently the meaning of these things in terms of the patient's psychopathology, and speak of her own unrealistic expectations that the patient will be able to change as quickly as she would like, the trainee is constantly irritated in the countertransference and I am constantly irritated with her, which makes me feel impotent, ungenerous, and unable to think. Is this a problem with the patient, the therapist, or the supervisor? As I try to process my annoyance at what I feel is the trainee's arrogance and scorn at this early stage of training, it becomes clearer that this is a projection of the patient's anger and refusal to accept what is given due to arrogance and narcissistic superiority that was not evident up to now in the material, which in turn is projected into me. As we work on the roots of these patterns in the patient, understanding these as defences in relation to childhood deprivation and the loss of her mother in early adolescence, the trainee is able to empathize more and to acknowledge and link with her own emotional patterns of not being appreciated. And I feel less irritated with her.

Difficulties in being a trainee

Early on, trainees frequently confound negative transference with their own feelings of incompetence as beginning therapists. It is often difficult to show the beginner that the patient's negative feelings of suspicion or mistrust, denigration of the therapist, or expressed hopelessness about getting help from the treatment is actually transference and not due to their inexperience. This negativity is part of the patients' internal world of experience with objects from the past who have let them down, exploited them or not been able to help them, and would occur even with the most senior therapist; this is negative transference that must be interpreted.

A thorny problem in teaching in NHS settings is theoretical difference. There are many different frameworks and models of how to do therapy in our pluralistic field, and there is no consensus regarding the best way, even within the same training institute. When a supervisee is in an analysis different from the supervisor's orientation, conflicting views on the importance of such things as interpreting the transference, the Oedipus complex, or even the emphasis on a mind having difficulty with thinking, can interfere with the learning alliance.

I will now give a detailed example of difficulty with a supervisee in one of my NHS groups, who appeared to be deaf to my supervisory guidelines. Lawrence, an honorary therapist, who was competent with his two other patients, was seeing an isolated, lonely young woman in her late twenties who worked for a dot.com company and spent most of her time in front of a computer. At assessment, although clearly there were sexual problems since she had had no boyfriends and hardly any sexual experience, there was no sign of the perverse sexuality that was later to emerge. After a good beginning, as the therapy proceeded the woman began to send e-mails to a man with whom she had had a one-night stand six years previously and who had suggested to her that they practise kinky sex, then treated her unkindly and dropped her. The therapy sessions became consumed by her desire to see this man again, even though he was now married and, although he answered her e-mails, he appeared not particularly interested in renewing contact with her. Nevertheless, her persistence led to his inviting her to see a film that contained perverse sex. In the supervision sessions, I suggested to Lawrence that he point out clearly what was happening and where this flirtation was going— that she was fascinated by the man's cruelty and was looking for a sado-masochistic relationship. I pointed out to the trainee that he needed to bring the energy into the transference by interpreting that the patient was finding the long gap during the week difficult and wished to have some contact with him between the sessions, perhaps even thinking of e-mailing him. Further talk of the patient's virtual relationship went on in the sessions without interpretative action by the trainee. In the next supervision I suggested that Lawrence remind his patient that the man was married, was not available, and to make interpretations of her wish to take the man away from his wife, thereby linking with her oedipal wishes to get in between her parents and to possess her father for herself.

In further sessions I said I thought the obsessive, excited talk about this wished-for relationship was a defence against the anxiety of being in the room with a male therapist, that the patient was fearful of intimacy and that she was afraid in the transference that the therapist would flirt with her and then drop her, treating her badly. Lawrence appeared to be deaf still to my words, but listened with interest to the patient's further plans to meet this man. I went on to try to convey that the patient wanted to excite her therapist by speaking of seductive ideas, and that she was using excitement as a defence against depressive feelings. The therapist duly wrote down my suggestions but no sign of them occurred in the material in the following weeks. Instead, he said to the patient things like, "and how did you leave it", and "and then what did he say", as if he was fascinated with how this tale would develop—sounding very much like a voyeur mesmerized by what would happen next, as hooked-in as the patient was. As I told him this I found myself getting agitated, saying that unless he began to show her what she was doing and bring it into the transference, she would act out unconscious sado-masochistic phantasies to her detriment, the very problem for which she had come into therapy to get help. His response was that he had been told in his coursework that making transference interpretations too early is ineffective and that they

would bounce off, that in his theoretical orientation explicit interpretations telling the patient what is going on are avoided—the
patient is meant to discover for herself, and he felt she was doing
that. I urged him to experiment, to try out interpreting how the
patient was tantalizing him in the transference and that if this
was wrong, no harm would be done. After urging him to speak, to
no avail, my tolerance was growing thin, and I finally said I would
have to stop the therapy, for which, in the NHS, I hold clinical responsibility, if he did not think about and do what I was
asking. The penny apparently dropped, and Lawrence came in the
following weeks having begun to put to his patient some of what
had been discussed, and the fascination with the man subsided; in
its place the patient spoke of her painful and sad relationship with
her father. The therapy now began moving on in the direction of
work around her anxious rejection of her femininity, her confusion
about her sexual identity, and the pleasure she gets from breaking
rules.

My belief about the supervisor's role can be taken from the
above vignette, that "the buck stops here", in the words of Harry
Truman. The responsibility for the therapy, not for the patient, but
for the conduct of the treatment, must rest in the hands of the
supervisor. However, doubts crept in and I began to question: was
I actually right in proceeding as I did? Did I help the trainee enough
with how scared he was to make transference interpretations, afraid
of the perverse or even non-perverse erotic transference? Did I
stress enough how interpretations in the transference reduce the
erotic content rather than increase it? Although I spoke from my
convictions of what I felt was a clear case of therapist voyeurism,
was I presenting enough options, holding the tension, or perhaps
even interfering in a unique therapeutic process? Why couldn't the
trainee understand me, were there unbridgeable theoretical differences? Should I have explored to a greater degree Lawrence's countertransference? How will our work together continue in view of
his attitude of "knowing best" and the obviously unresolved areas
of his sexuality? This sort of uncertainty and self-questioning in my
view needs to be a constant companion to supervision. The supervisory process itself, like all of our work, is full of uncertainties,
based as it is on a once-removed report of complex processes bound
to be imprecise and distorted in many ways. Fortunately, very few

supervisees are like Lawrence; most listen to, learn from, use, and are grateful for, supervisory input.

The supervisor as a transmitter of values

When working as a supervisor, it is important to keep in mind that trainees will be forming their professional identities based substantially on their experiences with you. Being perceived as a person who not only upholds standards of best practice and clinical competence, but who also has personal qualities such as integrity, persistence, and enjoyment of the work is vital. When supervision goes well, the therapist begins to reach a point where self-supervision is possible, a formation of what Patrick Casement (1985) has termed the "internal supervisor", but what I would rather call the internalization of psychoanalytic values. In our place as supervisors we are in a prime position to speak in a way that transmits professional values and core understandings of what it means to be a psychoanalytic psychotherapist.

To conclude, the supervisor has a crucial part in psychotherapy education; he or she is usually considered to be the main arbiter of whether a trainee is allowed to qualify. In spite of the inexactitudes of supervisory methods, the supervisor is in the best position to evaluate the quality of the trainee's work and to judge whether he or she has sufficiently taken in and consolidated the enduring psychoanalytic values.

References

Bion, W. R. (1970). *Attention and Interpretation*. London: Karnac.

Britton, R. (1998). Subjectivity, objectivity and triangular space. In: *Belief and Imagination. Explorations in Psychoanalysis*. London: Routledge.

Casement, P. (1985). *On Learning from the Patient*. London: Tavistock.

Dewald, Paul A. (1987). *Learning Process in Psychoanalytic Supervision: Complexities and Challenges*. Madison, CT: International Universities Press.

Eckstein, R., & Wallerstein, R. S. (1958). *The Teaching and Learning of Psychotherapy*. New York: International Universities Press, 1972.

Fleming, J., & Benedek, T. (1966). *Psychoanalytic Supervision*. New York: International Universities Press, 1983.

Ladany, N. (2004). What lies beneath psychotherapy research? *Psychotherapy Research, 14*: 1–19.

Malan, D. (1979). *Individual Psychotherapy and the Science of Psychodynamics*. London: Butterworth.

CHAPTER SIX

Some dynamics of supervision

Mary Twyman

It is only in recent years that the subject of supervision in psychoanalysis and in psychoanalytic psychotherapy has become the topic of study and of training. Before that it was assumed that any competent practitioner of sufficient seniority would possess the qualities necessary to carry out the supervision of students or junior colleagues. So the technique of supervision is a comparatively recent area of debate, and differing styles of supervision are beginning to be described. My own take on this in the current paper is a personal one, and I aim to explain my approach to supervision and the attitudes that inform it as I have developed over the years of supervising psychoanalytic psychotherapy practice in differing settings.

My primary aim is to help the therapist to become the practitioner s/he is capable of becoming. I do not think that my role is to impose my own style of work upon the supervisee. It is important to give due respect and recognition to what the therapist beings to the task, including life experience, previous work in related and unrelated fields. I view my task in supervising is to potentiate whatever ability, whatever talent, whatever sensibility the therapist brings to the encounter with the patient. This does not, however, preclude the aspect of the task that involves helping to correct aspects of the work that need to change.

In the early stages of getting to know the therapist one aim is to elicit what the therapist's implicit theory of mind is. They will certainly have one, made up variously of their own experience of analysis, previous supervision, seminars and lectures attended, reading and whatever brought them to the field of psychotherapy in the first place. For example, one group of therapists with whom I and a colleague were associated for three years in both teaching theory and clinical practice as well as supervising, had in its background training a quite specific orientation towards the object relation theory as propounded by Fairbairn and Guntrip. Each member of the group had a version of their theories and it persisted as a general tendency in the group. The introduction of other ideas presented something of a challenge to this established group theory of mind, as I am referring to it. However, once this is recognized by both supervisor and therapist, and the implicit theoretical orientation can be made explicit, there is an entrée to the supervisory process and a starting point for communication with the therapist in terms that are familiar to them. At the same time, the supervisor can seek to widen the framework of reference by introducing other theoretical and clinical ideas as may be appropriate to the cases brought. Initially, this challenge is often unwelcome, destabilizing and deskilling to the therapist so it requires both tact and firmness from the supervisor. Increasingly it stimulates the therapist to examine their own theoretical approach to their patient and the techniques they habitually employ, and how far these are or are not appropriate to the clinical picture now emerging. Therapists often need considerable support to find the confidence to use new ideas, new insights and theories, and to learn to judge the timing and appropriateness of untried lines of interpretation. These latter need to become the therapist's "own" and to carry conviction rather than be "applied" because the supervisor has suggested them.

This raises the question of how far is supervision a teaching and instructing activity. In some measure, of course, it is, but it is more than that. There will be times when the supervision has to be explicitly directive, perhaps in matters of technique, in the use of appropriate language for interpretation, in matters that pertain to the management of the setting of boundaries, of managing breaks, and of setting fees in private practice. There are also the requirements of the treatment setting in an agency whether NHS or other formalized agency. While these are integral to the supervisory process, I prefer to think of the supervision experience intrinsically as an educational one, and by this I mean in more than one direction. My view is that supervision is only really creatively effective if both members of the supervisory dyad are part of the learning experience. I expect to learn from the therapists I supervise as well as that they should learn from me. From a pragmatic point of view, as an analyst, there is a finite number of cases I have treated and shall treat in the course of my professional career in practice. One hears and reads of many cases from colleagues, in meetings, peer group supervision, conferences, etc., but there is a particular privilege in hearing week by week the work of analysis in an intensive psychotherapy case. This broadens my experience and challenges me to struggle along with the therapist to understand the myriad manifestations of unconscious processes, elusive and disguised as they are, by the resistances of the patient being presented, the therapist presenting, and my own as the listener. Supervision is hard work for all three of us.

Some of my observations on the dynamics of the supervisor–therapist relationship derive from working in a multi-disciplinary team in a NHS setting, in which intensive psychotherapy cases were undertaken by senior registrars, senior psychologists, and social workers, all of whom were being trained to staff psychotherapy posts in the health service. There were certain external factors that had consequences in affecting the relationship: for example, doctors being supervised by an analyst whose former status in the team was that of social worker—thus cutting across usual discipline boundaries. There were also represented in the department students from overseas with vastly different cultural norms, some with language limitations, students coming into a largely secular society from various religions, and from different ethnic and cultural backgrounds. They faced the difficulty of their confrontation with a complex British NHS organization and within that the theory and clinical practice of psychoanalysis. So, as well as the supervisor's search to glean a sense of the therapist's implicit theory of mind, this presented me as supervisor with the need to learn, as far as I could, the total setting the therapist brought within their mind, and that I may not be able to understand it. Issues of status, gender, and culture play their part in the supervisory relationship. I am reminded of the extremely deferential attitude of a Japanese male student who wished to be instructed, corrected, and generally directed at each stage. Contrasted with this was the macho over-confident approach of a young male European student who implied initially that he had little to learn, especially from a woman—a recognizable defensive stance in the light of his anxiety about losing a patient. This gives rise to the observation of the way certain regressive elements make their appearance in the way of working evidenced by some trainee therapists.

Perhaps I can illustrate. In the transition from working in one mode to beginning to work psychoanalytically, therapists tend to revert to their previous mode of working, with which they are familiar and comfortable, when they are confronted by difficult, often puzzling, situations, especially in the transference. A psychiatrist will call upon the psychiatric persona and techniques for reassurance in the treatment setting when at a loss to comprehend the patient's material in its symbolic manifestation. Students with an established counselling framework, perhaps with practice based on reflective techniques, mirroring, and verbalization of affect, will use these when they are struggling to move to a more psychoanalytic mode of containment and interpretation. The supervisor's task at this point is to identify the way in which the patient's material and the mode of the patient's relating to the student is felt to be baffling and undermining. The elucidation of this dilemma in terms of unconscious communication leads to the student's dawning appreciation of the continuous presence of transference elements in the session and how to address them. The same applies when a student is inclined to reassure a patient rather than to interpret. This is usually the student's response to anxiety in the patient (often also the student's fear of losing a training patient), such anxiety in the patient being frequently connected with the emergence of either hostile or loving/libidinal feelings in the transference. Both of these can present the student therapist with hitherto unfamiliar intensities. One of the difficulties inherent in the transition to a psychoanalytically based therapy mode is that the student finds it hard to understand how far he or she becomes a significant figure in the patient's inner world. There may be reluctance bordering on disbelief at the force of the patient's transference experience of their therapist.

What psychoanalytic ideas offer us are concepts that are among the most sophisticated available for understanding human subjective experience, especially in the areas of aggression and sexuality, and, more especially, in their unconscious manifestations. On taking a patient into psychoanalytic treatment, the patient usually being on the couch and encouraged to say whatever comes to mind, to free associate, something remarkable begins to happen. Thoughts, feelings, memories, and dreams emerge, with the patient partly talking to himself, partly communicating with the therapist, but overall bringing about the gradual revelation of the nature of the inner world. It is the slow realization, in the sense of becoming real in the transference relationship, that the momentum of the process of psychic change can be traced. So, with the patient and the therapist engaged in this maelstrom of unconscious phenomena and the defences that both employ, how does the supervisor figure?

First, the supervisor listens with evenly floating attention, as if listening to a patient, but also ready to focus on what is present and what is not being spelt out. As much as with a patient in treatment, the supervisor's unconscious response to what is being heard is of paramount importance—probably the source of the most effective help to the student therapist in alerting him or her to the unconscious content in the material. I am not sure that one can be taught how to do this. One might say that it consists of the development of the third ear, that it comes from a capacity to hear the music behind the words of the material, but these are metaphoric ways of expressing something hard to define. Its origins must lie in one's own experience of analysis and supervision, of being listened to and understood in ways that give meaning to experience of oneself and the patient one is trying to understand, but there is also the discipline of training oneself to listen. It is also about being able, as a supervisor, to be uncertain, to risk saying things to a therapist, an association to the material that on the surface may seem tangential but that turns out subsequently to have pinpointed something significant that arrives in following sessions. It is a matter of learning to heed unconscious promptings and to translate these into preconscious musings and then conscious thought. One may be wrong, but one is unlikely, following this process, to mislead the therapist. It is more likely that the supervisor will hear, "Remember what you said last week . . . well, it's rather odd . . . something on those lines came up in this week's material".

An example of this came when I was supervising a young male therapist whose female patient showed, to my mind, every sign of acting out in the coming summer break by becoming pregnant. The therapist was unsure of how to address this, as there was no explicit mention of pregnancy in the material. Against his cautious disbelief, however, he managed to raise the topic in relation to the break and the patient's wishes to give herself something or someone to provide an antidote to her therapist's absence. His courage was rewarded by confirmation that the patient intended to cease the use of contraception in the summer break and fantasies of how she would return triumphantly after the break to announce her achievement to her therapist followed.

A frequently described phenomenon in the supervisory process is that in which the dynamic occurring in the relationship between therapist and patient is re-enacted in the supervisor–therapist relationship. I think such projective mechanisms sometimes occur, occasionally to a remarkable degree, but in my view this is not the only dimension in which the supervisor–therapist dyad can be understood. Nor do I think that it can always provide a full foolproof definitive understanding of the patient's material. It can be an over-simplifying formula that bypasses a more thorough, cognitive examination of what is happening, and its inherent danger lies in giving too much weight to the therapist's emotional response to the patient. Its usefulness resides in the supervisor's use of unconscious responses, as mentioned above, as helping the therapist to expand insight about the session, but it also requires the conscious concentrated attention of the work egos of both supervisor and therapist. Its indiscriminate use, meaning its sole use as an indicator of the dynamic ongoing in the session, can lead to something intrusive for the therapist. My view is that from its inception the supervisor–therapist relationship must be guided by respect for professional boundaries carrying as much weight as those defining the analyst–patient relationship. The student therapist is a colleague, and deserves respect and treatment as such. By that I mean that, as supervisors, we should be extremely circumspect in offering views that might intrude on, for instance, the student therapist's own analysis. Trespass in that area is inimical to good practice as a supervisor, particularly when using the student therapist's work with a patient to infer "pathology" in the therapist. Tact is needed to convey the supervisor's perception of a blind spot in the therapist, and to correct faulty technique that this may have occasioned. There are times when firm insistence on a particular line of interpretation is necessary, especially when a student therapist appears to be unaware of the likelihood of serious acting out by the patient.

Some examples of problems encountered in supervision:

1. A young male therapist, who usually provided good accounts of his sessions with his female patient, began to come with sketchy notes and found he was forgetting much of the material. On examination, the supervisor discovered that a strong erotic transference had developed in the patient that the therapist was both embarrassed and gratified by, and thus was reluctant to reveal these responses to the supervisor. Once clarified, it was possible for him to contain the patient and help her to work through this phase of the work.

2. Having a background in counselling and being used to the more informal language of that mode, a therapist was reluctant to relinquish her entrenched position, finding the psychoanalytic mode too harsh, unfriendly to the patient, and lacking in what she perceived as helpful understanding. The supervisor's task here was to help the therapist, over some considerable time, to develop a new position in which the value of interpretation beyond the presenting problems of the patient could be appreciated, and a language for this kind of understanding be found.

CHAPTER SEVEN

Some personal experiences of supervision

Sue Johnson

W hen thinking about the subject of supervision I inevitably found myself reflecting on my own experiences as a supervisee over the course of my work. I have tried in this paper to capture the essence of them by giving a name to each of my supervisors. They are as follows:

Mr A—The Eye Opener
Mrs B—The Humiliator
Miss C—The Know-it-all
Mr V—The Facilitator
Mr W—The By-passer
Mr X—The Colleague
Dr Y—The Restorer

"The Eye-Opener" was the first person to open my eyes to the unconscious and its appearance in the consulting room. He was the Clinical Supervisor of the College Health Service where I worked, and clinical discussions with Mr A were the highlight of my working week for a number of years. I looked forward to them with eager anticipation and came out of each one with a sense of excitement at what I had learned. Mr A was gifted in his abilities to involve each member of the supervision group and to both name and contain the most pressing anxiety in the group in relation to the patient being presented. Although at the time I found his intellect awesome, I never felt inadequate or inferior in his presence. Instead, he seemed genuinely interested in each contribution to the discussion and demonstrated his respect for my colleagues and me by using our individual differences, reflected in our comments, to shed light on the material being presented.

I have called Mrs B "The Humiliator". Although I was initially very keen to go to supervision each week with Mrs B, I did not feel that my eagerness was reciprocated. Over time I experienced her as "doing her job" and often bored by it, and therefore my experience with her was quite a painful one. In retrospect, I believe Mrs B experienced my enthusiasm as tiresome and as a demand. Certainly I felt dependent on her, as I was inexperienced and the unconscious was still new to me. I remember buying an outfit that was identical to one she had and being shocked, embarrassed, and humiliated when I went into supervision and she looked at me angrily and made a rather cutting interpretation about my new outfit. She certainly did not experience imitation as the highest form of flattery! I did learn from her, but in contrast to the "Eye Opener", who enabled me to feel I had a valuable contribution to make, I sometimes felt belittled by "The Humiliator".

I have described myself as "dependent" in my supervision with Mrs B, and I think it was this that presented a problem for both of us.

The issue of dependence in supervision is controversial and influences the supervisor's technique. In writing about supervision with trainee analysts, Frijling-Schreuder (1970) writes about the importance of establishing a "working alliance" (p. 363) with the supervisee. He says that, from the outset, he tries to make the supervisee "aware that the supervisory situation, in contrast to the training analysis, does not stimulate regression. Supervisor and candidate work together at an adult and highly sophisticated level" (*ibid.*). In fact, when describing his personal use of supervision as a trainee, he says he was "co-operative but somewhat dependent" (p. 364), and later in the paper he acknowledges that the initial phase in supervision "may be marked by insecurity and dependency" (p. 365).

Searles (1962) believes that during certain phases of analytic treatment, the trainee-analyst's dependence on the supervisor may be "unprecedentedly great" (p. 595), and he likens it to the dependence of the nursing mother. He stresses the need for the supervisor to be sensitive to the trainee-analyst's dependence and says how important it is for the supervisor not to press for conscious acknowledgement of this.

I think my imitative outfit was an unconscious statement of both my idealization and my dependence on Mrs B, which at the time she herself found difficult to handle.

I have called Miss C "The Know-it-all" because that is how she always seemed. I had felt uncomfortable about my supervision with Miss C for some time. Her responses often seemed quite distant and to lack any emotional warmth, and my dissatisfaction was eventually highlighted for me over one particular incident. My patient had missed her session the previous week and Miss C asked me if I had written to her and what I had said. I replied that I had written and had said I was sorry not to see her at her appointment that week and that I would hope to see her the following week. Miss C did not respond with a spirit of exploration. Instead, she said I should not have used that wording—I should have written that although my patient had felt unable to attend her appointment that week I would be available for her appointment the following week. Of course, I could see what Miss C was getting at. Her letter was more neutral than mine, and was a reflection of her way of working. However, although I have since occasionally written letters in a style similar to that suggested by Miss C, I could not have written in that manner to that patient at that particular time.

Searles (1962) writes the following about his personal technique of supervision:

> I endeavour to keep to a minimum any interference with the student's own individual style of treatment; comparable again to the treatment situation itself, the other person must be left free to find that road to Rome which is most in keeping with his own capacities and interests. One is often tempted to try to indoctrinate the student with one's own individual style of conducting treatment; but respect for the other person's individuality is, in the long run, the only basis on which supervision, like analysis itself, will succeed. [Searles, 1962, p. 586]

I often felt in my supervision with Miss C that she was guilty of trying to indoctrinate me.

I went to Mr V for supervision early on in my career, and I have called him "The Facilitator". The patient I took to him for supervision presented me with the most challenging and anxiety-making experiences I had had to date. She had a long psychiatric history that included numerous incidents of suicidal behaviour. She gave minimal details about herself in her assessment interview and the full extent of her background only emerged during the course of her treatment. Mr V's treatment of my patient's material was always extremely thoughtful. His responses were considered and containing. In addition, I always experienced him as being concerned to look after me as a trainee. Our identifications were clear on one occasion before a break when I was very concerned my patient might kill herself. He and I pondered for some time what course of action I might pursue. Near the end of the hour I said, "I'm worried she may kill herself." He replied, "I'm not worried about that but I am concerned that she may drop out of treatment." I said, "I'm not worried about that." At that point we agreed she was probably contained.

On another occasion I remarked that my patient had felt a certain way about an interpretation I had made. Mr V said very gently, "You mustn't be omnipotent." This was a moment of learning for me. Although he could have said this in a manner in which I might have felt either criticized or belittled, I did not experience his comment in that way. Instead, I felt I learned something about the danger of holding an airtight view that left little room for wonder or curiosity. This was extremely refreshing, as it was in stark contrast to my previous experience with The Know-it-all. Because of the way I felt cared for by Mr V, this moment was one of revelation.

Whether the supervisor is working mainly with the patient's material or with the trainee therapist is a matter of debate. Searles' (1962) view is as follows:

> The supervisory orientation which I have found most effective and realistic is predominantly a lateral, rather than a vertical or hierarchical, orientation: I am not literally a supervisor, in the ordinary sense of the term, who is endeavouring to control the student's

treatment of the patient. I am, rather, a comparatively experienced colleague to one side, to whom he turns for help with his work. I am quite clear that I am working with him, not with the patient, and that I can be of maximal help to him to the extent that I can discover, with him, a larger and deeper understanding of what is going on between the patient and himself. [Searles, 1962, p. 585]

I have called Mr W "The By-passer" because his remarks often did just that—they passed me by. Mr W was an astute man who was very interested in the material my patient presented, but I felt when I was in his presence that only he and my patient were in the room.

Lebovici (1970) believes that the trainee therapist will inevitably develop transference reactions to the supervisor. My experience of "The By-passer" is of interest as it highlights the difficulty this can present in supervision, for I had a strong transference to Mr W. His snow-white hair reminded me too much of my father, and I always felt very young and foolish in my supervision sessions. In retrospect, I do not believe for one moment that Mr W actually thought me young and foolish. He was a very kindly man and was always interested and lively, but his comments often bypassed me. They bypassed me, however, because of my fear of seeming stupid. For that reason, it is incorrect to call him "The By-passer". Instead, I should call myself "The Fearful One". In relation to Mr W I behaved in the following manner described by Searles (1962):

> If he is relatively young, inexperienced, and unsure of himself, he will approach the supervision in a spirit of guardedness and of shame and embarrassment about his own style of personal responsiveness to his patient ... The supervisor's very designation, as "supervisor" or "control analyst" tends all the more to give him the significance, to the student, of a feared, hated, or despised superego. [Searles, 1962, pp. 584–585]

I have called Mr X "The Colleague". Although he was vastly more knowledgeable and experienced than I, he was the first supervisor who treated me as a colleague and enabled me to feel equal. He achieved this partly through sharing his own work with me, which was the way he taught. Through hearing about his work, what was clear to me was that he was a man of compassion, sincerity, and open-mindedness. And what always amazed me was how open and undefended his clients were with him. He, probably more than anyone, taught me, through example, that a lack of resistance and defensiveness in the therapist is matched by a lack of resistance and defensiveness in the client.

In his 1970 paper, "Problems of supervision", Grinberg (1970) writes about the importance of the supervisory setting expressing "quite clearly the difference between this educating situation and that of a therapeutic experience" (p. 375). He stresses the need for the trainee analyst to be treated as a colleague and says one way of doing this might be to offer the trainee a cup of coffee.

In a much later paper, "On transference and countertransference and the technique of supervision", Grinberg (1997) again recommends that the trainee be treated as a colleague, and says the following:

> It is helpful, therefore, for every encounter between supervisor and supervisee to begin with a brief chat, so that the relationship that is established is clearly between colleagues, without, of course, becoming too familiar and interfering with the specific task. [Grinberg, 1997, pp. 9–10]

In his paper "Psychoanalytic supervision of untrained therapists", Sedlak (1997) writes about supervising "therapists who have not had a formal, comprehensive training, part of which would have included psychoanalysis for themselves" (p. 25) and says this work illuminates aspects that apply to all psychoanalytic supervision. He seeks to show that psychotherapeutic work will break down at the point when the therapist is unable to deal with the countertransference, and particularly the negative countertransference. With regard to addressing difficulties with the supervisee's countertransference towards the patient, he says the following:

> I have found it helpful . . . to use the pronoun "we", as in "It is quite likely in such circumstances we lose our faith in interpretation . . .". This way of talking (I give it as an example of attitude rather than a technique) . . . communicates that one is talking about a professional difficulty inherent in the work and not a private, personal problem. Furthermore, describing a problem as one common to all of us helps the supervisee with his own difficulties about shame

and the narcissistic vulnerability that exposing oneself in supervision entails. [Sedlak, 1997, p. 36]

I have called Dr Y "The Restorer" as I sought supervision with her at a low point in my career. My narcissism and therapeutic zeal had been taking a battering through my work with one particular patient who had made me profoundly question my belief in psychotherapy. Dr Y had a formidable intellect and was highly regarded for her teaching ability, for the wealth of her theoretical knowledge, and also for her kindness and compassion, and when I went to her I believed her to be both omnipotent and omniscient. Because of my need to project these qualities on to her, I was sometimes unable to use supervision creatively. Instead, I went there to be spoon-fed. Again, at times when I felt particularly needy, I am sure she must have found me tiresome. Dr Y amazed me by her ability to hold both my patients and me in mind. She could be stern, humorous, lively, interested, bored, and tired, and because of the respect I had for her, she enabled me to tolerate those same psychic states in myself and to be able to use them in my work. I have called her "The Restorer" because she restored my commitment to and passion for psychoanalytic psychotherapy.

It will be obvious that in writing about my own experiences of supervision I am describing my personal development as a psychotherapist. On the whole, my experiences of supervision have been enriching and enlightening ones. It will probably not come as a surprise to hear that of the seven supervisors I have referred to, the two who were least qualified to supervise were "The Humiliator" and "The Know-it-all".

I will now give a vignette from my own supervision practice that demonstrates in some detail how I have behaved, and possibly been experienced by a supervisee, in a number of the ways I have just described. I will call my supervisee "Mrs Jones".

Mrs Jones came to a supervision session on a Monday morning looking unusually tired. She asked how I was. I replied that I was fine and asked after her. She said she had had a very difficult weekend. A close friend of hers had recently died, leaving her two little girls without a mother. With some distress, Mrs Jones told me about her friend's illness and about the funeral, and after a matter of a couple of minutes she began to apologize profusely for mentioning it in her supervision.

At this point she felt she had transgressed a boundary and she was ashamed of herself. Obviously, in the first few moments of the session Mrs Jones and I were behaving as colleagues, simply socially enquiring about each other. I believe that quite quickly I became "The Facilitator" in that I had created a space wherein Mrs Jones could tell me something of a personal experience she had had but the flip side of that was that I had also become "The Humiliator", in that Mrs Jones believed the personal information she had just told me belonged in her analysis— not in her supervision. I am not suggesting here that I actively humiliated Mrs Jones, but I am suggesting that she may well have felt humiliated by having shared this personal information with me.

Mrs Jones then went on to present her session from earlier that morning with her patient. This young female patient had been abandoned when she was a few months old by her mother, and the material of the session was related to the imminent break and to her transference experience of Mrs Jones as the abandoning mother. This material was not new and had been a recurring theme over the previous months. Although Mrs Jones had not failed to interpret her patient's transference experience of her previously, in this session when she interpreted it her patient had been moved to tears and had gone on to describe her experience of loss, both of her mother and of her own identity. Mrs Jones had herself felt profoundly moved by her patient's description of herself as a lost and abandoned child, as did I while listening to her account.

Near the end of this supervision session I said to Mrs Jones that it was perhaps clear how it had been possible for her to make the emotional contact with her patient that had touched her patient so deeply and why it had been important for her to tell me of her friend's death. Her experience of her friend's death and her compassion for the two motherless little girls had put her in an emotional position from which she had been able to interpret in a more meaningful way, and as a result her patient had felt she had made contact with her. This was clearly a moment of both revelation and excitement for Mrs Jones. She herself is a very experienced psychotherapist, and from time to time she and I marvelled together at the power of the unconscious. I think at this moment in the supervision I became a combination of "The Eye Opener" and "The Know-it-all", as I had been able to make a link she herself had not made. In addition, by putting her personal material into an appropriate supervision context, I hope I became "The Restorer" and enabled her to feel that the personal material she had revealed had served to contribute to the richness of the supervision experience we shared.

I do not imagine that what I have been describing is particularly unusual. As a supervisee I have been exposed to a wealth of emotions with a variety of supervisors, all of whom I have learned from but some of whom I hold in higher regard than others.

There is no getting away from the fact that supervision can be painful and will, at times, inevitably contribute to one's feelings of shame, humiliation, and stupidity. At its best, however, supervision is eye-opening, facilitating, and restorative.

References

Frijling-Schreuder, E. C. M. (1970). On individual supervision. *International Journal of Psycho-Analysis, 51*: 363–370.

Grinberg, L. (1970). The problems of supervision in psychoanalytic education. *International Journal of Psycho-Analysis, 51*: 371–383.

Grinberg, L. (1997). On transference and countertransference and the technique of supervision. In: B. Martindale, M. Morner, M. Rodriguez, & J.-P. Vidit (Eds.), *Supervision and Its Vicissitudes* (pp. 1–24). London: Karnac.

Lebovici, S. (1970). Technical remarks on supervision. *International Journal of Psycho-Analysis, 51*: 385–392.

Searles, H. (1962). Problems of psycho-analytic supervision. In: *Collected Papers on Schizophrenia and Related Subjects*. London: Maresfield Library [reprinted London: Karnac (pp. 584–604), 1986].

Sedlak, V. (1997). Psychoanalytic supervision of untrained therapists. In: B. Martindale, M. Morner, M. Rodriguez, & J. Vidit (Eds.), *Supervision and Its Vicissitudes* (pp. 25–37). London: Karnac.

PART III

ON ASPECTS OF THE
SUPERVISORY RELATIONSHIP

CHAPTER EIGHT

The supervision triangle

Denise Taylor

S eeing this title, one may well ask, *is* supervision a triangle? Two people, the supervisor and the therapist meet together to discuss a third person, the patient, who is never present yet is the central focus of the work. If we compare this to psychotherapy, there are again two people meeting in the context of significant but absent others with which the patient's world was peopled. The focus in both is to a large degree on the relationship between therapist and patient. So where do we place supervision? We can say that supervision adds a further dimension to psychotherapy, another layer of complexity, where the supervisor appears as the third other person in the therapist–patient dyad. It will not be surprising to find, with such basic common denominators, very similar patterns in both settings, and there is constant overlap. In fact, triangular situations abound in both and are indeed a universal phenomenon.

The antiquity of the triad concept and its symbolism pervades human thinking, from primitive societies to modern organizations, from different religions to folk tales and fairy stories. Bettelheim (1978), in his fascinating book, *The Uses of Enchantment*, has a lot to say about the symbolic, often mystical meanings given the triad, or the number three. He points out that in the unconscious the number three stands for the three visible sex characteristics in men and women, as well as the fundamental fact that male and female have to come together in order to create new life. In supervision this is translated into creating new insights that were not possible in the dyad.

Alternatively, let us look at the Biblical account of the creation of the world. God created the physical world and the animals, and then he created Adam and Eve. They lived in innocent bliss in paradise. Then, a third character enters the scene; the snake. The snake persuades Eve to eat the forbidden fruit on the Tree of Knowledge and Eve gives some of it to Adam. With this, their eyes are opened and they see that they are naked. In other words, they become aware of their sexuality and they try to hide it with leaves. It was the input of a third "other" that gave the couple insight. But there is a price to pay for knowledge: they now have to face the harsh realities of life, as well as feel such painful emotions as shame and guilt.

It may not be an attractive idea to view the supervisor as acting the part of the snake in the grass, but the supervisor *is* the third "other" who, because he or she is not part of the two-person relationship between the therapist and the patient, can shed light on what is going on, or, one could say, offer a different view. Without introducing a difference, there can be no change. Gregory Bateson (1980) anthropologist, philosopher, and leader of a research group into communication and schizophrenia which came up with the "double bind" theory, highlighted this fundamental fact in philosophical terms in his treatise on "Mind and nature". Differentiation lies at the heart of human development. We only become a person in so far as we define ourselves against another person. If the infant stays in symbiotic fusion with the mother, no separate self can develop. Symbiosis can never remain total, but to the extent that it persists, the personality will be stunted. At the other extreme, if there is never sufficient attachment from which differentiation can occur, equally disastrous results ensue.

The first differentiation is from the primary caregiver, usually the mother. To take the necessary steps towards independence, the infant needs to experience a difference. As Bateson points out, the necessary difference is not just any difference, it is a significant difference, a difference that registers a change. Perhaps the breast is not there just when it was expected to be; perhaps it was not mother's arms that picked up and held the infant but somebody else's—different, stronger, firmer, but also containing the infant's anxiety and rage, also gratifying, in a different way. There are all kinds of experiences from the moment of birth that impinge on the infant and help the child to realize that it is a separate entity. Differentiation means acknowledging separateness, requiring the ability to let go and to bear the pain of mourning the loss. In pathological narcissism the admission of separateness or anything good and of value outside the self is supremely threatening.

Winnicott's well-known formulation of mother's crucial position in the infant's development has more recently been augmented by contemporary Kleinians like Ron Britton (1989), who postulates that the triangular oedipal constellation confronts the baby from the earliest days in its life. What he emphasizes, in his paper "The missing link" is the link between mother and father from which the child is excluded. The child has to learn to tolerate this exclusion, while at the same time developing and sustaining separate links with each parent. This is, of course, a gradual process, taking place over time. It is also the ideal development, taking in its stride the later forms of the oedipal complex described by Freud. If the child can learn to tolerate this special link between the parents from which he is excluded "it provides him with a prototype for an object relationship of a third kind, i.e. not with one or the other, in which he is a witness and not a participant" (p. 87). Britton goes on to point out that this is the foundation of a capacity for observing and being observed, and for holding on to one's own integrity and views while being exposed to the opinion of others. I would say that this is a crucial test of maturity and very pertinent to supervision. As with so many other stages in human development, this is not a once and for all achievement but fluctuates with circumstances pertaining within and outside the person. It is not easy for a supervisor to maintain such a flexible stance and there could be a risk, for instance, of deteriorating into self-opinionated rigidity with advancing age.

In supervision, several layers of triangles come together: the therapist, the patient, and the patient's oedipal experience; the therapist, patient, and supervisor triangle; and the therapist's and the

supervisor's personal triangles. All these will influence the supervision process to a greater or lesser degree. The more self awareness
the supervisor and therapist can muster the more likely it is that the
distortions of skewed triangles can be avoided.

In supervision, we have primarily to look at two sets of material, one is that brought by the therapist, which is complex in its
own right, and the other the here and now process of interaction
between the therapist and the supervisor. In both, participants'
interactions will be heavily influenced by transference and countertransference phenomena, which will only be partially conscious.
The triangles meet, intermingle and overlap. For the sake of clarity
and to highlight the parallels, I will first give a simple schematic
outline of what I have called the Primal Triangle (Figure 1) and its
variations.

Mother and Father are at one level of a generational hierarchy.
The child is on another level. If the parents have attained sufficient
maturity to gain their own oedipal freedom, they will be able to
tolerate the tensions in keeping the generational boundary while at
the same time including the child in their relationship without feelings of jealousy or rejecting exclusion. Of course, the above pertains
to Western culture, which emphasizes the link between the parents.
This may not be so in other cultures, where the significant link may
be, say, between mother and son or between brothers.

In a less than ideal development, the equilateral Primal Triangle
becomes skewed to a greater or lesser extent. One example is shown
in Figure 2.

If a mother becomes too closely identified with her child and the
father feels there is no room for him, trouble ensues. This is often
the case when a baby is born and the mother is totally absorbed in
the infant, which may make the father feel shut out and fear that
he has lost his partner to the baby. It may lay the foundation of a

Figure 1.   The primal triangle

Figure 2. A skewed primal triangle, showing father excluded from the close mother–child relationship.

negative pattern that persists and interferes with the well functioning of the family and the adjustment of the child. One possibility in this vulnerable state is that the father may succumb to the temptations of a sexual encounter, much to the distress of others. If father can tolerate mother's preoccupation with the baby, this need be no more than a passing phase before father comes into his own.

James Fisher (1999), in his book *The Uninvited Guest*, gives Leontes, the king in Shakespeare's *Winter's Tale*, as an extreme example of a father and husband who has not negotiated his own oedipal separation and develops an insane jealousy of his wife, whom he is convinced has been unfaithful to him in begetting his own child. He cannot tolerate a third invading his own narcissistic space or sharing his symbiotic relationship with his wife.

An example shows the corollary to this (Figure 3), where the father becomes allied to the child against the mother. This is an equally unhappy situation that can have serious consequences. A supervisee brought for discussion a patient who was the father of twin boys. His whole life had revolved round the twins since their birth thirteen years ago. He married his wife because she fell pregnant, and not for her own personal qualities and attributes. The birth of twins was an overwhelming experience, and the father took

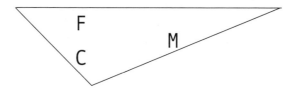

Figure 3. The primal triangle skewed to show an alliance between father and child against mother.

over most of the management of the twins while his wife was recovering her strength. His wife then returned to work, and they engaged some help for the house while he continued to play a major part in the care of the boys. They became devoted to him and assumed the rather denigrating attitude towards their mother that their father demonstrated to his wife. Eventually the father moved out and the boys with him, visiting their mother when it suited them. The mother seemed quite happy with this arrangement, although she complained that the boys never listened to her but were happy to accept treats. With the approach of the boys' adolescence the father, too, had lost the respect of his sons and became desperate, fearing that his whole life, including his work and money-making ability, was spinning out of control. In supervision it became clear to the supervisor that the therapist allowed herself to be controlled by this charismatic, forceful character and the therapy was in danger of doing little more than supporting father in his stance. In other words, she was colluding with perpetuating the skewed triangle.

In the next example the mother was the patient and felt painfully excluded from the close relationship between her husband and their son, aged ten years. In spite of holding down a good job and being the main breadwinner, she felt useless at home in the face of her husband's constant denigration. Her son was copying this and would have as little to do with her as possible, which was very painful. She felt that the "men" in the family were ganging up against her, and she became the bullied victim. This was not an unfamiliar state to her, as her father had been a very domineering, powerful man who inspired fear in her mother and herself. She left home as soon as she could and was determined to have a different family, and certainly her earning ability enabled her to be more independent. She had repeatedly tried to win some regard from her husband and son, for example by arranging interesting holidays, but these attempts had failed miserably. The two went off and enjoyed themselves, while she was left to trail behind. She now felt desperate enough to contemplate leaving the family, and hoped she could sort out all the strands in the failed relationships in the therapy. In supervision, the supervisor and therapist were both painfully exposed to the regressive pull of this skewed triangle and had to struggle to resist identifying with the masochistic wife or the highly defended, controlling husband and not allow this scenario to be played out in their own supervisory relationship. This gradually helped to establish a better balance in the family's triangular space.

In another common triadic scenario, mother and father are constantly at loggerheads, criticizing and accusing each other, perhaps making up once in a while. The child is tossed about in this confusing, erratic environment and uses what defences he can muster to cope. At an unconscious level the parents are in collusion and reject the child, who is then scapegoated (see Figure 4).

The child may either become cowed and withdrawn, or may act out by becoming self harming or hyperactive, destructive, and delinquent, so the parents can justifiably complain that the child is out of control. The parents appear puzzled, distressed, or appalled at the child's behaviour, while at the same time their rejection of him is denied. Frequently their preferred solution is to have the child removed from the home.

Skewed supervision triangles

The "primal triangles" described above are prototypes for triangles seen in supervision. In my first example (Figure 5), the supervisor identifies with the patient, feeling that the therapist is unempathic and does not understand the patient. This mirrors the skewed primal scenarios described above.

If careful analysis by the supervisor of his own possible interference from the past confirms him in his impression, he has to tackle the problem of how to combine the tasks of helping the therapist and helping the patient. The supervisor's ignorance of the therapist's "primal triangle" experience does not make an empathic

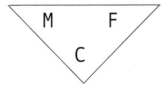

Figure 4.   Colluding parents and the rejected child.

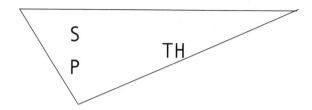

Figure 5. This triangle is skewed as a result of the supervisor identifying with the patient.

resolution of this conflict any easier. Even if the therapist, as some-times happens, is quite eager to reveal aspects of this, the super-visor has the delicate task of keeping intact the boundary between therapy and supervision and creating an opportunity for the thera-pist to explain some of her feelings about the patient, which can lead to insight and an easing of the problem. The key to unlocking such a seemingly fixed situation is to gather more information. In any deadlock, this usually supplies the crucial items that make a difference and make change possible.

In the next variant of the skewed triangle it is the therapist who overly identifies with the patient and feels that the supervisor is an outsider who does not understand the patient. The supervisor may be viewed as too rigid and expecting the therapist to act in ways that are alien to the therapist (Figure 6).

I can recall an example where these two states were combined and mirrored in supervision, a phenomenon usually referred to as the "parallel process", first identified by Searles (1955). The parallel process involves an unconscious replication of a patient's conflict in supervision, providing the supervisor with a graphic illustration of the patient's problem. The situation referred to above was provoked

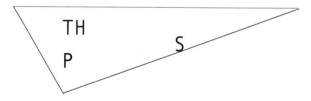

Figure 6. In this skewed triangle, the therapist is identifying too closely with the patient, with the supervisor seen as the outsider.

by a patient who knew well how to play off one parent against the other. In supervision, while I emphasized the patient's relationship with his father, the therapist thought the relationship with his mother was fundamental. It was not until we could reassemble the patient's triangular space and disentangle our roles in it that the two views could be combined in helpful interpretations to the patient.

The next example shows the supervisor and the therapist acting in concert, agreeing that the patient is too difficult, too damaged, and really unsuitable for the kind of psychotherapy on offer. While this may be a genuine, realistic situation, it may also hide collusion between the supervisor and therapist in rejecting the patient, in a similar way in which the parents can collude to reject a child. This situation often arises with therapists undergoing training, who become very anxious that they cannot cope with the patient; indeed, might lose the patient and have to start all over again with a new patient. At the same time they wish they were rid of the patient and had never started the treatment, although this can rarely be spoken aloud. The supervisor, for a variety of reasons, some to do with the patient, some with the trainee therapist, some of a personal kind, agrees that the unsuitability of the patient as a training patient should be presented forthwith to the Training Committee. Meanwhile, the resulting failure in containment can lead to the patient semi-consciously or unconsciously acting out, e.g., missing sessions, coming late, getting into trouble in his life—in short, by his remonstrations proving his unsuitability.

It sometimes happens that a conflicted primary triangle in either supervisor and/or supervisee leads to a rivalrous relationship in supervision, which not only makes it an uncomfortable experience but can also be to the detriment of the patient and even lead to the failure of the therapy. An idealized transference of the supervisee to the supervisor is equally detrimental to the learning process and can deteriorate to a state where the patient's therapy is being conducted by the supervisor rather than the patient's therapist. This may go undetected at the time, but the negative feelings that are suppressed in idealization are likely to emerge at a later stage and cause trouble for the therapist, who no longer has a proper arena in which to express them.

The deadly equal triangle

This is a variation of what at first sight appears as a perfectly balanced triangle and was first described by Janet Mattinson (1997) in a monograph bearing this title based on a casework supervision seminar run in the late 1970s at the Tavistock Marital Studies Institute. A drawing of it looks just like the primal triangle with which we began, with an important difference. Imagine the lines joining the three corners drawn very heavily to convey the rigidity that holds it in a rigor mortis-like grip. In fact, in the example cited, it was a fear of death of one or other party that Janet Mattinson identifies as making any movement impossible. The dread of a traumatic outcome in both the supervisor and the case-worker made any change impossible. This happened only gradually, against great resistance, after an intervention from outside the persons locked into the triangle; in fact, the authoritative order of a judge (Mattinson, 1997, pp. 10–14).

A variation of this I have called the "deadly protective triangle", with the same contours, and indeed it might be an alternative name for the above. In the primal family we see both parents unable to let go of the child, often an only child, or the last in line, or one with a handicap. The parents' acute anxiety over setting the child free and giving it some independence may result in the child becoming a "patient" with some psychosomatic disability, such as asthma, for example. Alternatively, they may need to cut violently free by going to live with another relative, or a boy or girl friend. In the supervision version of the triangle, the supervisor and the therapist can collude to keep the patient in an interminable therapy, or as an inmate in an institution, in the conviction that it is not safe to let the patient go. Supervisors need to be alert to this kind of collusion, which can readily develop when the relationship between therapist and supervisor becomes too cosy and they find themselves in agreement on most issues.

The "as if" triangle

This has the appearance of a triangle viewed from the outside but, when you take a closer look, you realize that it has no substance.

We may find this in severely deprived persons. There is such a need in the child in all of us for a safe container and for something solid to attach to. In the face of a lack of an attachment figure, one is created in phantasy, usually an idealized, make-believe mother or father figure. Anything seems to be better than facing stark reality.

John Steiner (1993), in his book *Psychic Retreats*, graphically describes variations of the phenomenon and links it to an exploration of the character of Oedipus in the two classic dramas by Sophocles: *Oedipus the King* and *Oedipus at Colonus*. The defences he describes are "turning a blind eye", i.e., not recognizing what should be obvious, and a flight into omnipotence, a sort of over-compensation, a triumph over despair. Oedipus blinds himself when he discovers that he has indeed killed his father and married his mother, who, on learning this, has taken her own life. Twenty years later he returns from exile and omnipotently declares himself a "Holy Man".

Similarly, therapy and supervision can go on in an "as if" manner. For example, in a supervision group for supervisors that I participated in, it gradually became apparent that the supervisor was blind, or chose to be blind, to the inadequacies of a recently qualified therapist. He did not want to fail as a supervisor, and adopted the role of the guru who could save patients and therapists even in the face of serious impediments. The unmasking of the firmly established parallel process presented a delicate task and was a gradual process.

Supervision is based on the supposition that the supervisor can get a reasonably accurate picture of what goes on in the therapy session on the strength of a supervisee's verbal or written reports. On this premise, process recordings are sometimes treated as if they were objective and, as such, are valued above a more "free" presentation. However, objectivity in observation and reporting can only be achieved in general terms, and will inevitably be contaminated by subjective factors. A process recording is written from memory after the session, and we all know what tricks memory can play on us. Bion (1967) speaks of "involuntary distortions" and suggests that "memory should not be treated as more than a pictorialised communication of an emotional experience" (pp. 1–2).

The account presented to the supervisor may therefore be heavily coloured by the supervisee's countertransference to the patient, by the feelings he or she has about the supervisor and the supervision process, or by such factors as extraneous events in the supervisee's life. Does this matter? Many supervisors think it does not, because what does get conveyed is more important than literal facts. It only matters when the supervisor treats the material as if it were objective fact rather than an emotional experience. For example, a supervisee with a new patient repeatedly came saying she found it very difficult to write coherent notes on this particular patient, especially as far as her own contributions were concerned. Looking back over a session the scene seemed to her to be covered by a thick fog, through which she could only make out vague shapes. Details had quite disappeared. When she would sit there, time and again, with an agonized expression, I would enquire "Foggy weather?", and this would usually release some of the tension and start her off, as often as not describing the feeling climate in the session and the inhibiting effect this had on her.

Such a state in a supervisee gives quite a powerful message to a supervisor that could have all kinds of meaning, depending on the context. In this case the patient had a strong inhibition about being known and hated being looked at. It may also have been that the supervisee had fears of being exposed and shamed. It is when denied blind spots in patient and supervisor coincide that stalemate results. The supervisor, while not in the position of the therapist's therapist, can, nevertheless, by showing respectful and sensitive empathy with the patient, also make the supervisee feel more comfortable. In fact, I often invite supervisees to join me in drawing on personal experience of the emotions touched on, without mentioning details, e.g., "We all know what it feels like to be acutely embarrassed". In this way one's own vulnerabilities are turned to good advantage. The origin of these vulnerabilities, of course, go back to one's own primal triangle experiences. As the therapy unfolded, the patient disclosed how her mother had always had an intrusive interest into her sexuality, first ostensibly to ensure cleanliness and, as she entered adolescence, to look for evidence of illicit sex by examining knickers and skirts for tell-tale signs.

The triangle of supervision mirrors the triangle of therapy, i.e. patient, therapist and the patient's primal triangle, and the fluidity and interconnectedness between them allow effective echoes to resound in this common space. That is how what one could call "therapy at one remove" can take place. The psychoanalyst Gerald Caplan (1970) made use of this technique after the Second World War when asked to give some support to the many orphaned and traumatized children in Israel cared for in Children's Homes. He saw individual staff for consultation about children that worried them, a process much akin to supervision, but the workers were not trained counsellors or therapists and were in many cases as displaced as the children. He later elaborated this approach and called it Mental Health Consultation. Many Mental Health Clinics were established across the United States and exerted a great influence on Child Guidance Clinics in Britain and Europe. It is a cost-effective way of helping many by consulting with a few key people. This approach has been further developed in staff consultation in hospitals, and with groups such as General Practitioners (Balint Groups) and groups for teachers by Gerda Hanko (1999).

The countertransference is often the arena where these triangular scenarios are re-enacted. Since Paula Heimann (1950) initiated the rehabilitation of the countertransference as a valuable source of information of the patient's unconscious state of mind, it has come to stand for *all* of the therapist's emotional response to the patient. We need to remind ourselves that this does not include our own unconscious blind spots, anxieties, and defensive needs, which have remained impervious to analysis, or which rear their head when specifically provoked. We must therefore remain cautious and not take our countertransference at face value as truth, but look for additional corroborative evidence before following our hunches. Sedlak (1997), in his paper entitled "Psychoanalytic supervision of untrained therapists", singles out a negative transference as being particularly difficult to cope with, and can often result in premature termination of therapy. It is also an ironic fact that in the public sector the most inexperienced and least trained workers often treat the most damaged people. However, even with experience, personal therapy, and supervision, a negative, belittling patient can put severe strains on our countertransference.

For example, I began to feel concerned over the fate of a patient assigned to a trainee counsellor whom I was supervising in a voluntary agency. The young counsellor was shocked and repelled by the patient's story (a man who had abandoned his family) and she began to behave very erratically by cancelling sessions at short notice, arriving late for supervision, or forgetting her notes. We managed to clarify that she really hated seeing this patient, who reminded her graphically of a significant figure in her past. She decided to suspend her training until she had some personal therapy for herself.

Gender and cultural issues

Both of these areas can cause skewing and provide a ready replay of the supervisee's personal triangle, but are often not given sufficient attention. A woman therapist being supervised by a male supervisor will feel and behave differently than she would if she were supervised by a woman. A paper entitled "Women supervised by men", by Marilyn Mayse and Paula Teague (1987), usefully distinguishes eight styles of relating, ranging from Passive– Deferential to Little Girl Helplessness, to Amazon, the latter being seen as a defence against fear of closeness and abandonment. The Amazon supervisee acts demandingly and in a hostile manner to the supervisor, thus provoking the very thing that is feared. Similarly, a male therapist with a woman supervisor will feel and act differently than he would if he were being supervised by a man. I have had male supervisees who were very cautious in expressing themselves and with whom it was hard to establish a robust relationship. I have also come across the male supervisee whose fear of intrusion (originally by the mother) is such that it is difficult for anything to be taken in from a woman supervisor.

Cultural issues are increasingly encountered as our society becomes more multi-racial and multi-lingual. Language differences, both in therapy and in supervision, are enormously important, and ignorance of the culture and mores in which the therapist or the patient grew up can sabotage the most well intentioned work. Dr Cecilia Batten (1990), a psychoanalytic psychotherapist who lived and worked for some years in Australia, in her paper entitled "Dilemmas of cross-cultural psychotherapy supervision", describes her supervision of a Vietnamese Medical Officer working with the local Vietnamese community. She outlines many dilemmas, such as the role of silence and the issue of politeness, which made it well nigh impossible for the patient to disagree with her therapist or the therapist to challenge the supervisor. A form of "as if" supervision is a ready outcome.

The organizational dimension

Therapists and supervisors often work as employees of an organization. How do triangles manifest themselves in such settings? In Western society, the primal family is organized along generational lines, as we have seen. In organizations this is replicated in administrative levels. In an organizational hierarchy, it is an unwritten rule that a manager must not become too friendly with one of his employees, which could lead to the accusation of favouritism among other staff, and in group supervision the supervisor has to remain equidistant between all members, as a parent with the children in a family. Another scenario from a "skewed" primal triangle that may be re-enacted would be a manager who abusively bullies, say, his secretary, with the personal assistant standing by helplessly or collusively, for fear of being the next victim, or for other self-interest considerations. The similarities with families where there is an abusive member are clear.

On the other hand, it is no longer unusual for a member of staff, usually a woman, to lodge a complaint about a boss for sexual harassment, bullying, or other discriminating behaviour. Such complaints may be perfectly justified, or constitute a vengeful displacement of anger held towards a tyrannical father. In supervision, it is also not uncommon to come across some unseemly coalitions of administrators with therapists against a supervisor, or some other cross-hierarchical alignments. This produces cynicism in staff and supervisees and promotes an insecure working climate.

A classic study undertaken some fifty years ago by Stanton and Schwartz (1954) entitled *The Mental Hospital*, almost accidentally stumbled across a phenomenon that they called "The special case". It was the first time that the role of triadic forms in conflict situations in organizations had been identified and described. They noted that problems in staff relations invariably occurred when a patient was singled out as the "pet" of a nurse or some other authority figure. For example, a hospital rule was waived with regard to a particular patient and this caused resentment. The more permissive authority, say, the nurse, would get into conflict with the stricter authority, such as, for example, the administrator, but they could not confront each other over this. Their unspoken battle was fought out via the patient, who acted as a conduit, much to the detriment of the patient's mental state. It is easy to see the parallel to the skewed primal triangle, where one parent is in permissive coalition with the child, leaving the other parent to take the role of disciplinarian and the child without a secure base. In the supervisory triangle, this dynamic can also become re-enacted within training organizations, where the supervisor might enter into permissive coalition with a trainee, as a "special case", while other figures in the organization uphold training standards in a particularly strict way.

The merit of the triangle concept

The triangular space of supervision has great scope. Once we have come to identify a pattern such as triangulation it is much easier to recognize it in other situations and to extrapolate from it a number of variations. This is of practical use to all who work in the mental health field, because it offers a short cut to recognizing connections and so enlarging possibilities for remedying the situation. The triangle offers a firmly delineated structure with definite reference points, within which there is the opportunity for free movement from one position to another and offering a choice of view points. It can lead us to the heart of the matter and unfold the drama to which the supervisor is the privileged witness.

References

Bateson, G. (1980). *Mind and Nature.* London: Fontana.
Batten, C. (1990). Dilemmas of crosscultural psychotherapy supervision. *British Journal of Psychotherapy*, 7(22): 129–140.
Bettelheim, B. (1978). *The Uses of Enchantment.* Harmondsworth: Penguin.
Bion, W. (1967). *Second Thoughts.* London: Heinemann.

Britton, R. (1989). The missing link. In: R. Britton, H. Feldman, & E. O'Shaughnessy (Eds.), *The Oedipus Complex Today* (pp. 83–101). London: Karnac.

Caplan, G. (1970). *An Approach to Community Mental Health Consultation*. New York: Basic Books.

Fisher, J. (1999). *The Uninvited Guest*. London: Karnac.

Hanko, G. (1999). *Increasing Competence Through Collaboration in Problem-Solving*. London: David Fulton.

Heimann, P. (1950). On counter-transference. *International Journal of Psychoanalysis, 31:* 81–84.

Mattinson, J. (1997). *The Deadly Equal Triangle*. London: Tavistock Marital Studies Institute.

Mayse, M., & Teague, P. (1987). Women supervised by men. *Journal of Supervision and Training in Ministry*, 35–41.

Searles, H. (1955). Problems of psychoanalytic supervision. In: J. D. Sutherland (Ed.), *Collected Papers on Schizophrenia and Related Subjects* (pp. 584–604). New York: International Universities Press [reprinted London: Karnac, 1986].

Sedlak, V. (1997). Psychoanalytic supervision of untrained therapists. In: B. Martindale, M. Morner, M. E. C. Rodriguez, & J.-P. Vidit (Eds.) *Supervision and Its Vicissitudes* (pp. 25–37). London: Karnac.

Stanton, A., & Schwartz, M. (1954). *The Mental Hospital*. New York: Basic Books.

Steiner, J. (1993). *Psychic Retreats*. London: Routledge.

CHAPTER NINE

The analyst's countertransference when supervising: friend or foe?

Jan Wiener

Introduction

We would surely all agree that transference and counter-transference dynamics operate in supervisory relation-ships. Supervisees have transferences on to their supervisors, supervisors to their supervisees. Both may have trans-ference and countertransference responses to the organizations in which they are trainees or members, particularly if reviews and evaluations are involved. However, although we may be in agree-ment that transference dynamics are alive and well in supervision, more difficult to assess is whether they are fostering or hindering the task of supervision. This will be the main focus of my chapter. I begin with an excursion to visit the concepts and processes of transference and countertransference as they operate in the super-visory relationship. Using two case examples, where transference projections from the supervisee, and their complementary counter-transference affects in the analyst either fostered or hindered this process, I then offer what I hope will be a helpful concept of my own about the particular nature of the supervisor's counter-transference.

Transference processes in supervision

There have probably been more words written on the subject of transference and countertransference from a wide variety of different perspectives than on any other subject within the domain of depth psychology. This is as true among psychoanalysts as it is for analytical psychologists. Today it remains as "hot" a topic for debate and dispute as it was between Jung and Freud almost a century ago. Our definitions of the concepts and the focus of these debates have evolved and changed over time and we now have a wealth of clinical experience and theoretical evidence built up during these years. We know a good deal more about how to define transference and countertransference, the dynamics of transference projections from the patient and their effect on the analyst, and technically how to approach and work with transferences in the analytic relationship (Wiener, 2004). The movement over time from seeing a phenomenon as a pathological process—an impediment to analysis—to seeing it as a normal part of all conscious and unconscious interactions is nowhere more evident than in discussions of transference and countertransference.

Different authors have defined transference in similar but actually subtly different ways. All seem to agree that transference is a form of unconscious projection from the patient on to the analyst and a universal phenomenon. In the Tavistock Lectures, Jung referred to transference as follows:

> The term "transference" is the translation of the German word Übertragung. Literally, Übertragung means: to carry something over from one place to another ... the psychological process of transference is a specific form of the more general process of projection ... that carries over subjective contents of any kind into the object. [Jung, 1935, par.153]

Jung's emphasis is a broad one on "subjective contents of any kind". From his definition of transference as something carried over from one place to another, the question arises as to how can we map out this process as it emerges in supervision? Supervisees' transference to their supervisors can range from the healthy, positive anticipatory curiosity that is aroused at the prospect of a new working relationship to more problematic transferences, for example, supervisees who idealize their supervisors or who are competitive, compliant, dismissive, secretive, withholding, or envious. Often, in my experience, the nature of the transference and my corresponding countertransference responses change and develop during the course of supervision. Supervisors themselves can become defensive and avoid examining their own transferences to their supervisees.

Theoretically, it is only since the late 1950s and 1960s that any real interest has been taken in transference processes in supervision. I imagine it was only when things began to go wrong that the impetus to examine the process heated up. It was Eckstein and Wallerstein (1958) and Eckstein (1960) who first took an interest in understanding the dynamics of the supervision process, taking account of the complex interactions between patient, therapist, supervisor, and institution. However, while they were interested in what could promote or inhibit the learning of the supervisee, they took little interest in the power of the unconscious in this complicated interaction.

It was Searles (1955) who first observed that the transference–countertransference dynamics between patient and therapist could influence interactions in supervision. He introduced the idea of a "reflection process". Searles thought that if this could be elucidated in supervision, then not only could the supervisee be helped, but also the patient–therapist relationship. Searles took account of the supervisor's personality and the emotional impact on both supervisor and supervisee, moving theory into an intersubjective context that would include the supervisor's countertransference and resistances.

It is in this domain that some theory about supervision now exists. Three terms, "mirroring", "parallel process", and "reflective process", have entered our conceptual vocabulary, making bridges from understanding transference in the therapeutic relationship to the supervisory relationship. Following Searles, Janet Mattinson (1975) took up the term "reflective process", showing how processes originating in one relationship are acted out in an adjacent area and unwittingly played out in a kind of mimicry. Hughes and Pengelly (1997, p. 84) prefer the term "mirroring" to "reflection process", and explain the process simply and rather well:

> mirroring is a secondary effect of countertransference that is not fully known about, but enacted . . . the therapist like the patient is

compelled to act rather than to feel or think and then, by a further projective identification, draws the supervisor into joining the enactment in supervision.

These three concepts are often confusing and can be used loosely as catch-all terms. For example, in reality, a mirror image is identical to its original, but its structure is actually reversed. I think that mirroring in supervision is complex and can take several different forms, with subtle reversals. I am doubtful whether the process of projective identification that takes place in analysis and then emerges again in supervision can be accurately described as a parallel process. In my experience, the process involves a temporary loss, or blurring, of boundaries, an experience of confusion, sometimes seduction, and certainly intrusion. This occurs because something has become dissociated in the patient, in the analyst, or within their relationship; anxiety is aroused and then defences against this anxiety. If what is dissociated is close to awareness, it is usually easier to deal with, for example, the supervisee who says, "I can see that this patient is triggering a complex of my own." Here, something not yet known can be integrated. More problematic is when a supervisee is defensive and unaware of an unconscious, split-off complex. Of course, any countertransference experience relies on there being related hooks or host areas (Symington, 1986, p. 330) in the supervisor for the projected dynamics to become attached. It is important not to forget that what happens in supervision can also travel in the other direction, reflecting itself back within the patient–therapist relationship.

Bringing the organization into supervision

The context that frames the supervisory relationship adds a further complexity to the transference dynamics to the supervisory process. Mirroring, or a reflection process, can also work downwards, when something from the organization can be mirrored or reflected in the supervision process (see Case Example 1).

Jung was suspicious about organizations as he saw them as the enemy of individuation, an introverted process where we face our own psyches in the privacy of analysis. He thought organizations

often try to murder our individuality because the idea of individuation threatens their dominance and authority. Stein (1992, p. 1),
describing working in organizations, remarks wryly, "organisations
can be murder. Is there anyone who has not been badly mauled
by one?"

The reality is, though, that most of us choose to work in an
organization. We both love and hate them, but we continue to be
dependent on them, often far more than we realise. A containing
and coherent organization supports us, yet we also hate, envy and
fear it because it holds power and very easily comes to represent
persecuting figures from our internal worlds.

Supervisors and supervisees working in an organization attend
to the unconscious dynamics between patient and therapist and
between themselves, but also have to process an additional set of
transferences to the organization. Four troublesome unconscious
forces are likely, more often than not, to inflame the supervisory
relationship from time to time.

1. Organizational defences (often to avoid the primary task).
2. Issues of power and authority.
3. Issues of accountability and responsibility.
4. Ethical concerns.

Organizational defences

Institutions, like individuals, develop defences against what is
painful or difficult. Defences can develop as a result of external
pressures, internal conflicts between colleagues, between groups
fighting for scarce resources, or because of the nature of the work.
Some defences are healthy; some hinder the development of the
organization and damage staff within it. As Jungians, we might
describe these defences as organizational complexes (Lepper, 1992).

There is by now a wealth of literature which has explored the
nature of institutional defences emerging in response to anxiety
but which often mean the avoidance of the primary task (Bion,
1961; Menzies Lyth, 1988; Obholzer, 1994a). Analytic institutes are
just as prone to institutional defences as other organizations. In
Kernberg's view (1986, p. 809), one of the reasons for this is because

psychoanalytic institutions tend to practise as a *trade school* (learning a clearly defined trade) mixed with a religious system on the *seminary model*, whereas they should be modelled somewhere between an *art academy* (expert crafts people, bringing artistic talents to fruition) and *a university* (generates knowledge and methodological tools for the creating on new knowledge).

Bion (1961) thought that much of the irrational and chaotic behaviour in groups comes from three basic assumptions:

- dependency; to seek someone to solve all the problems, to do the looking after;
- fight–flight; to find an enemy to create a sense of spurious togetherness;
- pairing, sustaining a vague sense that everything will improve in the future as a way of avoiding the present through a belief that salvation will come through a pairing

These basic assumptions are "defensive or regressive manifestations of group life and prevent effective thinking" (Stokes, 1994, p. 25). Dependency gives rise to a culture of subordination requiring obedience; fight–flight results in a culture of paranoia and aggressive competitiveness, preoccupation with the enemy within as well as without and aberrant pairing produces a culture of collusion supporting pairs of members in avoiding the truth. These are defences against the primary task, in our case, good supervision. For Bion, the task was to achieve a "work group" where primitive defences did not obstruct the task.

Authority and power

Authority is the right to make ultimate decisions that are binding on others (Obholzer, 1994a, p. 39). Formal authority derives from one's role in an organization and is sanctioned from below. If we join a system, we delegate personal authority to those in authority, so confirming the system. However, authority also has internal components. We may be ambivalent about delegating authority to those in charge. For example, we may not respect an individual supervisor.

Authority from within depends on our inner world and our experiences of past authority figures. Supervisors may be unable to exercise authority, or its opposite, they become authoritarian. Obholzer makes helpful distinctions here. To be authoritative, he thinks, is a depressive position state of mind. To be authoritarian is a paranoid–schizoid state, in Jungian terms, a complex, where we become cut off from the roots of authority and processes of sanction in our organization and fuelled by an inner world conflict. Obholzer defines good enough authority as "a state of mind arising from a continuous mix of authorisation from the sponsoring organization or structure, sanctioning from within the organization and connection with the inner world authority figures" (*ibid.*, p. 41).

Power is more of a personal attribute than a role, and refers to the ability to act upon others or upon organizational structures. It can arise from both internal and external sources. Power comes externally from money, privileges, promotion, etc., producing a capacity to rally others to one's side. Internally, it comes from a strength of personality, a state of mind, how powerful we feel and present ourselves to others. Power can be projected, leaving us feeling powerless. Authority without power will lead to demoralization; power without authority to authoritarianism. A well functioning organization, and presumably a good supervisor, actually require both.

Accountability

The question arises when supervising as to whom we are accountable? Is it to our patients, our supervisees, to our employers or managers in the NHS, to training committees or Directors of Training, or to society as a whole? Inevitably, there will at times be tension between professional/clinical and bureaucratic accountability, especially if the supervision has a formal evaluative component. The whole idea of accountability could be said in itself to be unanalytic when supervisors want to preserve a secure container for supervisees and their patients. Organizational documents outlining procedures can smack of fundamentalism in a profession where uncertainty and openness are paramount and individual creativity valued. As supervisors, we can easily "forget" that we are ultimately accountable to our training committees, or in the case of health service professionals to our managers.

Ethical issues

Ethics is a field that is not just about actions that are right and wrong, but also about the fundamental principles that lie behind these actions. Etiquettes and institutional structures we hope will help to contain us but, ultimately, they will not prevent the inevitable internal struggle for each one of us between the chaos arising from our archetypal shadow, usually narcissism or omnipotence, and the wish to behave ethically as supervisors in the face of adversity (Wiener, 2001a). When supervising, as much as when analysing, we turn to our inner private place of feelings, of intuitions and thoughts—the centre of the self—to search for subjective knowledge to foster an ethical search for reflection that facilitates ethical behaviour. Along the way we hope for support from our colleagues, our theory, and our codes of ethics to contain this intrapsychic process, but for sure, we will have to struggle with that shadow force of what is most unethical within us.

Solomon (2001, p. 452) thinks that "the analytic attitude is an ethical attitude and therefore we may say that the analytic attitude is embedded deeply within our humanness". I prefer to maintain a distinction between the analytic attitude and the ethical attitude. For me, the ethical attitude, all that concerns personal identity, provides the foundation for an analytic attitude to develop. The analytic attitude introduces the professional competence that allows meaning to be made without action. It can be fostered through training if the gift is there. It is affected by our theories and practice, can deepen with clinical experience, and is somehow more conscious.

The development of an "internal supervisor" begins when we are first in therapy or analysis, and is externalized eventually when we begin to supervise. An ethical attitude provides the foundation stone for the development of this internal supervisor but the professional training and experience that comes from an analytic attitude is also required (see Solomon, Chapter Three and Arundale, Chapter Five, in this volume).

Case example: supervising in the NHS

The supervisor works in an NHS setting supervising a group of honorary psychotherapists. Most have little clinical experience and are just getting going in their psychotherapy endeavours. The supervisee, Rhona, is thinking of presenting one of her patients in the large fortnightly case discussion meeting attended by all the clinic staff and honorary psychotherapists. This is normal clinic practice. Her patient is a very difficult borderline personality who has had periods of in-patient care for depression in the local hospital and sees the psychiatrist regularly. He was assessed by the Consultant Psychotherapist before beginning therapy. He is contemptuous and controlling of the therapist, who finds him exceedingly difficult. The supervisor discovers, outside the supervision sessions in a clinic staff meeting, that the patient is the user-group representative for the area and is due to sit on a panel to consider bids for a new service. These bids would include a presentation from the same Consultant Psychotherapist who assessed him. The supervisor wonders what to do with this information. Should any of it be revealed to Rhona? The supervisor also realizes that due to restricted space in the clinic, Rhona has been seeing her patient in the room of the Consultant Psychotherapist. In the next supervision session, Rhona relates that her patient came into the room, opening his session with the remark, "I have just turned down Dr X's [the Consultant Psychotherapist] bid for the new service." The supervisor is concerned to protect the patient's identity, as he is well known to some of the clinic staff, and decides to ask Rhona to present a different patient in the case discussion meeting. She encourages Rhona to interpret the patient's wish to triumph over the consultant.

We can use our analytic concepts to understand the process between patient, therapist, and supervisor. Rhona's patient is powerful. He tries to destroy the capacity of his therapist and the clinic to help him under the guise of confidentiality. He is a terrorist, trying to destroy the patient part of himself. His terrorism disempowers Rhona, her supervisor, and other members of the clinic team. His aim is to triumph over the clinic staff and, in particular, his therapist. He becomes vicariously excited, intoxicated in a sado-masochistic way with his own status and power, preferring to remain angrily inside the mother clinic, observing what is going on and actually trying to destroy it rather than face his own considerable need for personal therapy. We could hypothesize that he may still be angry with his original assessor, the Consultant Psychotherapist, who did not take him on himself for therapy.

The dynamics in an NHS organization are different to a training institution. There is an institutional superego with a particular agenda, which can contaminate the primary task. Supervising is pressured; too little for too many. Unconsciously, the agenda may not be to do with the patient getting better or the quality of the supervisor's work. In this case, there may be an unconscious wish to get rid of an extremely difficult patient in order to reduce the burden of work. Supervisors may have to become managers, limiting the length of time therapists can see their patients in order to meet targets set by the Health Authority. In organizations everyone has rights now, but patients are asked to surrender their authority for a while, or in this patient's case, authoritarianism, in order to benefit from personal therapy.

The patient's terrorism provides a ready hook for the supervisor's internalized terrorist in the form of the NHS Trust, whose managers constantly threaten budget cuts and closure of psychotherapy units. This internal object distorted the supervisor's countertransference, making her overprotective of Rhona, who is at the beginning of her career as a psychotherapist and naturally compliant to her supervisor's suggestions. Hughes and Pengelly (1997, pp. 31–42) conceptualize the work of supervision in terms of two triangular interactions, There is, first, the triangle of the participants: the supervisor, the supervisee, and the patient triangle, and second, the triangle of supervisory functions: managing service delivery, facilitating the supervisee's professional development, and focusing on the work. They point out how it is impossible to keep all corners of the triangle in mind at one time and, inevitably, one corner may be unconsciously avoided or neglected. In this case, the organization intrudes forcefully and inappropriately into the supervisor, meaning that both the patient's needs and the supervisee's professional development are neglected. This powerful projective identificatory process produced indigestible countertransference affects in the supervisor and prevented her from using the existing structures and boundaries within the clinic as a helpful space to think. The supervisor and the staff team knew something, but turned a blind eye, under the guise of confidentiality, to what was in the patient's best interests. Normally, there is an assumed confidentiality, which resides within the team, and it would have been in the patient's (pro-therapy) interests to be discussed at the clinic meeting. It remains a controversial issue as to whether the supervisor would be confounding an already difficult therapeutic relationship by telling Rhona about "facts" pertaining to the patient's dealings with the clinic as a user representative.

Case example: two trainees

I shall now present two brief vignettes from my work as the supervisor of two trainees, each training in a different organization. I will call them Susan and Brian, respectively. Each was working with a training patient who was frequently absent from sessions.

Susan

When I first began to work with Susan, she was very anxious, immediately deferring to me rather compliantly. She asked how I would like her to write up her notes, did I want copies, etc. I intuited quickly that Susan had a critical, rigid, and controlling superego that was being projected into me. I wondered to myself about her previous experiences in supervision. I felt she needed to find her own way of working and make her own decisions about how to present her work in supervision, and I put this explicitly to her at the beginning. She seemed to accept my remark with relief. Susan was working with a very ill young female borderline patient who frequently missed sessions, sometimes for two weeks at a time, but she always returned. During these periods, Susan was severely tested in her capacity to manage her feelings about the absences, but she and I used these times to explore her countertransference responses in relation to her patient, trying to understand what could be going on in the patient's mind when she absented herself. At times, Susan would write or telephone her patient to encourage her to return. These actions were based on an agreement between us that the patient had shut down, dissociated, as a defence of the self against unbearable existential anxiety. To interpret the missed sessions as aggressive would, at this stage, have been ill-advised, premature, and probably wrong. I enjoyed working with Susan and she was blossoming as a budding analyst.

The patient, who had attended regularly for several weeks, suddenly disappeared again. This time, Susan was very angry with her. Susan arrived at one supervision session, telling me anxiously that there was something she had to ask me. Would these missed sessions prevent her from qualifying? I was surprised at her direct question to me (something was being enacted?) as I had previously indicated to Susan in different ways, including on paper in reports on the work with her patient, that I did view the work they were doing in analysis as satisfactory. Having a patient who attends regularly is certainly easier when you are in training, but frequency of attendance is neither the main nor the only criterion of progress. Susan then blushed, telling me that there was something she wanted to say. She told me that as she had waited in her consulting room for her missing patient the previous day, she had a strong fantasy that she would be thrown off the training. She recognized this as a familiar personal response and she became tearful. I felt moved by Susan's revelation and received it without much comment, but I thought about it. Later, I suggested that perhaps this was not only a personal response, but also an identification with her patient's unconscious fear of being thrown out of the analysis if she did not attend a sufficient number of sessions. Susan had been able to tell me something about her own psychology—a personal complex—that felt shameful to her and was not, as yet, well enough integrated. I felt sure that she would be taking it to her own personal analysis, but the point is, that it sat comfortably between us in supervision and was a therapeutic experience for her. A personal complex had been painfully touched but it could help Susan, and later her patient, to move forward in their work together.

Brian

Brian was a trainee in a different organization. He came to me, telling me that Mrs A had suggested that I would be the best supervisor for him. I was flattered, and immediately inflated by this projection on to me. The transference and countertransference dynamic was alive and kicking from the very beginning. Brian, like Susan, asked me how I would like him to present his patient. I suggested he might like to find his own way to write up his notes and that we could discuss it if it was not working. Unlike Susan, Brian did not settle down or begin to find his own voice with his patient. I found him rather obsequious, always looking at me anxiously, agreeing with everything I said. He had a particular inflection in his voice and at the end of many sentences would say "yes" in such a way that made him sound as though he were asking permission from me. Am I getting it right? Am I being a good boy? Sometimes he would say, "yes, you have got it, that is brilliant". His aim seemed to be to make me feel a good supervisor, His gratefulness was, I thought, intended to support my narcissism as if every word I uttered was a precious object. My response was to veer between feeling extremely irritated in an alert but unproductive way to feeling sleepy and lethargic in an equally unproductive way. Neither of us could think much about his patient. This dynamic was immobilizing us both. I found myself wondering about Brian's problems with his aggression. Was I being fended off as a supervisor who could attack him?

Brian's patient was a very ill woman with a history of depression, suicidal ideation, and one hospital admission when she was extremely depressed. Her depression masked huge rage about an abusive relationship with her partner that repeated earlier childhood abuse. She would attend two or three sessions, then cancel some. Brian wrote to her on several occasions when she stayed away, sometimes phoning me between supervision sessions to ask how to phrase the letter. The patient arrived one day and told Brian she wanted to stop; the therapy was not helping and only making her feel worse. Brian managed to suggest that she return to discuss it further, arriving for the next supervision in an extremely anxious state. What could he do? How should he take it up with her? He was pressuring me and I felt furious with him. I felt that all my attempts to facilitate the development of an analytic attitude in Brian had failed and he could not think for himself. Although he appeared to value my input, what he took from me was usually imitated rather than integrated. I felt irritated with his therapist for not analysing him properly. As I gradually regained some capacity to think about what was happening between us, I reflected on the theme of unconscious, split-off aggression—in the patient, in Brian, and between us in supervision. What I wanted to do was to interpret to Brian his difficulty with his aggression, which was leaving him frightened of his patient and prone to enactments in supervision. As his supervisor, this seemed to me to be a delicate area to approach without encroaching inappropriately on his personal therapy. I felt on safer territory approaching the aggression through Brian's patient and hoping that Brian would realize for himself that the analysis with his patient was inflaming a personal complex that he would take to his own therapy.

Fordham (1963, p. 7) defines transference as "an unspecified number of [*unconscious*] perceptions of the analyst by the patient, caused by the projection of *split-off, or unintegrated parts of the patient onto or into the analyst*" (my italics).

He uses two words here, "onto" and "into", and although he does not differentiate between them, they seem to imply that the nature and power of the projective processes can be different. "Onto" conveys something less powerfully projected and introjected by the analyst, who seems in the traditional way to act more neutrally, available to "deal with" patients' projections. "Into" is more suggestive of a forceful projective identification that invades the analyst, who will be affected whether he likes it or not. Fordham also talks of "split-off or unintegrated" parts of the patient, showing his attempts to link Jungian and Kleinian ideas in developing his pioneering theory of the self and its development in infancy and childhood. These two terms (split-off and unintegrated) actually have rather different meanings (Astor, 1995, p. 63; Mizen, 2003, p. 292). "Splitting" was a term used by Klein and her followers to describe the primitive defence mechanism employed to preserve good experience and evacuate the bad and intolerable so that they cannot contaminate each other. This was the earliest process by which internal objects were formed. She has been criticized for developing a model of "normal" functioning using clinical data from her work with ill and damaged children. Fordham reserves the term "splitting" for disintegrative experiences that are pathological, threatening to overwhelm the infant or adult, preferring the more Jungian idea of deintegration and reintegration to describe the dynamic process where the primary self reaches out towards objects and internalizes experience. His phrase "unintegrated parts of the patient" suggests that he is referring to the not-yet-known rather than the pathological or defensive. Splitting is only necessary when this process is significantly interfered with.

Zinkin (1996, p. 1) called supervision the impossible profession: "we know that supervision can be a delight, but may often be a torment". The two case examples seem to me to illustrate how sometimes, as with Susan, an event, or a series of events, in supervision can allow a personal complex not yet integrated in the supervisee to become integrated. Supervision becomes for a brief time an experience of auxiliary analysis. The projective identification in supervision with Susan is an "onto" rather than an "into" experience. It can be worked with without undue discomfort. In other cases, such as with Brian, the supervisory relationship reveals a split-off area in the supervisee, activated by the work with the patient that is difficult to address directly in supervision. The projective experiences are much more intrusive, "into" as opposed to "onto", making for countertransference reactions that are more difficult to manage.

Countertransference in supervision

Countertransference is no longer regarded as neurotic and an interference to analytic work, but as Jung (1929, par.163) says, "a highly important organ of information". Although woven into the fabric of Jung's fundamental conceptions about the nature of the analytic process, it was authors such as Winnicott (1949), Heimann (1950), and Little (1951) who paved the way for the wealth of ideas about countertransference in the context of intersubjectivity and its related processes—projection, introjection, projective identification, containment, and enactment. Later authors (Fordham, 1974; Racker, 1968) focused on the inner experience of the analyst and how it affected work in the transference, distinguishing between countertransference affects that were neurotic, developing if the analyst becomes too identified with his own infantile feelings in relation to his patient, and "true" countertransference affects.

Jungian authors have contributed significantly to elaborating the shadow aspects of countertransference. Jacoby (1984, pp. 94–113) describes a range of potentially dangerous countertransference enactments by the analyst, focusing on money, power, erotic feelings, and the neurotic need for therapeutic success. Lambert (1981) warns of enactments in the countertransference when the analyst becomes caught up in the talion law, unconsciously treating attack with counter-attack when identified with the patient's hostile inner objects. Guggenbuhl-Craig (1971) and Groesbeck (1975) elaborate how analysts can become identified with the "healer" archetype, leaving their patients as the only "wounded" ones.

Generally, countertransference, like other aspects of mental functioning, is now acknowledged to be complex. As Jacobs (2002, p. 31) helpfully summarizes: "Countertransference, like transference itself, is a creation fashioned out of components that shift and change in response to the developing process and changes in the psychology of the analyst".

It is a joint creation between patient and therapist, implying as it does the significance of both the therapist's subjective responses and projected aspects of the patient's inner world. It both influences the process and also holds within it rich opportunities for its understanding (Wiener, 2004).

Exploring the role of the supervisor's countertransference in supervision, Marshall (1997, p. 79) points out that "the supervisor's emotional response can be helpful and facilitating to the course of supervision and therapy, just as we believe that the transference of the therapist can be of use". It occurs to me that the question of how to work with our own and our supervisees' countertransference experiences remains as pertinent today as it did in the heated debates among psychoanalysts and analytical psychologists in the 1930s and 1940s, whose main preoccupation was whether or not to separate the functions of analyst and supervisor. These debates centred on who could deal most effectively with supervisees' countertransference feelings, with some firmly believing that it could only be their personal analyst and others clear that they could be worked with in supervision. The two roles have gradually come to be separated, but this separation can still fuel a split transference between the supervisor and the personal analyst.

Astor (2000, p. 372, 2003) has strong views here: "I strongly disagree with supervisors who tell their supervisees to take such and such a feeling to their analyst. We are analysts, so let us proceed like analysts not traffic policemen". I agree with him and rarely issue such edicts to my own supervisees, as they can feel crude and allow me to neatly sidestep finding an appropriate way of dealing with questions such as, in my case examples, how do I address with Brian in supervision his difficulties with aggression without making interpretations? I think there is always some auxiliary analysis in supervision, and it is precisely because of this that ethical practice—how to work with such issues—is so crucial.

In supervision, the framework of practice is subtly different to analysis in terms of its *focus*, supervisors' *ways of responding* and also in terms of the dynamic *process*.

1. *The Focus* in supervision is on the patient and the patient–analyst relationship. If I cannot find the patient in what is being presented to me, then I know that something is wrong.

2. *Ways of Responding*: since as supervisors we have no licence to interpret our supervisees' complexes, we must find different perspectives to consider them when they arise in supervision. Astor (2003) deals with this by formulating questions, Urban (2003) offers what she calls translations.

3. *The Process*: I find that I often have to work harder to process my countertransference thoughts, feelings, and sensations when I am supervising than when I am analysing. I try to think carefully what to say directly and what to formulate indirectly to my supervisees, though what comes out has at times forced me to acknowledge the inevitable failures and enactments that come from being human. However, these enactments occur as a result of the particular dynamic process of unconscious and conscious relating in supervision.

Jung (1964, par. 852) in his essay on "A psychological view of conscience", makes the point that what happens in the therapeutic process is only a special instance of human relationship in general. As analysts, I think we would probably all agree that the kinds of experiences we have in common are to become psychologically mixed up with our patients through the unconscious processes of projective identification and unconscious identity leading to uncertainty about which affects belong to whom. To understand these emotional states, Jung goes on to remark that, "a special act of reflection is required".

I think we could easily replace his phrase "therapeutic process" with the words "supervision process" and it is this "special act of reflection" that goes on within the supervisory relationship that is particularly interesting to me.

Refracted countertransference

I have come to think of the gestalt of the supervision process as represented by a prism through which different kinds of information (light) pass from one medium into another. I would like to suggest that we use the term, *refracted countertransference* to describe the supervisor's experiences when receiving the multi-beamed narrative of reported experience when our supervisees talk to us about their work with a patient. The angle of refraction is different in supervision than in analysis, and the supervisor must deal with a spectrum of information that is particularly challenging, both to her ethical and her analytic attitude. When the supervisory relationship is going well, as with Susan, facilitating relaxed discussion and playfulness between supervisor and supervisee about the patient, the refracted component parts are dispersed in a manageable form. When the relationship runs into difficulty, as with Brian's personal difficulties and with the supervision of Rhona's patient in the NHS, the supervisor's thoughts and feelings become refracted too widely, leading to potential enactments, especially since direct interpretation of personal material out of the countertransference is usually contraindicated.

There is a more complicated process of projection, projective identification, and introjection in supervision than in analysis. At times, I have had to work extremely hard to process and understand what was going on and which of my own affects could be understood as belonging to me personally or to some aspect of the supervisee–patient relationship.

Conclusion

In a chapter called "What makes an analyst", Jacqueline Rose (2003, pp. 183–184) makes a profound point:

> it is a central part of psychoanalysis to ask how you come to recognise and mis-recognise yourself in what you are . . . wanting to become an analyst cannot be the endpoint of something, like discovering one's vocation, it can only be the start.

This paper has been about how analysts come to recognize and misrecognize their appropriate roles as supervisors. There is no end point, and the process of learning continues.

Rock (1997, p. 18) also emphasizes the role of experience:

> supervision is experiential . . . the question is one of the tact and sensitivity of the supervisor and the receptivity of the supervisee, and the willingness by both to question themselves and their assumptions. The aim is not to purify the process, rather to

stimulate curiosity, self-awareness and a striving for clarity ... A personality change in the supervisee is not the goal of supervision, but the supervisee may well realise change in himself as a result of experiential learning in supervision

These two extracts from Rose and Rock illustrate how the personal psychology of both supervisee and supervisor are inevitably touched in supervision by the complexity of the transference and countertransference dynamics. As supervisors, I think we are working at the crossroads or the interface where the ethical attitude (all that concerns personal identity) and the analytic attitude (introducing the realm of professional competence), cohabit. Culturally, the push to supervise ethically comes from both internal and external pressures, but there is always a need for a non-institutional space for the unconscious. The role of the organization plays a significant role—consciously and unconsciously—for the supervisor, often restricting considerably this necessary non-institutional space.

The "special act of reflection" that Jung refers to takes place within a relationship with those less experienced than ourselves. This must involve considerable self-reflection, often under the most taxing of circumstances. It has helped me to understand why supervising can sometimes seem more difficult than analysing. Without the "right" to interpret, the supervisor has to have a more developed capacity to process transference and countertransference responses. Using three clinical vignettes, I have put forward the concept of refracted countertransference—a more complicated process of projection and introjection—that comes from having more than two people in the room together involved in the particular relationship that is supervision. The character of this process of refraction will determine whether the countertransference affects of the supervisor are indeed friend or foe.

References

Astor, J. (1995). Ego development in infancy and childhood. In: J. Astor (Ed.), *Michael Fordham: Innovations in Analytical Psychology* (pp. 52–71). London: Routledge.

Astor, J. (2000). Some reflections on empathy and reciprocity in the use of countertransference between supervisor and supervisee. *Journal of Analytical Psychology*, 45: 367–385.

Astor, J. (2003). Empathy in the use of countertransference between supervisor and supervisee. In: J. Wiener, R. Mizen, & J. Duckham (Eds.), *Supervising and Being Supervised: A Practice in Search of a Theory.* London: Palgrave/Macmillan.

Bion, W. R. (1961). *Experiences in Groups.* New York: Basic Books.

Eckstein, R. (1960). A historical survey of the teaching of psychoanalytic technique. *Journal of the American Psychoanalytic Association*, 8: 500–516.

Eckstein, R., & Wallerstein, R. (1958). *The Learning and Teaching of Psychotherapy.* London: Imago.

Fordham, M. (1963). Notes on the transference. *New Developments in Analytical Psychology* (1974). London: Heinemann. Also published in S. Shamdasani (Ed.), *Fordham, M. Analyst–patient Interaction: Collected Papers on Technique.* London: Routledge, 1996.

Fordham, M. (1974). Technique and countertransference. In: *Technique in Jungian Analysis, Vol. 2.* London: Karnac.

Fordham, M. (1995). Suggestions towards a Theory of Supervision. In: P. Kugler (Ed.), *Jungian Perspectives on Clinical Supervision* (pp. 41–51). Einsiedeln: Daimon Press.

Groesbeck, C. G. (1975). The archetypal image of the wounded healer. *Journal of Analytical Psychology*, 20(2): 122–146

Guggenbuhl-Craig, A. (1971). *Power in the Helping Professions.* Zurich: Spring.

Heimann, P. (1950). On countertransference. *International Journal of Psycho-Analysis*, 31: 81–84.

Hughes, L., & Pengelly, P. (1997). *Staff Supervision in a Turbulent Environment.* London: Jessica Kingsley.

Jacobs, T. J. (2002). Countertransference past and present: a review of the concept. In: M. Mickels, L. Abensour, L. Eizirik, R. Rusbridger (Eds.), *Key Papers on Countertransference* (pp. 7–41). London: Karnac.

Jacoby, M. (1984). *The Analytic Encounter.* Toronto: Inner City.

Jung, C. G. (1929). Problems of modern psychotherapy. *C.W.*, 16. London: Routledge and Kegan Paul.

Jung, C. G. (1935). *Analytical Psychology. Its Theory and Practice (The Tavistock Lectures).* London: Routledge, 1990.

Jung, C. G. (1964). A psychological view of conscience. *C.W.*, 10. London: Routledge and Kegan Paul.

Kernberg, O. (1986). Institutional problems of psychoanalytic education. *Journal of the American Psychoanalytic Association, 34*: 799–834.

Lambert, K. (1981). *Analysis, Repair and Individuation*. Library of Analytical Psychology, Volume 5. London: Academic Press.

Lepper, G. (1992). The complex in human affairs. In: M. Stein (Ed.), *Psyche at Work: Workplace Applications of Jungian Analytical Psychology* (pp. 72–79). Wilmette, IL: Chiron.

Little, M. (1951). Countertransference and the patient's response to it. *International Journal of Psycho-Analysis, 32*: 320–340.

Marshall, R. J. (1997). The interactional triad in supervision. In: M. H. Rock (Ed.), *Psychodynamic Supervision* (pp. 77–107). Northvale, NJ: Jason Aronson.

Mattinson, J. (1975). *The Reflection Process in Casework Supervision*. London: Institute of Marital Studies.

Menzies Lyth, I. (1988). *Containing Anxiety in Institutions*. London: Free Association.

Mizen, R. (2003). A contribution towards an analytic theory of violence. *Journal of Analytical Psychology, 48*(3): 285–307.

Obholzer, A. (1994a). Authority, power and leadership: contributions from group relations training. In: A. Obholzer & V. Roberts (Eds.), *The Unconscious at Work: Individual and Organisational Stress in the Human Services* (pp. 39–51). London: Routledge.

Obholzer, A. (1994b). Afterword. In: A. Obholzer & V. Roberts (Eds.), *The Unconscious at Work: Individual and Organisational Stress in the Human Services* (pp. 206–211). London: Routledge.

Racker, H. (1968). *Transference and Countertransference*. London: Hogarth.

Rock, M. (1997). *Psychodynamic Supervision*. Northvale, NJ: Jason Aronson.

Rose, J. (2003). *On Not Being Able to Sleep: Psychoanalysis and the Modern World*. London: Chatto and Windus.

Searles, H. (1955). The informational value of the supervisor's emotional experience. In: J. D. Sutherland (Ed.), *Collected Papers on Schizophrenia and Related Subjects* (pp. 157–176). New York: International Universities Press [reprinted London: Karnac, 1986].

Solomon, H. (2001). Origins of the ethical attitude. *Journal of Analytical Psychology, 46*: 443–455.

Stein, M. (1992). Organisation life as spiritual practice. In: M. Stein (Ed.), *Psyche at Work: Workplace Applications of Jungian Analytical Psychology* (pp. 1–8). Wilmette, IL: Chiron.

Stokes, J. (1994). The unconscious at work in groups and teams: contributions from the work of Wilfred Bion. In: A. Obholzer & V. Roberts (Eds.), *The Unconscious at Work: Individual and Organisational Stress in the Human Services*. London: Routledge.

Symington, N. (1986). *The Analytic Experience: Lectures from the Tavistock*. London: Free Association.

Urban, E. (2003). Supervising work with children, In: J. Wiener, R. Mizen, & J. Duckham (Eds.), *Supervising and Being Supervised: A Practice in Search of a Theory* (pp. 67–82). Basingstoke: Palgrave Macmillan.

Wiener, J. (2001a). The sanctum, the citadel and the souk: confidentiality and paradox. In: F. Palmer Barnes & L. Murdin (Eds.), *Values and Ethics in Psychotherapy* (pp. 144–163). London: Open University Press.

Wiener, J. (2001b). Confidentiality and paradox: the location of ethical space. *Journal of Analytical Psychology, 46*: 431–443.

Wiener, J. (2004). Transference and countertransference: contemporary perspectives. In: J. Cambray & L. Carter (Eds.). *Analytical Psychology: Contemporary Perspectives in Jungian Analysis* (pp. 149–176). London: Brunner Routledge.

Winnicott, D. (1949). Hate in the countertransference. *International Journal of Psycho-Analysis, 30*: 69–75

Zinkin, L. (1996). Supervision: the impossible profession. In: P. Kugler (Ed.), *Jungian Perspectives on Clinical Supervision* (pp. 240–249). Einsiedein: Daimon Verlag.

CHAPTER TEN

The role of supervision (internal and external) in working with the suicidal patient

Joscelyn Richards

Introduction

I n my experience as a therapist and supervisor the most frequent situation in psychoanalytic psychotherapy concerning issues around suicide is not so much a patient committing suicide successfully, or even attempting to do so (though, sadly, both these events can occur), but rather patients conveying to the therapist, directly or indirectly, that they are experiencing compelling thoughts to kill themselves. It is this situation that I am addressing in this chapter. When patients announce their intention in a deadly voice I always find it chilling and heart stopping. It is usually very alarming for the therapist to hear this kind of news and, if not, should be. Because it is shocking it is often difficult to keep one's bearings and to think as well as feel.

Often therapists feel they have to *do* something. They can especially feel that they have to pass the anxiety on to someone else but, as they are the ones on the receiving end of the communication, they need to be able to receive and process the information rather than go into action mode. When therapists are working in a public health setting, or any organizational setting, the belief in taking immediate action, such as telling the patient's GP or some other relevant professional, is often supported by policies of the wider health care system, for example, policies concerning the prevention of suicide. Thus, there can be both internal and external pressures to act rather than think that may overwhelm the therapist, so that the need to work out the most appropriate response, including considerations about confidentiality, may lose out to the pressure to act without thinking.

The therapist is the person the patient has chosen to tell of an internal push towards suicide. Whatever possible meanings lie behind both the telling and the wish for death, I would suggest that one of the meanings of the telling is an act of trust by the sane part of the patient that the therapist will respond thoughtfully. The therapist therefore must not avoid the issue, but find a way to handle this communication in the patient's best interests. Essential in the process is responding very seriously and empathically to the wish to die and holding in mind that this is a real wish or intention that could escalate if not accepted as such. If not taken seriously the patient can get more urgent in the attempt to get the therapist to respond appropriately.

It is my experience that it is often the case that the situation does not require drastic action, but a capacity in the therapist to allow oneself to be pulled into the world of the patient in order to understand its meaning emotionally and then to find the capacity to step outside of this world in order to think about it analytically. To be helped to do this in the supervisory situation, supervisees need to have internalized the knowledge that their supervisor is available, supportive, and knows about their strengths and weaknesses as a developing therapist and cares about the patient–therapist couple.

What are the main problems for a therapist when a patient threatens or hints at the possibility of suicide during the course of their therapy?

The therapist's personal reactions

1.   A feeling of panic and helplessness that can threaten to overwhelm the therapist.

2. A worry, both in the session and after the session, about being blamed for not doing the right thing. I have certainly had some bad moments when I have heard the announcement coming out of the mouth of a patient that he or she must die: whole scenarios have flashed through my mind about being blamed and punished, taken to court, being ostracized by colleagues, and so on. Fear of being blamed, especially if the therapy is taking place in a culture of blame, can lead to therapists being more concerned with protecting themselves than thinking through analytically what is needed for the patient, though, ironically, thinking through will probably protect the therapist as well as the patient.

3. A belief, already mentioned, that the therapist has to do something or tell a third party immediately without thinking first. Such a reaction, or any automatic following of procedures with or without the patient's consent, can seem to patients that their therapist is "passing the buck" and is not interested in, or capable of, helping them with this dreadful situation of possible self murder. Of course, there are times when instant action has to be taken and supervisees need to know how to do this and that their supervisor will support them.

4. An opposite reaction can occur, i.e., a denial that the patient may mean business; for example, turning a blind eye and a deaf ear or trivializing the seriousness of the intention because it is unbearable to hear. Such a reaction will also be interpreted by the patient as a lack of concern in the therapist to hear this painful news and the patient may withdraw or become more desperate and more likely to act out in order to make an impact.

5. Colluding with patients' denials, following material suggestive of suicidal pressures, that they are experiencing serious urges to kill themselves and thus being lulled into a false reassurance.

6. Experiencing angry and sadistic feelings towards the patient that would make things worse if expressed without being processed and the basis of them understood.

Supervisors, too, can experience some or all of these reactions. They can paralyse thinking and the working out of the most appropriate response. However, they can also become useful tools for understanding the patient if monitored and processed, and can help the therapist make appropriate decisions. If not processed, the therapist or supervisor may contribute to patients' states of despair, anger, or guilt and push them to an act of suicide. It is therefore the supervisor's task to monitor and process their own reactions as well as to help supervisees to do the same.

The possible clash between the policies and procedures of the wider health care system and those of psychoanalytic psychotherapy and a related conflict between the therapist's commitment to confidentiality and the wish to do anything to keep the patient alive

Therapists working in the public sector (or private organizations) may find that the psychoanalytic psychotherapy system and values conflict with the policies and procedures of the larger organization around issues of patient care and the prevention of suicide. Managers may not be particularly sympathetic to, or knowledgeable about, psychoanalytic psychotherapy and issues of transference, countertransference, and confidentiality. Each policy may have very good intentions behind it and may be suitable for patients who are at the more disturbed end of the scale, but may undermine therapists' confidence in using their clinical judgement and thus prevent them from thinking about the particular situation and how to safeguard the therapy as well as the patient's life.

In this context it can be useful to think of patients in psychotherapy as being on a continuum between those with sufficient ego strength and resources to look after themselves and those with more severe and enduring mental health problems who need active care from mental health services.

At the Association for Psychoanalytic Psychotherapy in the NHS Annual Lecture in 2003 the speaker, Dr Carine Minne, a psychoanalyst and Consultant Psychotherapist at Broadmoor Hospital, presented a paper that explored ways in which the Care Programme Approach system could support the psychoanalytic psychotherapy system. She suggested that patients at the ego strength end of the scale, who are fairly used to running their own lives and seeking help when they need to, would feel surprised and undermined if every time they mentioned suicidal thoughts the local Community Mental Health Team (CMHT) had to be informed or their GP turned up on their doorstep! For such patients it would be a breach of confidentiality and could undermine trust in the psychotherapist, especially if they have not been consulted or informed. However, Dr Minne thought that at the other end of the scale there are patients who have relied on mental health services for most of their adult lives and could feel neglected if the therapist did not work with or have communication with relevant other professionals. They could feel it was a repetition of their childhood, where often the parents could not act together as a concerned parental couple.

Dr Minne thought that therapists could also be placed on a continuum. At one end of the scale are therapists who believe in interpreting only and never communicating with third parties under any circumstance, as it would be a breach of confidentiality. At the other end there are therapists who cannot tolerate any anxiety and either rush to tell others or blindly follow procedures without thinking about what is in the patient's best interests. The sensible practitioner, I would suggest, knows about their organization's procedures, knows from whom to seek help and advice, understands the need to protect the patient's psychotherapy as well as the patient's life, and uses their clinical judgement to decide how to handle a situation where they are concerned about the patient's safety.

For therapists in supervision, this means that by the end of a session where suicide has been mentioned they have to make a clinical judgement as to whether they have time to wait for their next supervisory session, should ring the supervisor immediately after the session, or take more drastic action by contacting a third party with or without the patient's or supervisor's agreement.

In their initial discussions of suicidal intent, the therapist and supervisor need to address the following aspects:

- the patient's depth of despair;
- the pervasiveness of the feelings of helplessness;
- the extent of the determination to carry out the deed;
- the degree of murderous rage, particularly with the therapist, which could be turned against the patient's body;

- the extent of depressive guilt;
- the patient's capacity to contain all these feelings, which includes knowing if the patient has a supportive partner, friends, family, or GP.
- the patient's recent experiences in his/her psychotherapy;
- the patient's life history.

What are the tasks of the supervisor and what resources, knowledge, and attitudes are needed to supervise appropriately the therapist whose patient becomes suicidal in the course of their psychoanalytic psychotherapy?

Supervisors' tasks

In the immediate situation of supervisees being worried about a suicidal patient, the first task may be to help them overcome any panic or self-blame and then regain their thinking capacities, whether the contact is over the telephone or in a supervision session.

After this, I think the main tasks of the supervisor are to help a supervisee

1. understand the meaning of the suicidal wish or plan;
2. assess the intensity of the wish;
3. assess the likelihood of it being enacted;
4. help the supervisee to work out, if the situation is ongoing (which it often is), when it is appropriate to make an empathic comment only, when to give an interpretation, when to carry out an action, or when and how to combine these responses.

If action seems necessary, it is preferable to help the supervisee explore with the patient how best to help the part that wants to stay alive look after him or herself at this point.

However, I would say that to be able to carry out these processes supervisees need the supervisor's support from the beginning of supervision in being open to experiencing the full impact of the patient's communications, however disturbing, rather than defending against them, and then helped to find a way to think about and process their impact. They also need to know from the beginning that their supervisor is not interested in blaming and judging, but in exploring difficult issues thoughtfully.

Supervisor's resources and attitudes

To sum up the supervisor's overall task, it is to look after the therapist–patient couple that he/she is supervising. To carry out this task the supervisor needs the following resources and attitudes, all of which are particularly relevant in helping a supervisee with a suicidal patient.

1. A reasonably clear and complex conceptual model of the mind, combined with an understanding of the vicissitudes of the psychoanalytic psychotherapy process, which will do justice to the many reasons that can drive a patient to attempt or to feel internally pushed or persuaded to take his/her life during the course of a therapy, including why this can happen when the patient–therapist couple is functioning well. The section headed "A conceptual model" (below) gives an example of a conceptual model useful with suicidal patients that I make use of in the clinical examples that I present later.
2. To be prepared to discuss the therapist's anxieties about their patient in supervision, on the telephone between supervision, or in an additional supervision session if judged necessary. In other words, to help supervisees know that they are not alone with their concerns about their patient and that the supervisor will listen to and not dismiss their anxieties as being inappropriate or due to lack of experience.
3. To have discussed with supervisees who else can be appropriately contacted at the times when the supervisor is not available, especially if the supervisor is away for an extended period.
4. To think carefully about the transition to another supervisor if the supervisor has to move away permanently.
5. To convey an attitude of interest and understanding of difficulties experienced by the supervisee so that he or she will feel able to bring to supervision the patient's intense negative or positive transferences and their countertransference reactions, however uncomfortable.

6.   To pick up and explore if the supervisee is denying the meaning of, or is cut-off from, a patient's disturbing communications.

7.   To know supervisees well enough to be aware of their resources and vulnerable areas; for example, whether they are in their own personal therapy or if they are going through major life changes that may impair their functioning.

8.   To know the history of the patient and his/her vulnerable areas; for example, separations, and whether there is a history of suicidal thoughts and/or attempts and when these have occurred.

Points 7 and 8, because they involve anticipation of vulnerability in either the patient, the supervisee, or both, can assist the supervisor to help the supervisee prevent an escalation of acting out by the patient. Successful suicide is tragic for the patient and devastating for those left behind, including the therapist, who may then experience crippling doubt about his or her capacity as a therapist.

Supervisors also need

• to understand the context in which the therapy is taking place; that is, the policies/procedures of the organization or clinic holding clinical responsibility for the patient's psychoanalytic psychotherapy;

• to know what other professionals to contact in the patient's wider health care system for support, guidance, or prompt action if required;

• to know whom to consult for support, advice, and good thinking in their own professional network when necessary. We all benefit by talking over a problem with a trusted colleague.

A conceptual model

Obviously, therapists and analysts work with a range of analytic concepts they find useful. Supervisors need a model of the mind that allows them to understand and conceptualize the pull towards life and the pull towards death and how these two approaches are played out in the analytic relationship. Otherwise, a supervisor may share a supervisee's bewilderment or anger at threats of suicide, especially following positive developments in the therapy or the patient's life.

Keval (2003) works with the concept of parts: there is a part of the person that wants to stay alive and is desperate for help, while there is another that wants to die and is planning how to achieve this. By recognizing the existence of both parts it becomes possible to work with a patient in mapping out how the part that wants to stay alive is being hijacked or sabotaged by the part that believes death is the solution to whatever the problem is perceived to be.

I have found it useful to take the concepts of parts further and to use Sinason's concept of internal cohabitation (1993) to conceptualize two separate selves that co-exist in the same body and have very different mental capacities and relationship with reality and to life and death. In summary, one self is capable of functioning in the world of reality and has the potential to make relationships and wants to have a life and not it cut short: this self is interested in having therapy. The other self functions as an internal adviser who, because it is essentially paranoid and thus incapable of perceiving situations objectively, gives ill advice. For this self, life, relationships, and particularly therapy, are dangerous and threatening and, thus, so is any change. Change that is welcomed by the well self is often seen as life-threatening by the ill self (Richards, 1999). The therapeutic task is to differentiate these two selves from each other. I mention the concept of internal cohabitation because I have found it particularly helpful in working with patients to make sense of experiences, such as the pressure to kill themselves, that otherwise seem puzzling and frightening. It has also provided me with a useful tool for identifying ill internal advice in my own head in these situations.

Clinical examples

Below are two clinical examples that illustrate some of the above themes. One (Mr L) is from my own experience as a therapist, where I had to draw on my internalized supervisors, and the other (Mr R) is from a case I have supervised. Both patients were in weekly psychotherapy in the NHS.

Mr L

Mr L was twenty-five, very intelligent, with a diagnosis of schizophrenia. Ever since he can remember he has heard voices that tell him he belongs to the devil, causes others to die, and deserves to die himself. His father died when he was young. He was admitted to hospital and then referred for therapy when his girlfriend at the time was killed in a car accident. The voices were very active and persecuting after that, and said he that was an evil influence on people and must die.

He arrived at his first meeting with me convinced that he must die, that he wanted to die, and that my role was to help him. There seemed to be very little room for any other thought. The pressure on me was constant and intense. Mr L seemed desperate and begged me to help him find a way to kill himself. At other times he was silent and seemed preoccupied with the voices in his head. Sometimes he would explain that they said he was evil, belonged to the devil, would be killed one way or the other, and that therefore it was better that he took control and planned his own death. According to this logic it would be an act of kindness on my part to help him die painlessly; to know he could successfully kill himself at any time would be a blessed relief. The only trouble was that he had to be successful, as he did not want a botched job where he would survive but be maimed and then be cast out by his family and the hostel where he was living. Taking an overdose would be best. However, it was very difficult in the hostel to store tablets because the staff kept an eye on him at all times and made it a condition of stay that he did not hoard pills.

I remember feeling really cruel that I was not agreeing to put Mr L out of his misery. I also remember my hope that in time the therapy work would help him to contain the voices and live his life better seemed completely feeble in contrast to the absolute certainty of the voices that death was all he could look forward to. There were times when he would look at me very suspiciously and wonder if he could trust me not to tell other staff "certain things" and I would wonder out loud what these "certain things" were. For some time he could not say directly but gave hints that it was something to do with his pills and taking an overdose. In my countertransference I felt I had to win his trust and that the only way was to say "you can trust me—I won't tell anyone". I would then feel worried that I might act on this internal advice and if either he did kill himself, or was found to have hoarded his pills and the hostel staff were to find out about my collusion, I would be seen at best as irresponsible and at worst as a murdering therapist, breaking all the Trust's policies on Patient Care and be punished, sacked, and ostracized. At the same time I thought that for the therapy to take place Mr L needed to be able to bring to the sessions whatever was on his mind and trust that it was confidential. I felt cornered and tortured as well as enormously sorry for this young man who seemed to be almost permanently persecuted in his head by psychotic voices. I was not at all sure how to resolve the confidentiality issue.

To handle the difficulties with this situation I had to address both the work with the patient in the therapy session and my relationship with the CMHT via the psychiatrist.

Work with the patient

I came to observe that every time we had some meaningful engagement, however brief, it would be followed by him looking at me very suspiciously or looking at his hand, where he was certain that the devil had put a mark to show he belonged to him, as if the voices in his head were warning him that he had made a big mistake to trust me enough to talk to me. However, one of the things that he was able to tell me in a moment of trust was about a recurring dream. He told me this quite early in the therapy. In this dream there are two people walking beside a railway line. He is not sure what sex they are. One of them suddenly breaks away and runs towards the line as if to throw him/herself under the train. The other person tries to stop them. The dream ends without the patient knowing the outcome. The patient himself said that he felt the dream represented an internal conflict between wanting to live and wanting to die. Thus we noted together that however strong the internal persuasion is to die there is always someone, even if very frail, who wants to live and not have his life cut short prematurely. In talking about this dream, I say the aim of the therapy is to help the person that wants to live his life to do so by understanding and containing the internal persuasions to die. At the time he nodded agreement but could not say more. After that we both found it helpful to remember this dream at various times. Knowing that he had acknowledged that he wanted help to stay alive, however much this would be denied and opposed when he was under the influence of the voices, gradually helped me to find a way to resolve the confidentiality issue.

I found myself empathizing, using my countertransference, with the person that felt persecuted, blamed, tortured, and cornered by the inner voices. It seemed to me that I had to do my very best to imagine and feel what it is like to experience voices in your head that are always telling you that you are evil, that you belong to the devil, that you bring bad experiences to everyone you have contact with, and that sooner or later you will be forced into a cruel death. I also realized that the patient felt there was no one else he could tell without dire consequences about the belief that he had to die. He believed his mother did not want to hear these beliefs as she always hoped Mr L was better and would accuse him of being cruel if he tried to tell her. Mr L felt he could not tell the hostel staff because of their rule that tablets must not be hoarded. He felt, there-fore, that he had to keep all these thoughts of killing himself to himself. Thus I realized that I was the person who had to hear them and find a way to bear them and then help Mr L find a different way of thinking about them.

On reflecting how tortured and cornered I felt by the relentless demand to help with the suicide plan, it became clear to me that I had to experience the same pressure from Mr L's internal persecu-tor as he was experiencing, in order to understand what he was living with and then find a way to help him to understand and manage the pressure differently. I had to do the opposite of trying to shut him up, despite a longing to do so. I had to help him know that I was aware of the pressure and that I was interested in hear-ing what he was bringing to the session in order to understand, rather than dismiss or ignore, the seriousness of what he was saying, or join in with the aim of killing him.

I said to him something like the following:

"I think you are letting me know that the voices are very strong in threatening you and making you feel that you are bad, that you deserve to die and that there is no escape. I think the voices come from a mind that lives in your head with you and presents itself as the devil and tells you that you have to do its bidding or you will be punished. I think you are letting me know that you feel desperate, that you can't think of any way to deal with this inner persuasion that you deserve to die except to plan your death yourself and enlist my help. You want me to know that when the voices are this active you feel it would be a relief to die. However, I think your interest in telling me about your dream—

where one person tries to stop the other one from jumping under a train—means you hope that instead of me joining in with plan to kill you, I can, instead, help you to find a better way to live with the voices."

Mr L listened very quietly but did not speak. A bit later I said,

"I am wondering if the first step in finding the way to live is to share with me, as you have begun to do, the thoughts that come into your head that persuade or insist that you are better off dead. You are perhaps looking to see if I can really listen to you and hear about the voices and your reaction to them without panicking and without denying how very frightening it is for you and without joining in the plan to kill you."

Each time I said something like this Mr L tended not to comment but seemed relieved and the pressure for me to join in with a suicidal plan would lessen. There came a point, though, when I thought Mr L was not sure where I stood because it seemed that the inner voices were telling him that I had been persuaded to join in planning his death. Thus, there was an occasion when I said,

"I think the voices are confusing you because they are telling you that I want you to die because I too think you are evil and that makes you feel I am dangerous. I think you need me to say clearly that, as much as I understand the belief that to plan your own death can feel like the only possible escape from the insistence of the voices that sooner or later someone will kill you, I am not here to help you do that but to help you find a way to live your life even though this is not an easy undertaking."

The pressure for me to join in the plan to help Mr L die was never as intense after that.

Further thoughts about monitoring the countertransference

There is value in monitoring the countertransference, especially anger, because I think it is quite common for therapists to experience anger when a patient either threatens suicide and/or succeeds. There are many other emotions too, of course, but anger is common. Like all emotions in the therapist it can be a useful tool if processed rather than repressed, denied, or acted out.

At certain stages I was aware of an anger and indignation in my countertransference that Mr L was dominated not only by an assumption that I would help him kill himself, but that I was being bludgeoned and coerced into having ideas about how he could do it successfully and painlessly. It seemed a complete subversion of what I was there for. To express the anger directly would have been damaging, but by giving it space I was alerted to the fact that in my sane self I was becoming persuaded (by my mad internal adviser and his) that I ought to help him with the plan to die. This helped me to realize that I had to monitor and identify other internal reactions. I became aware of an insistent belief that in order to win Mr L's trust I had to promise to help him commit suicide or get him the means to do so and not tell anyone, otherwise I would be rejected and dismissed as useless. By bringing the belief more fully into my awareness, I realized that if I went along with this belief I would be abandoning all my knowledge and experience as a therapist, which would also mean abandoning the sane patient who had come for help to stay alive and understand better how to do this.

I then realized that there was a parallel between the coercive pressures that I felt under to give up my knowledge and role as a therapist and commit murder and the coercive pressures that the patient felt under to give up his life. In my case it would be professional suicide. I assumed that just as it was awful for me to feel bullied and threatened into giving up my usual therapy role and analytic functions, it was even worse for the patient to feel internally bullied and threatened into believing that he would be better off dead. When I said I understood how much the voices threatened and bullied him to agree that he deserved to die, he sobbed and sobbed. He said later that he was surprised at his reaction but felt it was a relief to feel I understood about the power of the voices and how real they are and how hopeless they can make him feel. He said he was scared to have hope about his life but wanted to. This was the beginning of the patient feeling he could bring these pressures into the therapy to explore why they were happening rather than go along with them. We could then begin to think further about who or what was behind the voices.

Communication with the psychiatrist

Clearly, I felt very vulnerable seeing this patient and in danger of acting out, and decided that I needed to talk to his psychiatrist, Dr Y, to clarify what was appropriate to communicate and to see if he could be a support to me. I was wondering how to go about this when an opportunity arose in a session. Mr L wanted to know where the limits of confidentiality were and wanted to know whether it was safe to tell me "certain things" (such as hoarding tablets) or would I tell Dr Y, the hostel staff, his key worker, or even his mother. I said that usually everything he said was confidential unless he told me something that made me think his life was in imminent danger, in which case I would discuss with him how we could best handle the situation. I said this could involve one or both of us contacting his psychiatrist or key worker. This made sense to Mr L.

In discussing this issue further, Mr L said he knew that Dr Y sent me copies of the letters he wrote to Mr L following an interview with him, as they had my name on the bottom, and he sounded pleased about this. So I said that it sounded as though he knew his psychiatrist had similar concerns about him as I had and therefore he, unlike the voices or the mind behind the voices, felt it was important that Dr Y and I had contact to make sure all three of us could support each other in helping him learn how to take care of himself. Thus he and I agreed that Dr Y and I would meet to make sure we were in agreement about when I would contact him.

When Dr Y and I met I explained to him that Mr L and I agreed that I needed to be able to call on him if I was concerned about Mr L being taken over by the psychotic thoughts completely or planning his imminent suicide in a very convincing way. I added that I did not want to burden myself or Mr L with every thought he had that might result in him harming himself, as this would be nearly all the time and would undermine our therapy work and his trust that the therapy was confidential. He said that that sounded right, that we both knew that Mr L was at risk whether he had psychotherapy or not, that we could not control every facet of his life, and that the hostel was doing a pretty good job in helping him to keep off non-prescription drugs and not hoard his medication. Dr Y's understanding and supportive attitude enabled me to feel held in my work with him. Without it I would have felt too vulnerable. As it turned out, we needed very little contact after this, partly because the first contact gave me what I needed and partly because

Mr L listened less and less to the internal advice that he deserved to be dead.

Mr R

This is a case I supervised in a psychotherapy clinic in the NHS. It involved helping a supervisee (Ms X) work with a patient (Mr R) in contacting a third party (GP) in order to anticipate and contain urges to self-harm which might have escalated into a suicidal attempt during the therapist's break.

> Mr R had been in weekly psychoanalytic psychotherapy for nearly two years as the summer break approached. He had a history that particularly made him vulnerable to breaks, though he had become more vulnerable recently because of his growing attachment to his therapist and because of the death of his mother earlier in the year. He had become closer to his mother in the last few years and experienced her death as a real loss.

> Mr R had been born with a physical disability that had involved numerous unsuccessful and painful operations all through his childhood, adolescence, and adulthood. At his assessment he reported that, although the operations were painful, he liked being in hospital because the nurses and doctors seemed to care for him more than his parents, who never discussed his disability or the pain he suffered. He felt the family got on with their lives and forgot him when in hospital (later in his therapy, when he became closer to his mother, he reported that she confirmed his view and apologized). He took a serious overdose in his twenties after the break-up of a relationship and since then had experienced urges to harm his body with a sharp knife. He said he often felt suicidal but would never consider killing himself while his mother was still alive. At the time of his assessment he had been able to observe that he experienced these urges to harm himself whenever operations or appointments were cancelled at the last minute and none of the staff or his family seemed to understand or care how frustrating and disappointing this was. He was now in his late thirties, single and living alone.

> He had previously had two years of psychoanalytic psychotherapy in the NHS that ended prematurely when his therapist left London. He did not seek further therapy for some years as he did not want the pain

of forming an attachment that might end suddenly. However, he and his GP, whom it was noted in the assessment he found helpful, decided that he needed further therapy when he had to give up working due to becoming confused and forgetful. He had become very isolated. The GP thought his cognitive difficulties were due to depression as there were no signs of impairment from neurological tests or brain scans.

For the first eighteen months of his psychotherapy Mr R behaved as if the therapist was deeply unimportant. He could not remember previous sessions, forgot what was being said in a session and was never surprised or distressed by the therapist's breaks.

The therapist noticed that links could be made and that sometimes these led to a sense of continuity, but these would be quickly attacked or broken up, leaving the therapist feeling confused and disorientated.

The three of us gradually mapped out that Mr R seemed to be under the influence of an internal adviser (or harsh superego) who continually informed him that

- he did not matter;
- if his therapist behaved as if he did this was not to be trusted;
- his needs could never be met;
- no-one was interested in how he felt;
- to communicate any anger or feelings of let down was utterly unacceptable;
- his previous therapist had left him because he had become attached to her and she had found his needs too much;
- everyone was like he had believed his parents had been in childhood, who forgot him and did not want to discuss his difficulties and needs (or only pretended to).

He was thus internally advised never to let himself need anyone.

Owing, I think, to the therapist's capacity to hold the patient in mind and to help him to begin to think about the internal advice that he had up until now accepted as the absolute truth, the patient had begun gradually to allow himself to acknowledge that his therapist mattered to him and to begin to trust that she remembered him.

As the summer break approached during their second year the therapist began to note the patient was mentioning that the thoughts telling him that he must harm himself with a sharp knife by sticking it in his thighs and twisting it had returned. We realized that he was very vulnerable to believing the internal advice that his needs had become too much for the therapist and that this was the real reason for the break. We thought it was a development in the patient that he could tell his therapist about these thoughts. She helped him to examine the extent to which the internal adviser informed him that she would not want to know about any anger or disappointment towards her for going away at this stage.

We thought it was important that he had shared these thoughts and that the therapist had acknowledged them and had helped him to identify their source (the internal adviser). She had interpreted the immediate reason for them (the therapist going on leave) and had linked them with both his childhood memories of being left in hospital and the recent death of his mother, and the possibility of his feeling that he had nothing to live for now. However, we thought this was not enough to contain the patient. We considered he was still very vulnerable to believing the assumption of the internal adviser that he was being forgotten and that he had to attack his body to show what a bad person he is to have needs, and to demonstrate in a concrete way that he desperately needed help. We also thought that the urge to harm himself could escalate into a belief that he had no reason to live, now that both mother and therapist had seemingly abandoned him, and therefore to take an overdose that could result in his death would be seen to be a good idea. Thus, it seemed to us that the patient needed actual evidence that the therapist was able to understand, be concerned about, and hold in mind how difficult the break was going to be for him, and that he needed to participate in forming a plan with his therapist as to how he could take care of himself during the break. We anticipated that the internal adviser would keep informing him that if the therapist really cared for him she would not have gone away and that Mr R was still too vulnerable to know how to withstand this persuasion.

Thus, first, Ms X and I talked through the various options such as informing the CMHT, his psychiatrist, his GP, or informing him that he could contact someone at our clinic such as myself or his original assessor. We decided to communicate with his GP because Mr R had known him the longest and had ongoing contact with him, and we knew from the assessment that he saw him as a helpful figure in his life. We also knew that this GP was sympathetic to psychotherapy and to the patient.

We initially discussed writing the GP a letter or ringing him to inform him that Mr R's therapist would be away for three weeks and that, as he had begun to open up and become more attached, he would be vulnerable and might harm himself physically or take an overdose during this time. During this discussion Ms X pointed out that we were not thinking about how to discuss this with Mr R himself. Ms X was particularly sensitive to the need to do this because of her first-hand experience of Mr R and I realized that I needed to listen to her view. We thus decided that it was not appropriate to contact the GP without Mr R's agreement for the following reasons:

1. The supervisee knew that Mr R believed—under the influence of the internal adviser—that his GP saw him as coping and he would be embarrassed and uncomfortable to have to admit that he was feeling he could not cope without his support. He would feel his therapist had betrayed his confidence if his GP was contacted without his agreement or without taking his embarrassment into account.
2. For the therapist not to discuss options with Mr R and seek his agreement would not meet our view that he needed to know by an appropriate action that his therapist was concerned about him and did not see his need of her as a nuisance.
3. Finally, discussing options with Mr R would help him to have an experience of being supported in thinking about how to be proactive in asking for help when necessary.

Thus, we decided that Ms X would explore options with Mr R over the next couple of sessions and work out with him what he felt would be helpful in looking after himself, so that he could contain the urgent persuasions of the internal adviser.

Mr R confirmed that he felt very vulnerable and that his GP is someone he turns to but thought he would be disappointed to hear that he was admitting that he might not be able to cope during the break. He said he knew he would not contact him in advance of feeling he might hurt himself and yet would like to. Thus, he felt relieved at the thought of his therapist writing a tactful letter to the GP that he would see.

Ms X wrote the first draft, then we worked on it together, and this is what we wrote:

As you are aware I have been seeing Mr R for weekly psychoanalytic psychotherapy since ... [almost two years]. I am writing to you now, with Mr R's agreement, as I will be on annual leave from *x* to *y* [three weeks]. Mr R has been making good use of therapy and has formed a relationship with me as his therapist and because of this is feeling vulnerable about the prospect of three weeks without therapy.

We discussed how he might manage his feelings of vulnerability during the break and he decided that he would like to make use of your help but has anxieties about this. He is aware that he usually presents as capable and coping and that he has difficulties in asking for help. With his history, there is an idea in his mind that he is a "disappointment" if he needs help and that he should just get on with it by himself. In particular he finds it difficult to admit that at times he feels alone and desperate. At such times there is an insistent idea that the way to express the emotional pain is to hurt himself physically with a sharp knife.

He has been having these thoughts frequently in recent weeks but so far has been able to distract himself and hold on to the idea that he will be seeing me again. However, while I am actually away the thoughts of self harm may increase and we thought you should know this and how vulnerable he currently is in case he contacts you.

Mr R was given a copy of this letter and we later heard that on receipt of it he had felt able to book an appointment with his GP. The thoughts never became too pressing during the break and he did not harm himself or take an overdose. At his first session back he spoke to his therapist as someone he knew and had missed rather than as a stranger he had no connection with, as had occurred after previous breaks.

Concluding comments

In the clinical examples I have given I have tried to show that the most appropriate way for therapists to respond to patients under a pressure to kill themselves is to resist the desire to act and instead allow themselves to be open to patients' communications. Through processing and understanding their countertransference, especially strong internal reactions such as anger, therapists are in a better position to understand their patients' internal worlds and can then help them question the pressures to take their life and gradually understand and contain them rather than go along with them. Although Mr L may be more extreme than many patients, because of a more obvious psychosis, his situation usefully brings to life the pressures and difficulties involved in working with a suicidal patient and suggests some ways of handling them. As with other patients, Mr L was able to indicate, in his case through a dream, that he wanted help to stay alive despite overwhelming pressure that he should die. Some of my countertransference responses to the situation with Mr L are a reminder that therapists can receive poor internal advice as well as patients, and that this poor advice needs to be differentiated from helpful internalized supervision.

To generalize from the two cases, I would suggest that supervisees need emotional support and relevant analytic concepts from their supervisor in order to be open to the patient's communications about suicide and thus to be able to process and make sense of the pressures that both patient and therapist are under. This is likely to be a situation of pressure and anxiety for the supervisor. Therefore, supervisors need to know to whom they can turn, such as a trusted colleague or supervisor, to be able to get the support they need in order to listen to their supervisees' concerns and provide them with the containment they need.

Finally, therapists always have to bear in mind the need for confidentiality and weigh this against the policies of the wider healthcare system. A helpful way to safeguard the therapy as well as the patient's life is for supervisors to help supervisees explore with the patient when/if it would be appropriate for their therapist to have contact—and what sort—with other professionals involved in the patient's care.

References

Keval, N. (2003). Triangulation or strangulation: managing the suicidal patient. *Psychoanalytic Psychotherapy*, *17*(1): 35–51.

Minne, C. (2003). The Care Programme Approach (CPA)—internal and external support of psychotherapy. Paper presented to the Annual

Conference of The Association for Psychoanalytic Psychotherapy in the National Health Service.

Richards, J. (1999). The concept of internal cohabitation. In: S. Johnson & S. Ruszczynski (Eds.), *Psychoanalytic Psychotherapy in the Independent Tradition* (pp. 27–52). London: Karnac.

Sinason, M. (1993). Who is the mad voice inside? *Psychoanalytic Psychotherapy*, 7(3): 207–221.

CHAPTER ELEVEN

The effects of difference of "race" and colour in supervision

Helen Morgan

When S, an Asian woman, began her training to become an analytic psychotherapist, she joined a supervision group. The two other members of her group, the teachers, and her supervisor were white. At their first group supervision session the supervisor asked what concerns they might have in starting work with their first clients, and S said she had been wondering about the possible reactions for a white client coming expecting to see a white therapist who then discovers that their new therapist was black. The supervisor responded by saying "You poor thing!", and then moved on to the next member of the group and the matter was never raised again. For the next year S's experience was of being constantly criticized and undermined by the supervisor—an experience corroborated by the other members of the group. In her regular assessment reports the supervisor questioned S's ability to understand internal processes and criticized her work. S survived the experience by ensuring that she exposed very little of herself, she kept her head down and did not mention any questions or concerns she might have regarding difference in colour again. Fortunately, there was a change of supervision arrangements after a year and a new supervisor was able to help her think through how the matter of difference between herself and her client might be used to illuminate the transference. Regular assessments of her were positive and, having completed all the requirements, she qualified as a psychotherapist.

This supervisor's response of apparent pity to a matter of genuine enquiry by the supervisee served to patronize and undermine. Her failure to pursue the question openly in the group and her subsequent belittling of the supervisee to the point where she considered leaving the training, suggests that the issue of difference in "race" and colour was a problem for the supervisor but was made to be that of the supervisee. There was no overt racist comment as such, but the combination of the supervisor's "pity" for S and the consequent ignoring of the issue was a more subtle, but no less damaging response. S was not asking for sympathy, she was asking for help in thinking about how potentially difficult transference material might be worked with. The experience within supervision was bruising and may well have meant an able psychotherapist turning away from the profession. The problem would be seen as hers and the status quo would be reinforced.

"Race" and racism

The evidence that has emerged from recent development in the analysis of DNA confirms that the concept of "race" is a constructed concept with no objective basis in biology. It is, as Rustin puts it "... both an empty category and one of the most powerful forms of social categorization" (Rustin, 1991, p. 57). To acknowledge the emptiness of the category I shall refer to "race" in apostrophes throughout this paper.

While racism as a form of social categorization needs to be understood within a socio-political frame, given its tenacity within the individual psyche there is validity in applying a psychoanalytic lens to the phenomenon. A detailed exploration of the debates concerning how such a lens might be applied and what might be observed when it is, is beyond the scope of this chapter. Here I merely want to note that most tend to place the mechanisms of projection and splitting at the centre of their considerations. Fakhry Davids, for example, cites the three components of internal racism as:

1.   The perception of an attribute on which subject and object differ . . .
2.   The use of that difference to project into the object an unwanted/dreaded aspect of the subject's mind, usually something infantile/primitive; and
3.   Establishing an organised template that governs relations with the object (who now contains the projected part of the subject). The effect on the victim is that no matter how hard he might try he finds that he is not allowed to be an ordinary human being. This structure functions like a sort of mafia in the mind, promising protection in return for loyalty. [Davids, 1998, p. 4]

While the division into so-called "races" is a socio-political construction, the fact of these divisions provide a series of attributes by which the "other" can be distinguished, which in turn provides a receptacle for the dreaded aspects of the subject into the other. Such a powerful, irrational, and unconscious process is all-pervading and tenacious, with no one immune. It is by no means the prerogative of the white individual but, given the power asymmetry within Western culture, it is white racism that has the greatest impact. While extreme forms of overt racism may be abhorred by the liberal white individual, the internal racist will express itself in more covert and subtle ways. Because of this abhorrence and the need to maintain an image of ourselves as fundamentally good, this internal racist may itself be projected on to the more extreme racist elements within society.

Blindness

I have considered the question of racism within the dyad of psychoanalytic psychotherapy elsewhere (Morgan, 1998, 2002). In the supervisory relationship the conscious and unconscious dynamics concerning exposure, shame, judgement, etc. will be present to a greater or lesser extent. Power differentials will exist especially when the supervision is set within a training whereby the supervisor's view will have a substantial effect on the supervisee's career. When differences in "race" and colour exist within the triad of supervisor, supervisee, and patient, then an additional layer enters the relationship. This layer will include the unconscious and primitive dynamics of power, guilt, shame, envy, and fear. Being irrational and unwanted, these are difficult matters to think about and discuss. Instead the defences of splitting and projection may function as a protection forming what Davids calls the "mafia in the mind". This mafia is as likely to operate in the mind of the supervisor as in that of anyone else. Racist thoughts are unlikely to have been the subject of a training analysis and, indeed, the shadow aspect of the fact of having undergone an analysis is that the individual can maintain an internal position as if they were now free from the primitive defences of splitting and projection. It is the myth of the complete analysis. If the white supervisor does not allow the possibility that they might have racist thoughts, then the consequences for the black supervisee or the black patient may well be destructive.

There are black therapists who have written on the matter of racism in psychotherapy and they make some reference to their experience as black supervisors (Dalal, 2002; Davids, 1998; Evans Holmes, 1992; Thomas, 1992). In this chapter I consider the matter from the perspective of a white supervisor which, as a white person, is the only position from which I have any authority to speak.

When, on researching the matter of how differences in "race", colour and culture might affect the work of supervision, I was interested to note that, apart from those black psychotherapists mentioned above, I could find no mention of the topic in the books I read on supervision in psychoanalytic or Jungian analytic psychotherapy. This is in stark contrast to the modern texts on supervision in counselling and social work, where at least one chapter on the issue seems always to be included. However, on reading some of those chapters in the counselling supervision books, I found the majority to take a position of cultural relativism and, in my view, failed to address how the dynamics of "race" and racism can be understood from the perspective of their impact, if any, on the internal world of the psyche. It seemed that the deeper the analytic enterprise, the less the subject is considered of relevance until it is ignored completely in the analytic texts.

One explanation for this silence on the matter of "race" and racism offered from outside of the theoretical frame is that psychoanalytic theory itself is fundamentally Eurocentric and not applicable, therefore, outside of its own white, middle-class world. This is certainly a serious challenge that needs to be taken on more directly from within the profession, for these analytic theories imply a universality in their explanation of the human psyche and, if they offer a model of the mind that is true and valid, then it must be applicable to all human minds—or what are we saying about the world? Yet, to assume that the external world and matters of culture, experiences of racism, differences in social mores and customs have no impact on the internal world of the individual, results in a certain sterility within the theory itself, as well as increasing its isolation from more mainstream thought.

On the other hand, it may be that the theories themselves are sound but it is the psychoanalytic institutions whose job it is to train the next generations in analytic practice as to where the problem lies. The criticism might be that these organizations are too entrenched in a defensive, white, middle-class structure of politics and power that cannot allow the challenge of difference within its portals. Andrew Cooper defines institutionalised racism as:

> . . . a process whereby organisational policies and practices effectively exclude participation or service take-up by a racial or cultural group, although no individual or group intends this outcome. The institution is prejudiced in favour of the majority culture because it organises itself in ways which are accessible to and meet the needs of that culture. Because the organisation also has the power to give or withhold services, and to change its practices or not, its prejudice is allied to power. [Cooper, 1989, p. 19]

If the trainee S, whose experience was cited at the beginning of this paper, had not had a change of supervisor or was less willing or able to battle on with her training despite her experience, she would have been excluded from participation in the profession, not because of inadequacy as a psychotherapist but, in effect, because of her membership of a racial group. No one would have consciously intended this, nor would it be understood this way. The individual supervisor, the training organization and the profession as a whole would have continued without having to examine or challenge either position or practice. The "problem" would be seen as hers and the status quo confirmed.

Farhad Dalal describes his own experience as a black therapist in supervision:

> I was speaking about the theme of colour when my clinical supervisor (white) said that he was not usually aware of the person's "race" or colour in a session; it was not a significant issue for him. This surprised me as I am often conscious in groups, and in one to one situations, of my colour in relation to others, [Dalal, 2002, p. 219]

Dalal goes on to ask why he might be more sensitive than his supervisor on this matter and suggests that one can take an internalist position that would search for the cause inside of him:

> Thus it might be suggested that I am overly sensitive or have a chip on my shoulder. In effect this is an interpretation of paranoia in which I am projecting some internal difficulty into the territory of black and white, which is now thought of as an expression of this latent difficulty. [Ibid.]

By stating that he was not aware of a person's "race", Dalal's supervisor was implying that there was nothing objective and external of which to be aware. Thus, by raising the issue, Dalal was could be seen as presenting indications of an internal difficulty and the intimations of a paranoid state. Given the anxiety for any trainee, this semi-conscious implication by the white supervisor of "internal difficulties" in the black supervisee must be hard to manage. Instead of the subject being open for thought, the report of black trainees is that they respond by keeping their heads down and learning not to mention the subject again. Some may well leave the training. Either way there is a loss of potential development of the theoretical model that is being taught.

Dalal offers an alternative understanding this difference in perspective:

> The white, by virtue of their colour, is in the mainstream and near the centre, whilst the black is marginalized and nearer the edge. The closer one is to the edge, with the resultant danger of going over, the more one is aware of the circumstances that put one there—colour. Meanwhile, those at the centre have a vested interest (often unconscious) in maintaining the status quo by blanking

out the colour dynamic altogether: if it does not exist in the first place then it cannot be changed. Thus, the difference between the feelings elicited in me and my supervisor are not just because of our asocial histories, but to do with where we are located in the field of power relations. [*Ibid.*]

For her dissertation for the MSc course that is run jointly by the BAP and Birkbeck, Margaret James-Franklin (2004) interviewed some black psychoanalytic psychotherapists about their experiences in training. What emerges from this research is how hard it is for the black individual to get through a training in psychotherapy. On many occasions the trainee has to put aside and ignore their "blackness" if they are to survive. The colour-blind position that "we are all the same and differences in colour are, therefore, not relevant" was often that taken by trainers. This meant a failure to acknowledge the fact of difference and required the black trainee to ignore an important aspect of her/his own experience. Given that they were mainly working with white training patients, they were offered little help by their supervisors in how to work with some aspects of the transference and countertransference material.[1]

In a paper on multi-cultural issues and the supervision process, Angus Igwe uses a simple but rather useful concept familiar in professional education that suggests that in learning we move through the four following states:

1. Unconscious Incompetence (I don't know what I don't know)
2. Conscious Incompetence (I know what I don't know)
3. Conscious Competence (I know what I know)
4. Unconscious Competence (I don't know what I know). [Igwe, 2003, p. 217]

On most aspects relating to clinical work we would expect the supervisor to be at the stage of either conscious or unconscious competence, whereas the supervisee, especially at the start of their training, may be more at the stages of conscious or even unconscious incompetence. However, when someone white is supervising someone black, the latter is likely to be far more aware of issues relating to being at the margins and thus be more "knowing" regarding issues of "race" and racism. The white supervisor, dwelling as they do at the centre, is more likely to have "blanked out the colour dynamic altogether". Thus, we have a reversal of the expected situation where the supervisee is more aware, more knowing, more "competent" than the supervisor.

On the surface, of course, Stage 4, "unconscious competence" looks very much like stage 1, "Unconscious incompetence". Both are unconscious states. Thus, the white individual can reach the conclusion that there is nothing to be explored, nothing interior to the supervisor to be analysed, no problem of difference, since difference is ignored. Any problem that might surface belongs, therefore, to the black other. Should the supervisor be in a state of "unconscious incompetence", regarding his or her internal racism, for the supervisory pair to develop and for learning for both to take place, the supervisor needs to be able to move to Stage 2 and to become conscious that, on this matter, they do not "know". Even this apparently small move is not easy. Any racist feelings may be rejected from a need to maintain a benign sense of self. If the internal racist organization is denied it cannot be confronted. Add to this a power dynamic inevitable in any supervisory relationship, the pressure to sustain the place of "knowing" is considerable. If this is not struggled against by the supervisor, then the "unconscious incompetence" becomes projected on to either the black supervisee or the black patient. By perceiving the failure to be in the other, the internal racist remains unchallenged and this particular organization within the supervisor's mind is reinforced.

Bion describes the links that describe the emotional experience that is ever present when two people, or two parts of a person are in relation to each other. These "links" comprise Love (L) Hate (H) and Knowledge (K). Whereas L and H are rooted more in the paranoid–schizoid position, K is seen as an aspect of the depressive position. "The sign K . . . is used to refer to the link between a subject which tries to know an object, and an object which can be known" (Grinberg, Sor, & Tabak de Bianchedi, 1975, p. 64).

Bion writes of K in terms of the relationship between analyst and patient. The notion of a K link between supervisor and supervisee, between supervisor and the supervisee-as-therapist, and between supervisor and patient, assumes that there is a subject which is trying to know the object and the object which can be known. This is not a knowing that is a mere knowing of facts.

The K link is that linkage present when one is in the process of getting to know the other in an emotional sense, and this is to be clearly distinguished from the sort of knowing that means having a piece of knowledge about someone or something. [Symington & Symington, 1996, p. 78]

Now, clearly to acknowledge that I am white and you are black, or that we are white and the patient is black, does not bring a new fact into the room and nor does it necessarily mean a getting-to-know-someone in an emotional sense. What it does do, however, is acknowledge that this is a fact of difference that will have an impact on the business of getting to know each other. It allows the possibility of the supervisor's "unconscious incompetence", and offers the hope that the more paranoid–schizoid links of L and H within racism might be tempered by those of K. It is not blind to colour, but admits an awareness of the political and social backdrop to our encounter with each other. It acknowledges difference in colour and, therefore, a certain difference in experience and hence in vertex or perspective.

To fail to acknowledge difference, to assume colour-blindness, leads us more into the realm of $-K$:

K symbolizes knowledge, and $-K$ is its opposite. It symbolizes not only ignorance, but also a trend to remain actively in ignorance with the adoption of an attitude in which there is an advantage of avoiding awareness or a disadvantage to approximating to the truth. [Bion Talamo, Borgogno, & Merciai, 2000. p. 122]

Fear

A previous paper I wrote, which considered issues of racism in the consulting room as a white therapist, was entitled "Between fear and blindness: the white therapist and the black patient" (Morgan, 1998). The title proposes two major responses to the fact of difference in colour for the white individual responding to the black other. That of colour blindness, which I have touched on above, is the denial of difference or its potential consequences. There is nothing to be thought about or talked about.

The fearful response is not of the other as such, but of the dreaded aspects of the self that may be revealed in the encounter. I know of no other topic for discussion that can raise the temperature and the defences as high and as quickly as this one. It seems such a hard subject to think about—and even more so to talk about. It is hard to stay with thought rather than either retreat into a defensive position that denies the problem, or get enmeshed in what Lousada calls "an obsequious guilt which undertakes reparation (towards the oppressed object) regardless of the price" (Lousada, 1997, p. 41).

The following example is taken from work with a white supervisee whose patient, A, is a man in his forties who was born in the Caribbean. When he was six years old his parents came to Britain to find work and A was looked after by his grandmother and two aunts in the Caribbean. While there were constant phone calls and letters from his parents, because of the costs of travel he did not see them again until he was sent for aged thirteen. A did well at school and further education and was now a successful and well-respected business man.

As the therapy progressed, A experienced any feelings of dependency on his therapist as difficult. He always seemed to have good things to replace any breaks in sessions so they were never missed. The session we were discussing in supervision referred to the first one after a three-week break. A was recounting what he had done while the therapist was away—which included a consultation with an astrologist, visiting an alternative practitioner, and reading several self help psychology books—all of which he praised enthusiastically. The therapist made the interpretation that he was telling her how well he had done without her and how others had replaced her so that she was not missed because it was hard for him to acknowledge how abandoned he had felt. She then linked this to being left by his parents when he was young, and the replacement of his mother by his grandmother and aunts. A became angry, pointing out that what had happened to him was very common among his generation in the Caribbean, and that it was the failure of the therapist to understand his culture that had led her to interpret it as a problem for him.

Under this attack the supervisee abandoned her initial thoughts and her thinking became paralysed. For the moment she was no longer the therapist trying to make sense of her patient's inner world because his spoken accusations matched her anxiety that she could be identified with the abusive colonizer. It is certainly true that socio-political imbalances globally resulting from colonization and slavery has meant large numbers of people migrating to the colonial nation to seek work and a better life, and having to leave behind young families to the care of family elders. Nevertheless, the fact that this was perfectly understandable and on a large scale, and that the individual was well cared for by known and loved relatives, does not mean that there is no loss for the individual child, or that the surfacing of internal, unconscious consequences in the transference cannot be interpreted. It was as if the therapist feared that to stay in the analytic space and consider the interpretation in the usual analytic light would be somehow to pathologize a whole people and an entire generation. She moved instead to the apparent safety of anthropology and thus lost the task of the analytic work.

For the therapist to stay with her interpretation and then to make sense of A's response, she was required to hear his raising of the matter of difference, his need to assert that he was not alone and that there was a problem of understanding between them. In my view, what looked like a respect of the view of the "other" was, in fact, to fail to face the underlying questions raised by "otherness", to allow the patient to prevent the therapist functioning analytically as well as to desert the analytic responsibility to the inner world of the patient. The dynamic behind this abandonment of the analytic endeavour was the arousal of the therapist's fear of her own racism and, hence, of feelings of shame and guilt. Ironically, of course, the consequence for the black patient was that he would receive a second-rate therapy.

The case described is similar to one cited by Davids in his paper, which prompts the following comments:

> ... please note how easy it is for one, in an apparent attempt to keep an open mind, to embark on a road that leads inevitably, I think, to a position of cultural relativism that is clinically sterile. Today there is a genre of psychoanalytic writing, critical of our mainstream theories for their ethnocentrism, that advance instead alternative conceptualisations claiming to allow for greater cultural variation ... but on the whole the new concepts ... are meant to alert the clinician to the dangers of inadvertently overlooking the

influence of culture, and to provide theories that are "fairer" to the psyche of the culturally different patient. I would suggest that such approaches have the diagnosis wrong. The problem of ignoring the patient's cultural background is not so much due to defective theory as a to a reluctance on the part of the analyst to acknowledge the patient's difference, which in turn reflects a fear of entering the domain of internal racism—both analyst's and patient's—within the treatment situation. Providing one is willing to enter this terrain, I find that existing psychoanalytic theories are perfectly adequate for work with the culturally different. [Davids, 1998, p. 7]

This view is echoed by Thomas in his 1992 paper, "Racism and psychotherapy", where he gives the example of a white supervisee who has a black patient who "suffered at the hands of a tyrannical mother who totally dominated him and still attempts to do so". He discussed the point where a good working relationship is established with the therapist and, whie recognizing what he has suffered as a child, still wishes to protect his mother from "his wish to retaliate and attack". He moves to a new job where his immediate boss is overtly racist and abusive. The patient brings the pain of this to his therapy but his therapist is immobilized. She reports that "she feels paralysed and totally useless, not knowing how she can help him. She feels that his problems are real, external, and that there is nothing she can do in therapy".

Thomas makes the important statement that:

Here, it is difficult for the therapist to recognise that the unconscious does not distinguish between colour as far as the perpetrators of pain are concerned, and that in this case it was the some of the pain suffered at the hands of his mother that was now resurrected. This connection did cross her mind but she feared using it as a bridge for an interpretation: her patient's dilemma at work, she considered, must be a separate matter. She could not see that, for her it was a separate matter, while for the patient, still the child in pain, there was not such a distinction, only repetition. Of course, making the link was not going to be easy, but it had to be made. [Thomas, 1992, p. 138]

The negative transference is never easy to manage and helping the supervisee to work with it is arguably the essence of the work of supervision, for to avoid the negative material that is in the transference is to avoid critical aspects of the analysand's inner world. From time to time, the therapist and patient will unconsciously collude to keep the paranoid–schizoid elements of both Hate (H) and Love (L) out of awareness. By doing so Knowledge (K) is limited. A crucial aspect of the supervisor's role, therefore, is to use his or her countertransference to shed some light on these darker, more hidden shadow states. The fear of shame and guilt means that when there are differences in colour between the participants, even greater unconscious effort is employed in the defence against the acknowledgement of the racist thought.

But, according to the analytic literature, the racist thought is itself a defence—essentially of splitting and projection. By avoiding the issue not only do we avoid the "bad" thought we do not wish to own but we also miss a deeper conflict that the racist thought is a defence against. The question S tried to ask in her supervision about the white patient's potential responses to the colour of her new therapist raises the possibility within the analytic supervisory process that the observation of difference by the patient can be considered in ordinary transference terms. Indeed, the negative influences of racist responses can be thought about not just as difficulties that the black therapist needs to manage (or defend herself against) but as a potentially useful and important route into transference material.

Dorothy Evans Holmes, in her paper "Race and transference in psychoanalysis and psychotherapy" (1992), considers the way that references to race can give access to transference reactions in the therapeutic situation. In the following extract she refers to an earlier (1985) paper of hers:

> Often it is said that patients' racist remarks in therapy constitute a defensive shift away from more important underlying conflict and that the therapist should interpret the remarks as defence and resistance. Whilst it is the therapist's ultimate aim to help the patient understand the protective uses of defences, this aim can best be achieved *only after* the defences are elaborated. [Evans Holmes, 1992, p. 3]

When a black supervisee is working with a white patient, it is likely that the racist defences for the patient will take subtle and secret forms. Because of the guilt attached to these responses, the patient will work hard to keep such feelings from surfacing openly in the room and, indeed, these are likely to be swiftly repressed even as they surface in the mind.

A black member of a supervision group was working with a white man, D. D, while insisting that the therapy was very helpful to him, was consistently late and missed sessions from time to time. The therapist frequently reported feeling irritated and despairing in her countertransference, and when he began saying that maybe it was time to end therapy, she recognized her own wish for him to leave. During the reporting of a session I found myself wondering whether this therapist was able to do the work and I had the thought that another (white) member of the group would have been a better "fit" for this patient, that she would have provided a better container for him. Behind these thoughts was a sense of disparagement of the therapist. I was seeing the therapist as inferior, not up to the job, and that this particular therapeutic pairing would not be able to work.

Initially, when D started his therapy, the matter of differences between them was raised and he was keen to assure his therapist that this was no problem for him. Unless the racist defences are very open and conscious (in which case a white patient is unlikely to start therapy with a black therapist in the first place) anything but this denial of a problem is unlikely. However, conscious denial does not mean that something does not exist. There may be an idealization and/or a denigration of the blackness of the therapist. Guilt, shame, and the rejection of shadow aspects result in the attempt to turn away from, to disown such disagreeable, "bad" feelings and thoughts.

What the white supervisor may be able to offer here is a recognition through identification of the patient's situation. In the supervision session my own countertransference reactions needed to be understood as mirroring the contempt of the patient. It was the therapist who was no good. She needed to be got rid of by lateness, missed sessions and eventually giving up altogether. My thought that she was inadequate as a therapist (when in fact I had considerable respect for her work with other patients) was a clue that there was a projection of these unwanted aspects on to her. If I could convince myself that the problem was her and not my hated and hateful feelings, then she could be rejected and I would be relieved of feeling badly.

By thinking this through in the group discussion we began to see that D's dismissal of the therapist and of the work should be seen as his need to denigrate her as a black woman, and that this hid a deeper internal conflict. The denigration and the racist defence needed elaborating before that underlying conflict could be brought to light. In the next session the therapist made an interpretation along the lines we had discussed. Not unexpectedly, D replied that there was no problem, that her being black was fine with him, was she accusing him of being racist, etc. The next session he phoned and cancelled. However, he arrived visibly shaken to the following session. He had started out late and had to run for the bus, but as he reached the bus stop the black driver, despite having seen D coming, closed the doors and pulled away from the bus stop. D "lost it" and began yelling at the bus, shouting at the driver. What shook him in particular was the raw, racist nature of the insults he heard himself shouting.

At first D found it difficult to speak about this incident to his therapist and was clearly overcome with shame at what he had said. The therapist was able to work with him to surface these feelings and to gather them into the transference. Again, his shame was excruciating but, seeing that his therapist was able to withstand these disparaging, attacking thoughts that were now in the room between them, he gradually was able to allow them to exist. Complex transference material began to emerge concerning his experience of a depressed mother who was constantly despised and belittled by his father and by whom he felt abandoned. Hiding behind his need to hold his therapist as inferior were his own feelings of worthlessness and self-disparagement.

None of this is straightforward, of course. Aspects of D's contempt for his therapist related to gender rather than "race", and we do not know how he might have been with a black male therapist. The point, perhaps, is that we are not blank screens, as certain facts concerning gender, age, "race", etc. are clearly visible to each other. Each of the members of the supervisory triad brings with them social connections as well as internal dynamics that will affect their responses to what is seen of the other. What is seen includes the colour of the other and whether that is perceived as the same as ours or different will inevitably "colour" our responses, both consciously and unconsciously.

Being white, I am only able to write here from that perspective, and limitations of space have meant I have only been able to focus on a couple of the permutations possible within that triad. Other dynamics may well arise when both the supervisee and the patient are black. The term "black" includes an almost infinite variety and complex dynamics may emerge when, for example, an Asian therapist is working with an Afro-Caribbean patient and the supervisor is white British. The combination that is very rarely spoken of is when all three, the supervisor, the supervisee, and the patient are all white. If we follow the analytic assumption that racist thoughts are defences, then they need to be worked with like all other defences. I suspect that they are often unnoticed within this particular triad and it is more likely that they will be reinforced by assumptions such as seeing black figures in dreams as negative symbols.

On the one hand this whole matter is extremely complex and difficult to explore. On the other it is really quite simple as long as one is able to stay within the analytic frame. It is colour blindness and fear of shame and guilt that will take the supervisor away from our task of working with the supervisee within that frame. For the effects of "race" and colour within the supervisory triad to be worked with as an ordinary aspect of analytic work, the internal racist has to be faced. The fact of difference has to be remembered in order that it can be forgotten.

Note

1. "Acknowledgement". Many of these interviewed by James-Franklin reported being told that, because this was depth, analytic work, the difference in "race" and colour was irrelevant. Very few experiences were reported of the fact of difference being raised by white seminar leaders or supervisors. When anyone other than themselves acknowledged the fact of difference their experience was one of relief. *Chambers Dictionary* defines "to acknowledge" as: "to admit a knowledge or awareness of; to admit to or recognize as true, genuine, valid or one's own . . .'

References

Bion Talamo, P., Borgogno, F., & Merciai, S. (2000). *W. R. Bion Between Past and Future*. London: Karnac.

Cooper, A. (1989). Getting started: psychodynamics, racism and anti-racism. *Journal of Social Work Practice*, 3(4): 15–27.

Dalal, F. (2002). *Race, Colour and the Processes of Racialization: New Perspectives from Group Analysis, Psychoanalysis and Sociology*. London: Brunner-Routledge.

Davids, F. (1998). The Lionel Monteith Lecture, Lincoln Centre & Clinic for Psychotherapy (unpublished).

Evans Holmes, D. (1992). Race and transference in psychoanalysis and psychotherapy. *International Journal of Psychoanalysis*, 73: 1–11.

Grinberg, L., Sor, D., & Tabak de Bianchedi, E. (1975). *Introduction to the Work of Bion*. London: Roland Harris Educational Trust [reprinted London: Karnac, 1985].

Igwe, A. (2003). The impact of multi-cultural issues on the supervision process. In: A. Dupont-Joshua (Ed.), *Working Inter-Culturally in Counselling Settings* (pp. 210–231). London: Brunner-Routledge.

James-Franklin, M. (2004). Processes of adaptation in black trainee therapists. Unpublished dissertation, MSc in the Psychodynamics of Human Development, Birkbeck College, University of London.

Lousada, J. (1997). The hidden history of an idea: the difficulties of adopting anti-racism. In: E. Smith (Ed.), *Integrity and Change, Mental Health in the Market Place* (pp. 34–48). London: Routledge.

Morgan, H. (1998). Between fear and blindness: the white therapist and the black patient. *Journal of The British Association of Psychotherapists*, 34: 48–61.

Morgan, H. (2002). Exploring racism. *Journal of Analytical Psychology*, 47: 567–581.

Rustin, M. (1991). Psychoanalysis, racism and anti-racism. In: M. Rustin (Ed.), *The Good Society and the Inner World* (pp. 57–84). London: Verso.

Symington, J., & Symington, N. (1996). *The Clinical Thinking of Wilfred Bion*. London: Routledge.

Thomas, L. (1992). Racism and Psychotherapy: working with racism in the consulting room—an analytic view. In: J. Kareem & R. Littlewood (Eds.), *Intercultural Therapy* (pp. 133–145). Oxford, Blackwood Scientific.

CHAPTER TWELVE

The many "ifs" of group supervision

Margaret Hammond

"There was a little girl, and she had a little curl,
Right in the middle of her forehead.
And when she was good, she was very, very good,
And when she was bad, she was horrid"

(Longfellow, 1807–1882, *Concise Oxford Dictionary of Quotations*, 1981)

G roup supervision might be like the little girl with the little curl. When it is good, it is very, very good, and when it is bad, it is horrid. I think every therapist will empathize with both of these experiences. Sometimes, an experience of group supervision can create an atmosphere of connection and illumination, in a supportive environment. Sometimes, on the other hand, the shadow, as described by Jung (1950[1948]), takes over and the experience is more one of attack or belittling. The therapist feels that their patient has been misunderstood and they themselves have been sidelined. Donald Kalsched (1995) wrote about both these possibilities in a paper entitled "The agonies and ecstasies of casework supervision". In this chapter I try to discuss some of the factors that can turn a potentially unique area for learning and growth into a nightmare. I focus on three areas: the frame and structure of the group, the process of the task, and the outlook of the leader, and I look at what might help and hinder in each category.

First, we need to define the task of a supervision group. One of the problems that beset supervision groups lies in the multi-faceted task they are expected to carry out. Such groups may have to carry an element of administration, which can be complicated and time consuming. Politics within the organization in which the group takes place can often influence the membership. Both administration and politics can be used by the group as a defence against the anxieties stirred up by the work with patients. This process has been described in an institutional context by Isabel Menzies Lyth (1959), in her paper "The functions of social systems as a defence against anxiety", where she describes how the anxieties aroused by emotional relatedness can be avoided by concentrating on bureaucracy, so denying the importance of the individual. On the other hand, groups are made up of individuals, each with their own psychology, and so, either through the attempts to make sense of the clinical material by considering countertransference phenomena, or perhaps fuelled by envy of the attention given to the patients under consideration, there is a tendency towards transforming the group into a therapy group for its members. In the midst of these competing forces it becomes the task of the group supervisor to safeguard a space for the primary task, which is, as Kalsched describes, first to understand as much as possible what is going on within the presenting therapist's patient and second, to try to understand what is going on between the patient and his or her therapist. Ostensibly, this may sound a simple task, but in reality it is extremely difficult.

The diagrams below (Figure 1a, b) illustrate these points visually.

Figure 1a shows how politics and administrative matters can almost engulf the transitional space within the group—the space to play in Winnicott's terms (Winnicott, 1971). The space at the centre has been quite consumed, perhaps an extreme example of what I am trying to describe. The circles representing the group members are there to suggest each personal psychic space, which again can be subsumed in defensive group (a).

By contrast, Figure 1b emphasizes the spirit of enquiry ideally to be encouraged at the centre of the supervision group. The spirit

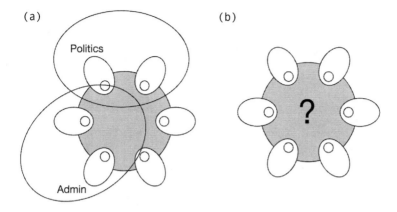

Figure 1.   (a) The political/administrative group.; (b) the group.

of enquiry is crucial, and can make the difference between enlightenment and a nightmare. In his paper "Supervision: the impossible profession" (1988), Louis Zinkin wrote in the postscript,

> What I suppose we shall go on calling "supervision" is actually a shared fantasy. It is the resultant of the trainee trying to imagine what he and his patient have been doing together and the supervisor trying to imagine it too. It works best if both remain aware that what they are jointly imagining is not true. But both can profit enormously, both can enjoy the experience as well as suffer and there is teaching and learning to be found in this joint imaginative venture . . . [p. 24]

This imaginative, enquiring attitude is even more important in the group situation. Kalsched speaks of a mystery at the heart of each of us, patient and therapist alike, supervisor and group members. These enigmas meet in the transitional space of therapy and also in the transitional space of the group. For meaning to emerge it is important for a spirit of enquiry and play to prevail, unencumbered by any notion of getting to the truth, or of judgement, or criticism. In a way, the whole process is an illusion and we can only see anything in part.

Having identified the primary task of the supervision group and emphasized the importance of a spirit of enquiry, what are some of the factors that may help or hinder group functioning? These are: the frame, including group size and composition; the task and group process; the roles of the group leader.

The frame

What is the optimum size for a supervision group? In my work with groups, both as a member and a leader, where the membership has varied from between four and ten members, I have found advantages and drawbacks in the differing environments. There are a number of ways in which group size may influence the effective functioning of a supervision group. There is the question of the number of people the presenter, leader, and group members can each hold in mind while presenting clinical material. There is a need for enough minds to hold the material, but not so many that there is insufficient space for individuals to think and contribute. When a group becomes too large, powerful competitive dynamics can take hold, which in their turn may terrify quieter members into silence. The exposure of participating can feel too great. On the other hand, too few participants bring other difficulties. If a group is too small, there can be nowhere to hide and work will be affected. There can arise the primitive fear of "not going on being" (Winnicott, 1958), that the life of the group is held by a thread, and any absence becomes a cause of anxiety. Irregularity of attendance has a greater effect in a group of four than in a larger group. On the other hand, there is the opportunity for more frequent presentation of work in the smaller group, which gives greater cohesiveness and can redress this balance.

The next issue to bear in mind is the frequency of meeting. Just as too many members in a group can make it difficult for individuals to hold colleagues and the material in mind, so meeting too infrequently can make it hard to hold on to the feelings and continuity of the sessions. This may mean that themes are forgotten and feelings are managed elsewhere, or a pressure may build up that is hard to contain. As in therapy, a secure supervision group needs a consistent environment, with regularity of meetings and personnel.

I will illustrate these matters with a case example.

A supervision group with four members had suffered a great deal of disruption since the arrival of a new leader. The previous supervisor, who was described as charismatic and greatly missed, had retired, but still took training days for the organization and was individual supervisor to one of the group members. Two members had recently left the group, both to join groups that met at different times. Their places were then filled by two new members. When the group met at the beginning of term after a break, the energy among them was extremely low, to the degree that they were hardly able to engage in the task of supervision at all. First, there had been too many changes in personnel. The group had hardly mourned the previous leader and accepted the new one before two more important losses occurred. They could not accept and allow in two new members, when there were only two of the old group and the new leader to manage this transition. The two new members could not participate in the mourning, because they had had no relationship with the previous supervisor. In addition, there had just been a four-week break for the Christmas holidays, when the group did not meet. The group was in the grip of a primitive anxiety of "not going on being". Acting out with irregular attendance then followed. The safety of the group had been disrupted and so people stayed away, and people staying away disrupted the safety of the group. In this parlous state it was necessary to negotiate spending a part of each session on group issues, a kind of therapy for the group. They needed to address their fantasies about the change of leader, about the lost members, about the new members, and about their expectations of each other. In this way, they gradually managed to establish a new group in which the energy and ability to work could return.

In this discussion of the frame and group membership, we need to give thought to the balance in the group between experienced and inexperienced therapists. Many counselling agencies place newly selected counsellors in mixed experience Case Discussion groups from the outset. This provides a good learning environment in which one can truly learn from the experiences of others. It especially offers an opportunity to think about the work of colleagues, without the anxiety attendant on exposing one's own work, and to consider clinical concepts and understandings in action. However, a strength may also be a weakness. A disadvantage is that such a mixed group may give credence and external evidence to strengthen the fantasies and anxieties that accompany the exposure of something as intimate as clinical work. Hence, the tendency to identify with roles such as "the new girl", "the expert", "the rebel", and "the dunce" may be enhanced. Experienced people may be idealized and those in training may feel overwhelmed by their lack of experience, perhaps for longer than is necessary. Experienced members may also feel resentment that they become part of the training environment, which may not provide the depth of thinking they require.

However, I am not suggesting that such roles only get established in a mixed experience group, because they represent the cast of characters that inhabits the internal worlds of us all, and can become projected in any human group. Powerful dynamics from a training group, in an organization to which I was training consultant, are illustrated in the example below.

The group consisted of four members, all at roughly the same stage of training, but with different abilities and capacities for linking experience to theory. Their task was to present their clinical material. The group worked for two years with a gentle, containing leader, but painful destructive dynamics became established where rivalry and pairing were common, and where one member became increasingly marginalized. There was an atmosphere of attack, which another member tried to alleviate by becoming the joker. These dynamics were discussed outside the group, between the group leader and myself as consultant, where it was understood that the anxiety around trying to qualify had caused a regression into a Basic Assumption group, as described by Bion (1961). Rivalrous pairings were set up to protect a fragile sense of adequacy, which was also enhanced by the creation of a scapegoat who carried the inadequacy. This dynamic was challenged in the group and partially understood, but was resistant to change. After two years, the leader changed to a younger, more confronting personality. The rivalries very swiftly dissolved and the dynamic reorganized into a protective alliance against the newcomer. The "other" was no longer a member of the group, but was now the new leader, the outsider. Interestingly, in this new situation, the trainee who had been marginalized felt able to form a kind of pair with the new leader and so come in from the cold.

This example illustrates the powerful influence that the anxiety of training can exert on a group, heightening defences and exacerbating the differing capacities of members, until it can be a daunting task for the leader to maintain a facilitating environment for learning.

The task and group process

The group leader needs to consider some of the group processes that may add to the difficulty of maintaining an atmosphere of learning and enquiry when one therapist presents clinical material for supervision in a group.

First, we need to keep in mind the prevailing group culture that has developed over time. Every group develops an underlying culture. I have already described such a culture in my previous example, in terms of a Basic Assumption. A slightly different way of thinking about the dynamic of this group is to think of the degree of competitiveness. This is a normal part of the group situation and has some very positive aspects. It can generate energy and vitality, a willingness to challenge, and creativity. However, on the shadow side it can easily slide into a wish merely to demonstrate one's own perceptiveness, skill, and ability, which has little to do with a wish to add to understanding. In this atmosphere feelings of envy and inadequacy are likely to prevail rather than enlightenment.

There are also groups where the opposite culture takes hold. In these situations competitiveness is suppressed, in the interest of remaining similar and denying difference. In such an atmosphere it can be hard for group members to discover their potential and find their own individual level.

For instance, I was with a group of supervisors discussing a prevailing attitude of low self esteem, in a group that recently had a new leader. It seemed unsafe to express any positive attitudes in this group, no confidence, hope, or satisfaction. The only emotions allowed were the opposite, as a defence against attack, envy, or disillusion. A new leader coming in was able to see and question this, whereas the previous leader had been part of that system. How it developed we could only conjecture, wondering whether the group had internalized an over-anxious leader. However, it was clear that it was affecting the primary task.

Second, supervisors need to be alert to the dynamic processes present from moment to moment in a group. When clinical material is presented by a therapist, every other group member is being invited to act as supervisor, which can easily lead to the presenter feeling attacked. Members may respond to the case and the material as if it were their own case, and consider what they might do. In one way, this is in order to empathize and access individual feelings, the countertransference, to try to gain more understanding. However, the pitfall comes when it is forgotten that this is actually a colleague's case and that the task is to reflect on the patient as brought by his own therapist. It is helpful to compare this with the task of the marital therapist, who tries always to address the relationship between the couple first, before considering the dynamics between the individual spouses and the therapist. Supervision is a similar process. The primary area for consideration needs to be the feelings and dynamics between the presenting therapist and their patient. The individual responses of group members are important but secondary. The discussion will inevitably oscillate between these two positions, where group members respond as if it were their own patient, and where they remember that it is, in fact, a colleague's patient. However, if the balance goes down in the former position, the therapist is likely to leave feeling robbed and attacked. It is important that the group supervisor is alert to this dynamic, and prepared to address it when necessary.

My third consideration of what may transpire when clinical material is presented to a group is to do with the dynamics of the case itself and how these may resonate with the group. This was written about by Janet Mattinson (1975) in *The Reflection Process in Casework Supervision*, and Hugh Gee (1996) in "Developing insight through supervision: relating then defining". The reflective process has been further developed recently in the growing interest in infant observation and infant research. Emphasis has been placed on the minute-by-minute interaction that goes on between mother and baby and is mirrored in the analytic situation. Beebe and Lachmann (2002) describe this as a process of mutual cueing, which can then be internalized by the patient. In a paper by Brown and Miller (2002), this idea is extended to supervision. They describe a "triadic intersubjective matrix" in which the personalities of the patient, the therapist, and the supervisor intersect. It is this point of interaction that provides the material for exploration in the supervisory container. When a patient is brought to a group for supervision, a similar process can be evoked. Unconscious or overwhelming feelings, which are to do with the pathology of the patient, are experienced by the therapist in the group situation and individual group members take up the positions of internal objects of the patient. An interaction is then in place which corresponds to the internal world of the patient. This can then provide a rich medium for containing and understanding, at this extended point of interaction, but only if the group supervisor can comprehend what is happening and interpret it. If this does not happen, the presenting therapist will feel overwhelmed and misunderstood in whatever way is syntonic with parts of her patient.

For example, I presented a patient of mine to a seminar group: a young man who was very sensitive, with many unintegrated parts of his personality. Throughout his childhood his mother was acutely depressed, leaving him convinced that his affects were too overwhelming for her, and that he must find a way to cut them off from her, or manage them somehow himself. In trying to present my patient to the group, in order to be the voice he tries to silence, I found myself presenting an overwhelming half hour of material and, as I delivered it, I could feel my colleagues sinking. This was fascinating, because when I prepared the material, I felt it was quite inadequate to express the affects involved. Some members of the group expressed their sense of being overwhelmed, whereupon I felt anxious and damaging, just like my patient. I was now personally in touch with an aspect of his inner world, through the reflection in the group. It was now very important for this group experience to be understood and linked with the inner world of my patient. That way, I could have an experience in which the overwhelming aspects had been felt, survived, and transformed through understanding. Without that vital processing, it was possible that the fear around being uncontainable would be reinforced and I would be left less able to contain my patient. It is necessary for the leader to link the group dynamic with the internal world of the presented patient for the learning to take place.

The role of the group is especially interesting and complex when a couple rather than an individual is presented for supervision. The material then includes the conscious and unconscious interaction of two people, as well as their internal worlds, all of which can resonate in the group. A therapist may well bring a couple to group supervision when there is a problem in holding both partners firmly in mind. Embarking on marital therapy by definition evokes an oedipal triangle, with all the possibilities for rivalry and alliances. As we all tend to use our relationships as places to project unwanted parts of ourselves, the dynamics in the group may be especially powerful as members identify or disassociate with the material. In this situation, it can be effective to really use the group, noting who is silent and perhaps inquiring about their thoughts, or what perhaps it is difficult to express. The feeling tone around what is said by vocal members needs to be reflected on, to encourage as full a picture as possible of countertransference reactions to the material. It can then be possible to reach understandings previously inaccessible from experiencing their resonance in the group.

Figure 2 illustrates this in diagrammatic form. The complexity of the marital relationship, both conscious and unconscious, is mapped in (a), which illustrates the interactions between the husband and wife at conscious and unconscious levels. This complex situation is then put into a group (b), where the individual members may then identify with one or other of these dynamics, evoking them most powerfully in the group situation.

The roles of the group leader

How can the leader help the group in the performance of the task, and how may he hinder?

First, it is vital that the group supervisor attends to the group process in its many aspects. This will include the dimension

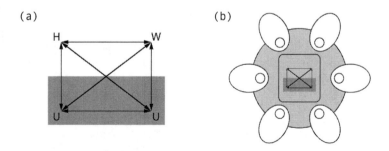

Figure 2.   (a) The couple; (b) the couple in the group.

described above, that is, being alert to the effect the inner world of the presented patient has on the dynamic in the group and being prepared to bring this to the group's attention. In this way, the presenter and the whole group can be helped to make sense of an experience and hopefully gain access to unconscious elements as they have been re-enacted. If the leader does not have this dimension in mind, the presenter may be left exposed, in a position where defences against certain affects may increase and the therapist's capacity for managing them may decrease. This dynamic becomes even more powerful when the patient under discussion is a couple.

Second, the leader has a responsibility to bear in mind the basic assumptions (Bion, 1961) and the prevailing atmosphere in the group, especially when it begins to affect the work. Sometimes, some specific work on the group process may be necessary, as in my previous examples, when there was a need to focus on loss, excessive rivalry, and anger. It may fall to the leader to initiate such discussion, or it may come up in the case material, when unconscious processes influence the choice of the case that emerges for discussion. For instance, in the first meeting of the group I mentioned earlier, where there had been fantasies about a charismatic predecessor, the first case presented was about a resented step-mother.

It is the task of the group supervisor to foster appreciation, and to support the skills of the members whenever possible. Therefore, it is helpful to try to address issues through the case material. A remark such as "I wonder what was going on between you and your patient when you made that comment?" supports an atmosphere of enquiry rather than criticism and is likely to encourage the supervisee to open up and be frank, rather than close down defensively. There is always a risk in a group of a critical atmosphere taking hold, which may settle into criticism of the patient as well as the therapist. Again, the leader can help to keep alive a spirit of curiosity by being aware of critical attitudes when they arise, and bringing them out for discussion.

We also need to consider the role of teaching and assessment in a group supervisory situation. Much has been written about assessment elsewhere, for instance by Edward Martin (2003). It complicates the dynamics and enhances the anxieties in the group about being judged. As for teaching, I do consider it is important that the leader offers some theory and teaching, but it will be much more valuable if linked to experiences in the group. There is a danger that theory can be used as a defence against the anxiety of not knowing. Kalsched (1995) wrote about this in relation to his experience of group supervision,

> Individual "theories" were not coherent systems, but represented the "personal equation" of the therapist—a way of formulating what was seen, a lens through which otherwise chaotic information came into focus for him or her. [p. 108]

A supervisor who offers too much theory may be an over-anxious supervisor who needs to know, and may therefore demoralize the group rather than inform them. However, some theoretical concept that emerges from a presentation or from an experience which happens at a feeling level in the group may truly link thinking with affect and so be more readily understood. Patrick Casement (1990) wrote,

> This conflict, between a search for certainty and a need to remain open to the experience of still not-knowing, can become the source of a patient's greatest potential for change and creativity. [p. 15]

My job specification for a group supervisor sounds a bit like Kipling's "If":

> If you can keep in mind your position as leader, neither denying it, nor succumbing to idealization, or its twin, demonization;

> If you can hold inside yourself your own experience and learning, as a resource, with which to help the group learn from their own experience;

> If you can assess, when you must, but with an open mind, always aware of the context;

> If you can remember that it is the therapist who is seeing the patient, and you are seeing the group; and that it is your task to try and facilitate an experience in the group in which it will be possible to learn more about the patient and the therapeutic process;

> If you can achieve this impossible task, you should get by as a good enough group supervisor.

References

Beebe, B., & Lachmann, F. (2002). *Infant Research and Adult Treatment.* New Jersey: Analytic Press.

Bion, W. (1961). *Experiences in Groups.* London: Tavistock.

Brown, L., & Miller, M. (2002). The triadic intersubjective matrix in supervision. *International Journal of Psychoanalysis, 83*: 811–823.

Casement, P. (1990). *Further Learning from the Patient.* London: Routledge.

Concise Oxford Dictionary of Quotations (2nd edn) (1981). Oxford: Oxford University Press.

Gee, H. (1996). Developing insight through supervision; relating then defining. *Journal of Analytical Psychology, 41*: 529–551.

Jung, C. G. (1950)[1948]. The shadow. C.W., 9(*ii*). R. F. C. Hull (Trans.). London: Routledge & Kegan Paul.

Kalsched, D. (1995). The agonies and ecstasies of casework supervision. In: P. Kugler (Ed.), *Jungian Perspectives on Clinical Supervision* (pp. 107–118). Zurich: Daimon.

Martin, E. (2003). Problems and ethical issues in supervision. In: J. Weiner, R. Mizen, & J. Duckham (Eds.), *Supervising and Being Supervised* (pp. 135–150). Basingstoke: Palgrave Macmillan.

Mattinson, J. (1975). *The Reflection Process in Casework Supervision.* London: Institute of Marital Studies.

Menzies Lyth, I. (1959). The functions of social systems as a defence against anxiety: a report on a study of the nursing service of a general hospital. *Human Relations, 13*: 95–121.

Winnicott, D. W. (1958). *Through Paediatrics to Psycho-analysis.* London: Tavistock.

Winnicott, D. W. (1971). *Playing and Reality.* London: Routledge.

Zinkin, L. (1988). Supervision: the impossible profession. *British Association of Psychotherapists.* Papers from a Public Conference. London.

CHAPTER THIRTEEN

Janus as a metaphor for the assessment process

Maureen Chapman

The aim of this chapter is to consider the function of assessment and how best we can fulfil this purpose within the various settings we might find ourselves in as supervisors of both trained and trainee therapists. It seeks to illustrate the function of the assessment process and the qualities looked for when preparing an assessment. The Formative and Summative approach to assessment is discussed. Using myth and metaphor the chapter explores some issues, illustrating the power of the unconscious that might blur the judgement of the assessor.

The Romans associated Janus with beginnings. January takes its name from Janus, marking the beginning of a new year when we reflect and assess the last year and make new resolutions. Using the story of Janus as a metaphor draws attention to the complexity and the "confrontational" nature of the supervisory relationship during assessment. I see the assessment process as a marker, a moment when the future is barred until the confrontational process of the assessment is complete.

The image of Janus found on a Roman coin shows his two faces pointing in opposite directions, allowing him to simultaneously guard both the front and the back doors of his double-gated temple in Rome. His title was the God of Doors and Gates; sometimes he was thought of as the guardian of the Gate of Heaven. His power as a gate keeper is important, as symbolically a house may only be as strong as its doors.

In supervision we can think of this as symbolizing the appraisal of both inner and outer worlds of all those involved in the assessment process, a constant alertness at every step of the way. As an assessor, the supervisor needs to look in two directions at once, to the profession and the standards expected for entry and to the supervisee and the level they have reached, acting as a connection between one and the other. A poor connection carries the potential for time consuming difficulties and painful disappointments erupting between the training body and supervisee that further analysis prior to training may have avoided.

Janus also has two insignia, a key, to open the Gate of Heaven and a stick, which his porters used to fend off those who had no right to pass the threshold. The supervisor, like Janus, often has a pivotal role in the decision-making process when permission is sought to enter the professions as a qualified psychotherapist or counsellor.

When we think of making assessments we can be affected by our own personal experience. We bring to consciousness a defining moment, thus creating a space within which to reflect, and frequently to express, and perhaps protest, about the effect the power our supervisors and assessors' perception of our competence can have on our professional and financial lives.

The most difficult question for me is the following. How do we know the criteria we have to relate to when making an assessment? Our primary experience is of our own trainings. How does this compare with other trainings? How do we as supervisors from varying trainings apply a criterion in relation to other trainings we might not have experienced? How do we make a benchmark when supervising trainees from other orientations? Supervisees are individuals; their rate of progression is also individual; likewise all trainings are unique. Herein lies one of the major difficulties encountered in assessment, for it is as if we have a moving target with an indefinable object.

Defining the function of assessment is necessary to ground and contain it. Implicitly, the assessment acts as a "gate keeper" with a triple function.

Primarily, it becomes the protector of patient care by sustaining standards and accountability. Second, it determines the professional ability and the continuing development of the supervisee. This culminates in a third function, that of signifying a rite of passage into the respective professions, where external approval from assessment connects with an internal healthy narcissism and sense of self worth on the part of the supervisee.

The assessment, then, is the nucleus of supervision. With this in mind, why is such an important and indispensable aspect of supervision treated with such discord amongst psychotherapists? Although there are many parallels between working as a therapist and as a supervisor, a significant difference is that of making a clinical judgement about a colleague's work. As therapists, we are trained to accept our patient's limitations, and to facilitate their growth through our interpretive skills. However, as supervisors our focus is facilitating integration and reintegration within the supervisee in relation to his or her analytical work with the patient. Supervisors therefore become decision-makers and, when necessary, demand change from their supervisees to fulfil criteria. Supervision therefore creates a dissonance.

What is being assessed and by whom?

Historically, an aspect of a supervisor's work has always been one of monitoring or assessing, either periodically or as a continuum. The *Shorter Oxford English Dictionary* (1959, p. 109) describes the verb *to assess* as *to make a valuation,* and we would apply this to a valuation of the complex cost benefits in relation to the patient, the profession, and the supervisee.

Plaut (1961) pointed out what may be a ubiquitous phenomenon in assessment, saying, "It seems a fact that each successive generation tends to establish ever more exacting criteria of selection and acceptance into the organisation as long as advantages accrue from being admitted" (p. 98). Therefore, it is those who belong who set the price and who determine the criteria for the succeeding generation.

However, there are those who question the legitimacy of evaluation and lack a sense of entitlement to act in the role of Janus, as cited by Bernard and Goodyear (1992):

They do not think they should or can judge another. Further, they are oppressed by conflicting, ambiguous evidence of performance and by imprecise, vague standards available for judging performance. Not feeling "without sin" they are reluctant to cast the first stone. [p. 153]

The supervisor's identification with the supervisee in this instance creates a dissonance, which can affect the task of clear and fair evaluation of a professional colleague. This, along with the scarcity of studies that separate out and specify therapeutic competency, contributes to the subjective reaction to assessment, which should aim to be an objective process. Holding in mind the diversity of trainings, the individuality of assessors, and the differing states of readiness found in supervisees, how do we do this, what is the "Key to the Kingdom of Heaven"? Being a mere mortal at this stage is helpful, as there cannot be a perfect solution. All we can think of is to achieve good enough guidelines, keep constantly alert, and hope the porters with us are vigilant and attend to challenges early before the key unlocks the gate.

Wampold and Holloway (1997), amongst others, have made various studies attempting to measure clinical competence in relation to skills, knowledge, experience, and the personal characteristics of therapists, all with mixed results. However, intuitively most professionals believe from collective understanding that experience matters, good clinical skills and knowledge matter, and importantly, the relationship between supervisor and therapist matters in developing clinical competence. Therefore, accumulated wisdom and experience form the matrix of assessment and supervision. All of these criteria are necessary when making a judgement that opens up a debate about a trainee's competence.

In 1991, a symposium of Jungian supervisors from the SAP addressed the question of qualities they valued in a supervisee while assessing their competence. They produced a number of key points, all demonstrating the development and integration of the supervisee:

1. Evidence of ongoing development in the trainee during the course of supervision, especially increased emotional flexibility in relation to his/her patients.

2. A developing capacity to empathize and be affected by patients without over- identification.
3. Evidence of a growing capacity in the use of the transference and countertransference.
4. The capacity to sustain a negative countertransference without retaliation.
5. A capacity for a growing independence and responsibility without too much anxiety.
6. Sufficient insight about their current limits of competence to seek help when needed.

Perhaps every training course requires such a symposium on a regular basis, in order to ensure that common criteria and standards are being applied by common consensus.

Wharton (2003) later commented that therapists are born not made. She highlights the all-important quality of a therapist as the intuitive understanding of another's inner world, which she says is probably a gift (p. 96). However, undifferentiated intuition can be quite disturbing and must be grounded and checked by one of the remaining functions: observation, sensation, thinking, and evaluative feeling. There are clear research findings through psychometric tests using the Myers–Briggs Type Indicator (Briggs Myers & McCaulley, 1988) that a high proportion of psychotherapists are likely to be intuitive types whose secondary function will be evaluative feeling.

Regardless of our skills, experience, and aptitudes it is impossible to get all assessments correct every time, but what we must seek to avoid is letting the supervisee down by our difficulty in acknowledging our concerns and making a judgement, or by offering too little too late. In my experience this dilemma is more dominant in trainings where trainees have had insufficient therapy for the work they are training to do, and where the training body delegates clinical experience to outside agencies and relies on the trainee to find their own supervision.

Although the choice of supervisor is usually an individual issue, we need to explore the reasoning behind such a choice. If we omit to do this we might find that unanalysed problems remain unnoticed and the choice of supervisor may be more related to working through or avoiding personal issues in the supervisee than the treatment of the supervisee's patient. Equally, it is important to monitor the choice of patients, as this may indicate weaknesses in the trainee's development, or mirror personal issues to the extent that identification with the patient impinges on the work, or becomes a way of avoiding issues of race, sex, abuse, authority, etc.

When doubts arise about a supervisee's competence, a serious problem ensues for everyone involved. We really need to explore where things went wrong, to pre-empt repetition. Wharton (2003) emphasizes the importance of a good assessment. She reminds us to trust the training body. This implies, I think, a need to trust the training body to select from within its members those with special-ist training, experience, skills, and qualities as assessors. They represent the Janus of the training body. Fairly and without preju-dice, the assessors attempt to expose and explore the potential for the trainee to develop a training alliance. Accepting the training alliance implies a level of psychological mindedness necessary to facilitate ongoing discussion and assessment.

Not all trainings go according to plan, training patients leave and life events frequently intervene. However, if the assessment has been made with care and concern for both training body and trainee, the mutual commitment to the training will allow for the flexibility needed. Through discussion and ongoing assessment a developmental resolution to the issues of concern becomes achiev-able. I see it as part of the commitment of the training body in such circumstances, to provide the trainee with whatever time it takes for the trainee to reach the required standard of the training orga-nization. There is a greater possibility of this happening in the more intensive atmospheres of analytical trainings.

*   *   *

Just as we listen to the story of a patient coming for assessment and take into account their family history, so, as supervisors, we can begin formulating and assessing the capacity of our supervisee to make meaning and understand their clients' inner world by listen-ing to their professional story and training history. What we have to seek to prevent by our clinical assessment is the possibility of overwhelming unanalysed personal pathology being expressed unconsciously within the transference and acted out within the supervisory space or projected on to the agency the supervisee is working in.

A difficult Janus situation presented itself when a counsellor came requiring supervision of agency work. On meeting, I felt very uneasy and confused; in fact I began to wonder if I had made a mistake; was this person actually seeking psychotherapy? We had a conversation about her experience, training, and her present placement. None of these experiences seemed to ignite any sense of pleasure; in fact they all seemed in some way to have let her down. It became clear to me that she was probably so depressed that her margin of competence as a counsellor was in jeopardy. Tentatively, I suggested that she might think about whether she had brought her clinical work, which she was feeling overwhelmed by, to me as a guise for her own troubled self to be taken seriously. Her relief was profound and we spent the rest of the session thinking about how she could go back to the agency, which she felt she could not abandon, to arrange for time out and to get herself back into therapy.

This person had become lost in a training system that had delegated clinical training outside the college, where I suspect the agencies used had various assessment levels. The assessment process had let this person down, accentuating her sense of inadequacy, which had brought her into training. Such tricky situations can be avoided by early intervention and care on the part of the training body. Many trainees find the need for further analysis difficult to hear; however, we need to remember that the emphasis of the treatment remains for the benefit of the trainee's patient. Supervisors in this respect have a wider Janus role, as guardians of the repute of the profession as a whole.

Assessment and the dynamics of the supervisory relationship

It is important to pay attention to the dynamics of the context within which a supervisee works, clarifying procedures and clinical responsibility. Boundary issues are vital for supervisees, particularly those in trainings who have to find their own placements, as they may be unaware of the significance of boundary issues if they have not addressed them within their own therapy. It is not uncommon to discover supervisees unwittingly disclosing fragments of their own personal life while holding conversations with their clients to and from consulting rooms. One trainee thought it was nice of her colleague who, while waiting for her own patient to arrive, chatted with my supervisee's client. They could compare notes!

As supervisors we need to role-model the boundary observances of Janus to our supervisees, creating a space of containment within which to work.

The supervisory relationship, unlike that of the analytical relationship, is generally more spontaneous in that the supervisor is essentially relating to a colleague, be it that the relationship is asymmetrical due to the experience of the supervisor. Fordham (1961) said, "I wish to propose dogmatically that it is the supervisors role, together with that of the seminar leader, to treat the candidate actively as a junior colleague, not as a patient, right from the beginning" (p. 98).

This important nuance pushes the supervisee into a more objective space of reflection on the dynamic relationship they have with their patient, a space for shared observation helped by the more collegiate relationship of supervisee and supervisor. Unlike analysis, where the therapeutic alliance supports work in "Child Time", i.e., the transference, the supervisory relationship predominantly takes place in "Adult Time", in the here and now. Problems arise when the supervisee's unanalysed neurotic material is triggered by the inbuilt asymmetry of the supervisory relationship. Such issues require analytical treatment by the assessing supervisor, through drawing the attention of the supervisee to the fact it is the supervisee's countertransference that is counter to the patient's transference. This keeps the focus on the patient's material and forces the supervisee to think about the patient's projections. If these issues are not treated analytically by the assessing supervisor, the patient is likely to experience a repetition of past experiences acted out within the therapy.

This process reminds us of the "confrontational" nature of the assessing supervisor, who at the same time frees the supervisory space to allow for creative thought and exploration to happen. It is a place where learning can safely take place through the testing of ideas and honesty of presentations. The supervisor requires the sensitivity to maintain a relationship that is neither too close or too strained, but one which is supportive, objective, professional, and not personal. A relationship that is lacking in trust will also be one of avoidance, risking censoring of material and the delivery of mixed messages, providing poor material with which to make objective assessments.

Formative and Summative assessments

It is necessary that the assessment process is bedded into supervision and is not just a form-filling process by the supervisor every six months or annually. Most training bodies develop their own format, incorporating verbal consultation and full written reports, while some use rating scales and questionnaires. In my experience the greatest difficulty is where and how to pitch the first assessment. A structure is needed to which the assessment can be related. A common structure in social work, counselling, and psychotherapy trainings is the use of the Formative and Summative assessment process.

The Formative assessment is when the assessor becomes like a porter at the gate of the Kingdom of Heaven; alerting concerns early, through the ongoing verbal feedback between supervisor and supervisee that stresses progress and process. This is much more compatible for the supervisor, as the process is experienced as less decisive and judgemental than Summative assessments, because its role is not about outcome. However, the assessment needs to be systematic, objective, and accurately based on specific examples of the supervisee's practice, which have been observed and identified as a focus of development or a need for change.

When offering feedback as part of the Formative assessment process, it is important that the feedback is given close to the situation in question, before the impact is lost. The language used is mutually shared, explicit, and clear and to the point to avoid misunderstandings, not ambiguous and tentative. It is also useful to seek clarification with the supervisee as to what they have heard one say, particularly if the supervisee is very anxious and defended. We, as supervisors, may think we have offered a congruent input, but there are times when we do not know what impact we have had until we hear from the other what they have heard us say.

The success of this form of assessment depends on the communication skills of the supervisor to offer observations in a congruent manner, taking into account the supervisee's levels of anxiety and psychological mindedness. Potential for ongoing development is generated, in an atmosphere where a sense of play and creativity facilitates ongoing learning from experience. A balance is required, as too stern an atmosphere and a fear of making mistakes may engender censorship, as discussed earlier. An added advantage of consistently using this method of evaluation in the assessment process is its use to prepare the supervisee for the more definitive Summative assessment. It acts as a safeguard, offering the opportunity for early problem solving and timely intervention to forestall the build-up of issues over time.

The Summative assessment should be the culmination of an agreed evaluation period, not the commencement of it. It is important as it creates a baseline and a reference point to which following assessments can be related. The Summative assessment is a formal marking-down using documentation, following a face to face discussion with the supervisee of standards reached and standards to be achieved, as required by the training body. The written form of assessment is more stressful for both the supervisor and supervisee. This assessment metaphorically sets the price that enables the trainee to gain admission, having passed the criteria set by those who hold the keys to the kingdom. The supervisor has to take a step backwards, devote time to the task, take stock of the situation in an objective manner, and report on how the supervisee measures up. If all has gone well with the Formative assessment process there should not be any surprises for the supervisee. It is also an opportunity for the supervisor to assess her own skills as a mediator and communicator, in enabling the supervisee to comprehend and integrate the information that was offered during the Formative assessments. In the case of consultative supervision post qualification, the focus could be the recognition of areas of weakness, which collaboratively are chosen as areas for future development.

Summative assessments are frequently a lonely task; they take time, usually with low financial remuneration. They require great care because Summative assessments are those that play a direct part in major administrative decisions, occasionally bringing to consciousness what others have turned a blind eye to. An important safeguard against a difficult Summative assessment is to invest considerable care and thought into the Formative assessment process, to ensure there are no surprises. In other words, to take the Janus approach, to pay attention to the inner world of the supervisee through analysis, and the supervisee's perception of her patient's inner world within the supervisory space.

Unconscious processes and the judgement of the supervisor

So far we have focused on the assessment of the work between supervisee and patient; to complete the assessment process we have to take a Janus look in the opposite direction, i.e., towards the supervisor. As supervisors, we carry the responsibility of being in a position of power and influence over the supervisee.

A supervisee chooses a supervisor for many conscious reasons such as location, cost, time, orientation of training, and personal recommendation. However, separation anxiety, sense of self, control, envy, oedipal issues, idealization, and identification may be some of the unconscious motivations beneath these reasons and require special thought in relation to countertransference within the supervisory alliance. The process of assessing a supervisee starts with the supervisor. It is to be hoped that we have substantial knowledge of our inner world and recognition of those tertiary parts of our pathology that, like the tail of the evolving frog, remind us metaphorically of previous unconscious states that can still become activated when we are overwhelmed by the pressures of our present day living. We need to ask ourselves what it is that motivates us to make the transition from therapist to supervisor.

Guggenbuhl-Craig (1971) writes, "No one can act out of exclusively pure motives" (p. 10), and again, "The greater the contamination by dark motives, the more the therapist clings to his alleged objectivity" (p. 9). Exploring our motives involves us facing the shadow side of our helping impulse, including our lust for power. Guggenbuhl-Craig goes on to point out that most of us have an attraction for the healer–patient Archetype. Our overwhelming need to continue as a healer can stifle our supervisees from discovering their own internal healer. It also enables us to feel good about surrounding ourselves by those more fearful than ourselves and it can feel powerful when we are able to direct parts of their lives. We may delude ourselves into feeling extra special, becoming addicted to praise and fearful of blame. As assessors and supervisors we act as trouble-shooters. The very nature of our work implicitly implies an expectation that a problem exists in someone. Thus, we offer the parent–child Archetype the opportunity to infer that every person who seeks help is an aspect of one's own wounded childhood, needing its wounds attended to by good enough parental care. A countertransference may be set up before we have a supervisee.

The same parent–child Archetype affects us by needing to correct and punish. The mythological story of the ogre Procrustes, who lured travellers to his castle, reminds us of the ideals and values of the Archetype of conformity. The fear of change and the envy of the freshness of ideas a supervisee may offer can lead the supervisor to "clip the wings" of the trainee, much like Procrustes putting the travellers to bed and, if they did not fit, chopping off their long legs or stretching them if they were too small. Clearly it is the supervisor's insecurities that can lead to adherence to theories like adhesive attachments, turning them into dogmas.

Acknowledgement

I am indebted to Jan Wiener for first drawing my attention to Janus in a then unpublished paper some years ago.

References

Bernard, J., & Goodyear, R. (1992). *Fundamentals of Clinical Supervision* (2nd edn). Boston, MA: Allyn and Bacon.

Briggs Myers, I., & McCaulley, M. H. (1988). *A Guide to the Development and Use of the Myers–Briggs Type Indicator*. Palo Alto, CA: Consulting Psychologists Press.

Fordham, M. (1961). Suggestions towards a theory of supervision. *Journal of Analytical Psychology*, 6(2): 98–102.

Guggenbuhl-Craig A. (1971). *Power in the Helping Professions*. Dallas, TX: Spring.

Plaut, A. (1961). A dynamic outline of the training situation. *Journal of Analytical Psychology, 6*(2): 98–102.

The Shorter Oxford English Dictionary (3rd edn) (1959). Oxford: Clarendon.

Wampold, B. E., & Holloway, E. L. (1997). Methodology, design, and evaluation in psychotherapy supervision research. In: C. E. Watkins (Ed.), *Handbook of Psychotherapy Supervision* (pp. 11–27). New York: Wiley.

Wharton, B. (2003). Supervision in analytic training. In: J. Weiner, R. Mizen, & J. Duckham (Eds.), *Supervising and Being Supervised* (pp. 52–99). Palgrave: Macmillan.

INDEX